T0374724

The publisher and the University of California Press
Foundation gratefully acknowledge the generous
support of the Joan Palevsky Endowment Fund in
Literature in Translation.

The Selected Letters of
Cassiodorus

The Selected Letters of Cassiodorus

A Sixth-Century Sourcebook

Cassiodorus

Edited and translated by M. Shane Bjornlie

UNIVERSITY OF CALIFORNIA PRESS

University of California Press
Oakland, California

© 2020 by Shane Bjornlie

Library of Congress Cataloging-in-Publication Data

Cassiodorus, Senator, approximately 487–approximately 580,
    author. | Bjornlie, M. Shane, translator, editor.
Title: The selected letters of Cassiodorus : a sixth-century sourcebook /
    Cassiodorus; edited and translated by M. Shane Bjornlie.
Other titles: Variae. Selections. English
Description: Oakland, California : University of California Press, [2020] |
    Includes bibliographical references and index.
Identifiers: LCCN 2020004116 (print) | LCCN 2020004117 (ebook) |
    ISBN 9780520297357 (cloth) | ISBN 9780520297340 (paperback) |
    ISBN 9780520969728 (ebook)
Subjects: LCSH: Cassiodorus, Senator, approximately 487-approximately
    580—Correspondence. | Ostrogoths—Italy—History—Sources. |
    Italy—History—476–774—Sources.
Classification: LCC PA6271.C4 Z48 2020 (print) | LCC PA6271.C4 (ebook) |
    DDC 945/.01—dc23
LC record available at https://lccn.loc.gov/2020004116
LC ebook record available at https://lccn.loc.gov/2020004117

Manufactured in the United States of America

29   28   27   26   25   24   23   22   21   20
10   9   8   7   6   5   4   3   2   1

CONTENTS

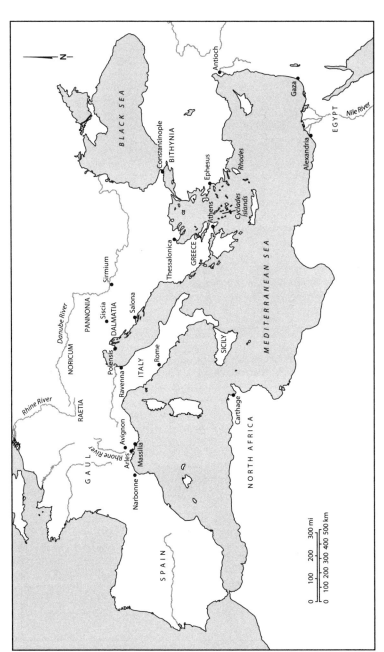

MAP 1. The sixth-century Mediterranean.

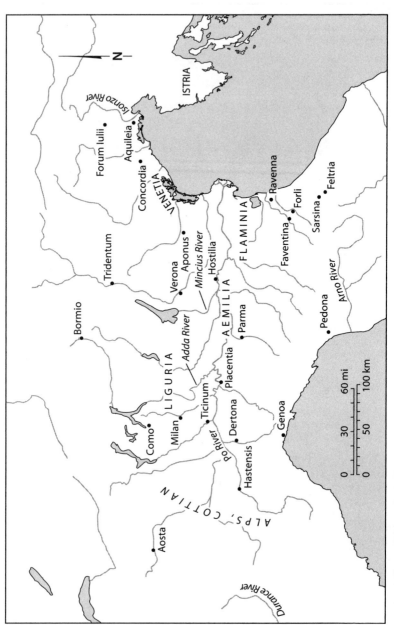

MAP 2. The northern region of Ostrogothic Italy.

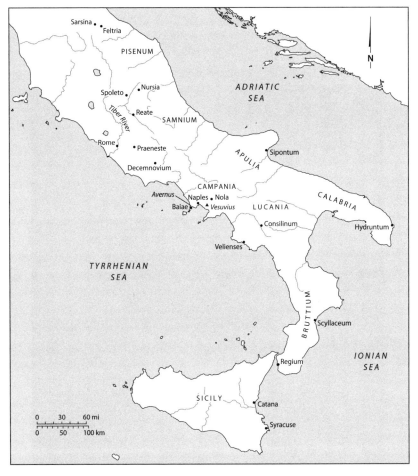

MAP 3. The southern region of Ostrogothic Italy.

Introduction

CASSIODORUS, THE *VARIAE,* AND THEIR WORLD

The *Variae* are an important source of primary evidence for the study of late antiquity. Cassiodorus, their author, wrote toward the end of a period in which the Mediterranean world assumed striking differences from what we consider a classical Roman Empire. In general terms, late antiquity (ca. 300–600) is characterized by the coalescence and then the fragmentation of political unity on scales not previously experienced under the Roman Empire. At the beginning of this period, the Roman Empire reached its greatest extent, spanning from the deep hinterlands of North Africa to the Rhine and the Danube in Europe, and from Britain and the Atlantic shores of Europe to the culturally fertile crescent of the Tigris and Euphrates rivers at the Persian frontier in the east. Although these far-flung regions were initially treated as conquests, by the time of Emperor Constantine's reign (306–37), people from every corner of the empire self-identified as Roman: peasants lived their lives in accordance with the diverse customs and languages of their own provinces, but from the Rhine to the Euphrates the members of the empire's governing and military classes could at some level identify themselves as Roman. The expansion of military and civil service facilitated this to a great degree. Where the emperor Augustus and his successors (a dynasty known today as the Julio-Claudians, who ruled from 27 B.C. to 68 A.D.) had relied on a coterie of senatorial appointments made in Rome and the support of soldiers conscripted largely from Italy to govern their subjects, by the fourth century the Roman Empire drew men to state service from cities across the Mediterranean and recruited soldiers from the villages and fields of every province, and even from beyond imperial borders. In this sense, the fourth century was a period of grand cosmopolitanism. It also saw the empire reach its greatest accumulation of wealth, as the now-massive imperial bureaucracy enabled tax collection on a scale never witnessed before. Late antiquity is also when Christianity emerged as the dominant religion of the Mediterranean world, slowly but ineluctably eroding the traditional partnership between the state and what were increasingly thought of as "pagan" gods. Thus, the fourth century may be seen as the high point of the Christian Roman Empire. By contrast, the fifth century witnessed increasing fragmentation: civil wars fractured the unity of the military and bureaucratic establishment, the rise of Christian bishops and clergy as political leaders altered the orientation and culture of the classical city, and new immigrants to the empire offered alternatives to traditional government at the regional level. Only in its eastern provinces, with the imperial seat firmly anchored at Constantinople, would the Roman Empire resist the forces that tore at the social and political fabric of the western provinces.

Thus, scholarship uses the term *late antiquity,* with increasingly wide scope, to demarcate a period in which the Roman Mediterranean's cultural, religious, and political characteristics transitioned from what we generally recognize as "classical" to what we think of as "medieval." Upon even cursory examination, however, it becomes clear that there were many late antiquities from the fourth to the seventh century. The grandeur of imperial power in the mid-fourth century, for example, contrasts markedly with the disintegration of imperial boundaries evident at the end of the fifth century. And, almost inversely, the modest ambitions of Christianity at the beginning of the fourth century contrast, again markedly, with the deeply entrenched position of the church at the end of the sixth century. Furthermore, regional differences in the Roman and former Roman world become increasingly evident in this period. Whereas Italy, for example, shared political, religious, and material cultures with the rest of the Mediterranean in the second century, in the sixth century it bore the marks of profound economic and cultural differences from other regions of the western Mediterranean and from the eastern empire, its partner during the last Roman centuries. In a setting where not only discontinuity, rupture, and transition but also continuity were the norm, it is difficult to identify definitive watershed moments, let alone sources that can be said to typify a particular late-antique moment. One of the rare exceptions is the *Variae* of Cassiodorus.

The letters of the *Variae* represent approximately thirty years (507–40), during which their author served as a senior magistrate of the Ostrogothic kingdom in Italy. Cassiodorus was thus a privileged participant in the peninsula's political, economic, cultural, and religious life in the first half of the sixth century. The 468 letters that he collected and published under the title *Variae* originally served as political and administrative instruments, correspondence with other high-placed officials in the last Roman-style government in Italy. More than official documents, however, they are also the literary product of a highly educated individual author, and as such they reveal an extended and nearly continuous period with a level of detail and variations of texture not found in any other late-antique text.

The circumstances in which Cassiodorus produced the *Variae* also make it one of the rare witnesses to a regional watershed moment. When he assembled his collection, the Ostrogothic kingdom, as the final stage of the centuries-long transformation of the western Roman Empire, had preserved elements of the Roman Empire completely absent from other regions of the western Mediterranean. Indeed, "Ostrogothic kingdom" and "Ostrogothic Italy" are terminologies of modern convenience; contemporaries such as Cassiodorus simply referred to their state as *res publica,* a locution designating the Roman state. However little the *res publica* of sixth-century Italy may have resembled the earlier Roman state, it is significant that the Ostrogoths self-consciously attempted to project their state as continuing this imperial tradition. But any pretense to preserving the *res publica* came to an abrupt end in the lifetime of Cassiodorus, when the eastern emperor Justinian attempted to "reclaim" Italy for the "Roman" empire in 535. The ensuing Gothic War lasted nearly twenty years and wrought havoc on the political and economic life of Italy. Societal changes already in process were exacerbated by the conflict and became so entrenched that the Italy which emerged toward the end of the sixth century was no longer a single state, but a mosaic of dislocated regions, contested by a variety of powerful forces: the rising papacy, the Lombards who held power in the north, and the remaining imperial authority. In a very essential sense, Italy had become "medieval." Thus, Cassiodorus's life straddled the transition from classical to medieval, and the *Variae* serve as witnesses poised on the precipice of that change.

Although this transformation was profound, so was the continuous process of wide societal change beginning in the early fifth century that culminated in Ostrogothic Italy. Thus, the *Variae* are also important witnesses to the difference between sixth-century Italy and earlier phases of late antiquity. In political terms, it is often convenient to fasten upon the deposition of Romulus Augustus by the warlord Odoacer in 476 as the end of the Roman Empire in Italy, but in fact the matter is far more complicated. It could be argued that the end began with the death of Emperor Theodosius I in 395 and the subsequent permanent division of the empire into eastern and western states. Although these successor empires tended toward cooperation, and most fifth-century western emperors received the support of Constantinople and even shared the appointment of consuls with it well into the Ostrogothic period, the development of independent states in the provincial territories of the western empire (in North Africa, Spain, Gaul, and Britain) diminished the financial and political resources of Italy's central imperial authority. Thus, when Odoacer deposed Romulus Augustus (who was an imperial appointment of questionable legitimacy by another rogue military commander), he assumed control over an Italy that had long since lost its extended political, military, and economic apparatus. For all that might have been "barbarian" about Odoacer, he enjoyed the full support of the Senate and the Roman army in Italy, in addition to the tacit acquiescence of the eastern emperor Zeno (ruled 474–91), for a prosperous span of thirteen years.

Before that, Odoacer's career in the western Roman military had been shaped by events beyond the frontiers of the Roman Empire that would also contribute to his eventual ruin and the rise of the Ostrogothic state. In 454, the confederation of Germanic and Hunnic peoples maintained during the lifetime of Attila (d. 453) ended with the Battle of Nedao. The *Life of Saint Severinus* by Eugippius portrays the Germanic Odoacer as a young adventurer en route to Italy through the frontier province of Noricum, and it seems very likely that he, and many others like him, offered himself, whether as a refugee or an opportunist, for military service in the Roman Empire. (The same circumstances brought the family of Theoderic, who eventually overthrew Odoacer, to the Balkans later in the 450s.) Gothic and Germanic peoples conquered by the Huns had quickly become instruments and partners of Hunnic power. After these formerly subject peoples rejected Attila's heirs at the Battle of Nedao, one of the Gothic groups that had enjoyed success under the Huns was incorporated into the Roman Empire and settled in the province of Pannonia. In the sixth century, this people became known as "Ostrogoths," to distinguish them from the "Visigoths," who had entered the empire in the late fourth century.

The Ostrogoths' official status within the empire was *foederati,* or "federated peoples," bound to the Romans by treaty (*foedus* in Latin), and although they were not technically citizens, they were expected to act as soldiers in the Roman army. As leading members of this new military reserve, Theoderic's family, the Amals, soon rose to prominence in the political affairs of the eastern empire. Theoderic himself spent much of his childhood as a political hostage in Constantinople, at the court of Emperor Zeno, who later appointed him consul and senior field commander of the military in the Balkans. By 488, Theoderic had acquired authority over most of the federated peoples in the Roman military who were settled along the Danube and in the Balkans. Facing the prospect of having to allocate even more authority to him in the eastern empire, Zeno settled upon the expedient of offering him the governance of Italy, which Odoacer had been enjoying as the emperor's nominal regent.

Theoderic entered Italy in 489 with a diverse collection of federated soldiers and their families, who had served the Roman state for well over a generation. The military forces with which Odoacer opposed Theoderic were "Roman" in the very same terms: federated peoples who had been systematically settled as military reserves, in this case primarily in northern Italy. The war lasted four years, with successes and losses on both sides, but Theoderic managed to secure the support of the Roman Senate early in the conflict, likely as a result of Zeno's support. He eventually deposed Odoacer, executing him in Ravenna in 493, and from that point set about establishing the Amals as the new ruling dynasty in Italy. In political terms, probably very little differentiates Theoderic's rule in Italy from those of Odoacer and previous fifth-century emperors, except perhaps the length of his reign (491–526) and its overall success. The *Variae* refer to Theoderic and to each of his Amal successors as *Princeps,* a Latin word meaning "foremost or most prominent," a designation appropriate for an emperor, and other sources use the similar terms *imperator* and *augustus.* Theoderic established a tenuous diplomatic balance with Zeno's successor in the east, Anastasius, which in part depended upon allowing a degree of autonomy, although only limited participation in government, to the traditional senatorial elite in Rome. Ruling for the most part from Ravenna and northern Italy (as had Odoacer and the last generation of fifth-century military commanders), Theoderic primarily relied upon elite families from the Italian provinces outside Rome, such as the family of Cassiodorus, to constitute the apparatus of civilian government. The military comprised the federated soldiers whom Theoderic had either brought with him from the Balkans or incorporated from Odoacer's forces and had settled, along with their families, as landowning communities primarily in northern and central Italy. This heterogeneous group, collectively known as the Goths, became part of a political ideology, prominently represented in the *Variae,* whereby the "Goths" preserved the state with arms and the "Romans" preserved it with peaceful citizenship.

In a very real sense, Theoderic was a western Roman emperor to the same extent as the others of the fifth century: he was familiar with the political culture of Constantinople, had been elevated to positions of public rank, and supported the rule of Roman law. As a result, civilian government in Cassiodorus's Italy assumed a style very similar to that of the fifth century, with appointments to traditional high offices and bureaucratic departments made by the king (emperor) and his representatives. By contrast, the military assumed an ethnicized identity, as "Goths," despite the fact that the Goths' service as "Roman" soldiers did not differ from that of other Roman federated peoples. This rhetoric—that the state was clearly divided into two distinctly different peoples, Goths and Romans—has promoted the modern view of Ostrogothic Italy as a barbarian state that entertained Romanizing traditions, while it would probably be more accurate to understand Theoderic's Italy as a continuation of the fifth-century Roman Empire with adaptations to the scale of government operations. Some of what appear to be "ethnic" differences between Romans and barbarians beginning in the late fifth century were, in fact, social differences between civilian and military populations that became formalized under Theoderic. It should also be noted that there is much disagreement among modern scholars concerning the proper definitions of Gothic and Germanic ethnicity, and the *Variae,* as the chief source of information for the former, often serve as a focal point for these debates.

As the ruler of Italy, Theoderic furthermore forged relationships with ruling families across the western Mediterranean and with peoples of the former Hunnic Empire. Marriage alliances with the Vandals of North Africa, the Visigoths of southern Gaul, the Franks of northern Gaul, and the Thuringians of the eastern Rhine lands are visible in the *Variae.* Although many of these unions proved to be less secure than intended, it is certainly the case that, at its height, the Amal family exerted influence over Italy and Sicily; Dalmatia and Pannonia, on the frontier with the eastern empire; Raetia and Noricum, at the Roman Empire's former northern frontier; and southern Gaul and Spain. Over the course of Theoderic's lifetime, the state he ruled came close to realizing the former dimensions of the Roman Empire's western expanse, but that ended with the Gothic War.

Theoderic died in 526, leaving his throne to his grandson Athalaric, whose mother, Theoderic's daughter Amalasuntha, served as regent. Upon Athalaric's premature death in 534, Amalasuntha proved incapable of commanding the loyalty of Italy's military nobility, so she appointed her cousin Theodahad as co-ruler to appease them. This proved disastrous for the Ostrogothic state. Theodahad murdered Amalasuntha within a year, and her death provided a convenient pretext for the eastern emperor Justinian to send his forces to invade Italy. After his troops took Sicily and Naples, Gothic soldiers assassinated Theodahad and elevated Witigis as the next king, initiating what would become a twenty-year succession of Gothic rulers, who held power throughout the Gothic War. Witigis, however, was the last one to whom Cassiodorus offered allegiance. When Witigis surrendered Ravenna in 540 and was removed to Constantinople with the core of what remained of the Amal court, Cassiodorus's public life ended and he turned to the publication of the *Variae.*

Cassiodorus was probably born around 485, hence at the height of Odoacer's reign in Italy. His own writings, primarily the *Variae,* are the basis of the majority of what is known of his biography. The *Variae* report that his father, grandfather, and great-grandfather all held elevated positions in the western imperial government, beginning in the reign of Valentinian III (425–55), and an eastern branch of the family was apparently prominent in Constantinople in the late fifth century. The family's patrimonial estate was located in the southernmost district of Bruttium (in the area of modern Squillace, in what is now Calabria), where Cassiodorus retired at the close of his public career. That career probably began in 503, when his father assumed the highest-ranking public appointment in the realm as praetorian prefect and Cassiodorus served as *consiliarius,* or aide, to his father's official role. Subsequently, Theoderic appointed him *quaestor,* from 507 to 512, during which time he drafted most, if not all, of the Amal court's official correspondence. His services earned him a consulship in 514, which he may have celebrated in Rome, or perhaps Milan or Ravenna. At the time, Rome and Constantinople each appointed one consul every year; Cassiodorus was named consul without colleague, perhaps an indication of tensions between Italy and the east. In 523, Theoderic appointed Cassiodorus master of offices, the position that administered palace personnel and the daily affairs at court. Cassiodorus was tapped to fill a vacancy resulting from the downfall of the previous master, the famous senator and scholar Boethius, who was accused of treason and executed along with his father-in-law, the prominent patrician Symmachus. Because of these circumstances, Cassiodorus's elevation could not have been well received by the established families in Rome, and there is evidence in the *Variae* of opposition to his increasing influence at court.

Theoderic died in 526, and Cassiodorus continued in the role of master of offices under Amalasuntha and Athalaric. After stepping down in 527, he may have returned to his family estate and held some position of local leadership, perhaps as governor of Bruttium. In 533, however, he was recalled to the capital (Ravenna) as praetorian prefect, the most demanding of civil offices in Italy, formerly held by his father. While Cassiodorus was serving in this capacity, Athalaric died, followed swiftly by the accession of Theodahad, the death of Amalasuntha, and the outbreak of war with the eastern empire. The final years of Cassiodorus's prefecture, when the new king Witigis was campaigning against Justinian's imperial agents, including a year-long siege of Rome (537–38), must have been the most trying of his career. After Witigis finally surrendered in Ravenna in 540, it is generally assumed that Cassiodorus accompanied the captive Amal court to Constantinople, where many émigrés had already sought asylum from the turmoil in Italy. Papal sources place Cassiodorus in Constantinople as late as 551, and it may have been Justinian who finally conferred the rank of patrician upon him. In 554, Justinian issued his Pragmatic Sanction, declaring an end to hostilities in Italy, and Cassiodorus may have returned to Bruttium then, where he founded a monastic community and spent the remainder of his life, until perhaps 580, in scholarly and religious retirement.

While Cassiodorus's public career demonstrates dedication to the Amal regime in Italy, he was just as committed to his life as a writer. He is known to have written, and likely recited before court, three panegyrics: one to Theoderic, another to Athalaric's father upon his receipt of the consulship in 519, and a final piece on the occasion of Witigis's marriage to Amalasuntha's daughter Matasuntha during the Gothic War, probably in 536. Additionally, Cassiodorus composed a chronicle of Roman consulships and a history of the Goths at Theoderic's bequest. The latter work, now lost, is the basis for the surviving *Getica,* written after the Gothic War by Jordanes in Constantinople. The *Variae* was compiled as a tribute to the end of Cassiodorus's public career, sometime between 538 (the year of the latest datable letter in the collection) and the 540s, after the fall of Ravenna as the Amal capital. Cassiodorus's location while he worked on the collection—whether Rome or Ravenna, or perhaps Constantinople or Bruttium—is not known. Before completing it, however, he composed a treatise on the soul, a traditional philosophical work known as the *De anima.* Although he is best remembered today for the *Variae,* throughout the Middle Ages Cassiodorus was widely renowned for his religious writings. At least one of these, a massive spiritual analysis of the Psalms (*Expositio Psalmorum*), had its origins in Constantinople. Others, such as the bibliographical *Institutes on Divine and Human Learning,* an ecclesiastical history from Greek sources, and several biblical works, were completed at the Vivarium, the monastic community that Cassiodorus founded on his familial estate.

THE *VARIAE* AS A LETTER COLLECTION

In its original, intended structure, the *Variae* is a collection of 468 letters arranged in twelve books (or chapters). The first five books consist of letters written by Cassiodorus in Theoderic's name. Books 6 and 7 comprise *formulae* for appointments to public offices, the granting of honorary titles, and particular legal and administrative enactments. In Books 8 and 9, Cassiodorus gathered letters written on behalf of Athalaric. The final selection of letters, written in the names of Amalasuntha, Theodahad, and Witigis, constitute Book 10. Cassiodorus reserved Books 11 and 12 for the letters that he wrote in his own name as praetorian prefect. Each book contains between twenty-five and fifty letters, of considerably different lengths and with content that varies widely from that of the other books. Most letters fall between 200 and 250 words, but some barely manage a terse fifty words and more ornate ones swell well beyond a thousand words. In general, Cassiodorus observed a tendency to bookend, placing letters notable for the recipient's prominence at the beginning and end of each book: diplomatic missives to emperors or western kings, addresses to the Senate, appointments of illustrious men to high honors.

Within each letter, Cassiodorus observed a particular regularity that generally conforms to the administrative style of the day. Most commence with a *proemium* that introduces the subject matter in a highly abstract form, often in terms of an ethical or legal principle, followed immediately by the particular circumstance attracting the court's attention (for example, a complaint or report that had reached the king) and then a decision or command for the recipient of the letter (the *sententia*). Not infrequently, letters conclude with *exempla,* or moralizing intended to elaborate on the court's decision. Topics include appointments to honorary offices in Rome and clerical positions at the palatine *scrinium* of Ravenna; conflicts and alliances with the eastern empire and other western states; taxes, the allocation of resources to the military, and the maintenance of urban infrastructure; legal decisions concerning civil disputes and criminal cases; and formal edicts addressed to urban or provincial populations. Although most letters have the formal structure of administrative writing, their level of detail varies widely. Some, such as *Variae* 5.39 (see Section 5), concerning fiscal arrangements in Spain, offer the kind of dense detail expected of a formal edict. Others, such as 3.35 to Romulus (perhaps the same Romulus Augustus who retired from the imperial throne in 476), offer only a few lines vaguely confirming the undisclosed decision of a magistrate. Still others were clearly intended to be literary works in their own right. A handful of letters in each book unfold lengthy disquisitions on encyclopedic topics (geography, nature, history, the arts and sciences), which, while providing fascinating insights into the intellectual culture of the sixth century, actually obscure the purpose of the letter.

Thus, the formal and thematic structure of the *Variae* is quite complex. It also includes two fairly elaborate prefaces (not in the current translation) at the beginnings of Books 1 and 11, both sophisticated literary compositions. The first explains that Cassiodorus accepted the task of compiling the *Variae* at the request of colleagues, "so that the coming generation might esteem both the disinterested deeds of a clear conscience and the burden of my duties, which I had endured for the sake of common advantage." It then elaborates a staged exchange between the author and his interlocutors. Cassiodorus initially declined the request because the daily circumstances of public service had not allowed him to exercise the kind of style that would boost his reputation. His colleagues protested, citing the trust that Gothic kings had placed in him, the prestige of his office of praetorian prefect, and the enhanced value of letters written under genuine, as opposed to rehearsed, circumstances: "it will happen that those who are situated in more tranquil circumstances will more happily obtain the habit that you practiced while tossed about amid the dangers of various altercations." Additionally, this preface claims that these colleagues reasoned that Cassiodorus's letters would preserve a record of the moral character with which he and those appointed by him had served Gothic kings and, furthermore, that he should not fear censure from an audience that so approved his history of the Goths. Cassiodorus yielded, out of affection for his associates, but advised others not to model their efforts on his own hurried writing. Hence, the preface explains, his twelve books represented a more polished version, titled *Variae* as a token of the variety of materials contained within. The first preface then ends with a discussion of the ancient precepts of literary style and their relation, in general terms, to the topics discussed in the collection. The second preface, introducing Books 11 and 12, opens with the curious observation that a preface often allows an author to anticipate the objections of an audience. Cassiodorus then picks up the main theme of the first preface: the censure or approval that his style of writing might garner from different audiences. This preface, like the first, ends with a discussion of precepts of style, this time related to Cicero's recommendation to improve composition with diverse reading. Both prefaces end with Cassiodorus excusing himself for having written at unseemly length and inviting readers to judge the collection's merits for themselves.

In addition to their relative novelty among epistolary collections, the two prefaces are remarkable in letting Cassiodorus use his own voice. In a collection where the majority of letters are written in the names of various Gothic rulers, the prefaces signal to the audience that Cassiodorus's role went beyond merely collecting and compiling state documents. The topic of literary style, addressed in both prefaces, is particularly suited to anchoring Cassiodorus's authorship of the letters. Treatments of rhetoric had for centuries viewed style as an index of interior character. As Cassiodorus's interlocutors in the first preface reminded him, "it is scarcely possible that speech is found inconsistent with character," and, more pointedly, the letters contain "the image of your mind." Similarly, the preface to Book 11 draws explicit attention to the authorship of letters that Cassiodorus wrote in his capacity as praetorian prefect, "so that I, who have acted as the royal spokesman in ten books, should not be considered unknown for my own role." It is also noteworthy that the two prefaces mirror each other in both function and themes, despite the fact that they introduce letters written under the cover of different names. Both express concern about the collection's style of writing, its reception by different audiences, how it represents the moral integrity of persons involved in the Gothic government, and the extent to which its potential repudiation shaped Cassiodorus's presentation of its letters. Literary presentation and historical reality are carefully balanced in these prefaces, as befits a collection with the primary purpose of portraying ethical virtue as the active agency in government. As Cassiodorus noted, he wanted to portray the merits of those in state service "in some measure with the color of history."

The art of depiction in the *Variae* is also present in the encyclopedic knowledge that forms one of its major themes. Cassiodorus placed letters representing aspects of this learning in each book: histories of different liberal arts disciplines, explanations of geography and natural history, and discussions of the importance of various arts and sciences. Cassiodorus's strategy of selectively scattering these digressions throughout the collection conforms to an established discursive mode, part of a coherent intellectual tradition, for representing universal knowledge. Importantly, such representations in the wider literary tradition were often tied to moral, and therefore ideological, depictions of the world. The *Variae* participate in this tradition to present the government of Italy as "enlightened" and informed by universal ethics. Each of its digressions unfolds a topic from the encyclopedic tradition to justify the government's actions or decision in a particular case. Especially prominent are the themes of nature and antiquity, which Cassiodorus wove into a network of legal, governmental, and philosophical ideals based on the legitimating forces of natural order and tradition. Thus, he paints landscapes of local geographies to explain the fiscal capacities of particular regions; the flocking habit of birds sets the example for civil order in Italian towns, the constancy of sea snails demands the regular production of the dye used to make imperial purple, and the regularity of the Nile provides for the mirrored regularity of court documents produced on papyrus; the perfection of mathematics demands precision in the payment of soldiers, and the long history of land surveying anticipates the preservation of property rights. Many of these excursuses are performances of a reverence of antiquity, not only discussing the age of, but also referring to the venerable authorities on, the topic at hand.

The sheer variety of the collection allowed Cassiodorus to interlace the daily concerns and functions of the state with sometimes passing, sometimes profound meditations on virtues, ethics, the balance of nature, and the inheritance of the past. The connection between the *Variae* and the *De anima* puts the philosophical basis of this matrix of concepts into high relief. The *Variae*'s second preface explains that Cassiodorus's colleagues compelled him to embark upon another project after completing the letter collection. This new project, the *De anima,* would offer speculation on the substance and capacities of the human soul, particularly as the instrument which allowed Cassiodorus to declaim so much in the *Variae*. The introduction of the *De anima* reiterates the completion of the *Variae* and makes it clear that the topics apprehended by the soul that so interested Cassiodorus's interlocutors were the same as those found in the digressions of the letter collection—that is, the encyclopedic topics, including natural history, which the *Variae* mobilize so prominently to represent a government that follows the principles of natural law. According to the *De anima,* which Cassiodorus appended to the *Variae,* only a soul of good moral conscience was capable of the kind of perception that would reveal the secrets of nature and allow an individual to lead a truly ethical life. Thus, this work reinforces the notion that Cassiodorus and his colleagues had acted with moral character in supporting the Amal government of Italy.

The *Variae's* literary nature runs much deeper than the mere adoption of a particular style of exposition. Studies have located the collection within a tradition of late-antique administrative writing, at least at the levels of terminology, sentence structure, and legal style. Nonetheless, it also represents something entirely novel: Cassiodorus was the first to combine the an epistolary collection with the administrative style of the late-antique chancery and the longer tradition of encyclopedic exposition. The *Variae's* differences from other epistolary collections are apparent enough: two elaborate prefaces, supposedly official documents as opposed to personal letters, the first body of *formulae* in antiquity, and the appendage of a treatise on the soul, which acts as a philosophical underpinning for material embedded in the letters. Similarly, the encyclopedic interest present in the *Variae,* although visible to less-pronounced degrees in other epistolary collections, is comparatively absent from any tradition of administrative writing. Some pretense to enlightened learning may be found in the *Novellae* that serve as later additions to the *Theodosian Code* and in Justinian's *Novellae,* but nothing on the scale of the *Variae's* topical treatments, such as would warrant calling encyclopedism a habit of administrative writing. Indeed, far from it: the *Theodosian Code* and various successors produced in the West clearly privilege a more restrained and direct style of exposition. Similarly, other examples of official composition from the sixth century (e.g., the *Edict of Theoderic,* the *Collectio Avellana,* and the *Epistolae Austrasicae*) lack the *Variae's* idiosyncratic features, which represent, as we have seen, something unique to Cassiodorus's authorial aims.

A NOTE ON THE PRESENT TRANSLATION

The *Variae* are crucial to understanding Ostrogothic Italy and its distinctiveness from other regions of the sixth-century Mediterranean;

nonetheless, previous English translations have offered limited utility. The first, by Thomas Hodgkin (*Letters of Cassiodorus*, 1886), was doubtless a brave work, but it provides only a paraphrase of the complete collection, fails to reproduce the style of the *Variae*, and even omits much material that he deemed unnecessary to a student of sixth-century Italy. By contrast, the recent translation by S. J. B. Barnish, for the *Translated Texts for Historians* series (*Cassiodorus: Variae*, 1992), offers a masterful rendering of the spirit and letter of Cassiodorus's collection, but with the limitation of including only 110 letters. A selection of the *Variae* naturally prevents the entire collection from being read as Cassiodorus intended, from start to finish, negating some of the purposeful connections between individual letters and rendering impossible an understanding of the overall structure. Similarly, although many of the letters in Barnish's translation are duly famous (e.g., those to Boethius), much that is important to legal, religious, economic, literary, and cultural historians did not find a place in his version. The current volume is also a partial selection, but it has been organized into the kinds of thematic groupings that complement modern course study of late antiquity and the early Middle Ages (for a full translation by this author, see *The Variae: The Complete Translation* [University of California Press, 2019]). Students of this period will find sixth-century examples of such topics as political culture, law, gender, and economy, useful artifacts of comparison for understanding either the end of late antiquity or the beginning of the early Middle Ages.

Cassiodorus's style is both literary and bureaucratic. It is arguably totally unto itself: partly a construct of learned reading meant to resonate with a kind of received classicism, partly a construct of a world of legal and administrative language that had to be rendered understandable to the collection's wide intended audience. Cassiodorus thus wrote within two distinctive received traditions. Late-antique bureaucratic style, on the one hand, ensured consistency of meaning by preserving mainly legal habits of expression. On the other hand, literary correspondence was often purposefully ambiguous, in order to invite the reader's exploration of a range of interpretations. As an author, Cassiodorus had at his disposal exemplars of Latin that ranged, on the literary side, from the classical golden age of Cicero to the late silver age of Tacitus and, on the legal side, from third-century jurists to Theodosian and Justinianic *Novellae* of the fifth and sixth centuries. And while he did classicize by drawing from authors who were ancient by his day, he was also embedded in the contemporary professionalized use of Latin by sixth-century civil servants. Thus, translating his late-classical Latin into English requires sensitivity to several registers of meaning (classical literary and sixth-century bureaucratic). Although his Latin may appear idiosyncratic, it is important to note that, for Cassiodorus, all Latin usages, whether ancient or contemporary, probably collapsed into the great fecundity of the *lingua Latina* that he had inherited and that he continued to modify. A simple tally of the incidences in which Alexander Souter's *A Glossary of Later Latin to 600 A.D.* relies exclusively on examples from the *Variae* is a good indication of the extent to which the text represents a unique development. Although Cassiodorus had a propensity for contemporary usages, there are notable cases where he inclined to the classical sense, such as *debitor* as "one obliged to an oath" (as opposed to the postclassical sense of "sinner") and *pietas* as "familial obligation" (as opposed to the later "piety"). Additionally, his Latin achieves what may be thought of as syntactical irregularities through the inclusion of *clausulae,* rhythmic ends to phrases, which was not standard in late-antique administrative writing.

The present translation renders Cassiodorus's text word for word, as closely as possible, according to the meaning best suited to a given Latin passage. In most cases, care has been taken to preserve his sometimes baroque syntactical structures, to convey something of the voice and assumed grandeur of administrative writing of the period. At the same time, certain verbal constructions for which Cassiodorus had a penchant, such as the future perfect and perfect infinitive, have been translated into more readily legible English usages. Conversely, where an English equivalent of specific words—such as *imperator, princeps,* and *comitatus*—would be unsatisfactory, the Latin is retained (for which, consult the Glossary). Finally, Cassiodorus at times uses the demonstratives *ille* and *illa* to substitute for specific information, such as the names of the envoys who would have delivered a letter, the names of properties, or indiction (tax cycle) years; the current translation replaces these place holders with "x" or "x and y." The titles of certain offices and ranks have also been left in Latin where attempting to find an English equivalent would only cause confusion for students (for which, again consult the Glossary).

The dates assigned to individual letters, which are often ranges of years, are based on the reign of the ruler in whose name the letter was written, biographical information known from external sources about the recipient or other mentioned individuals, and rare references to specific events or indiction years. Indictions occurred in a repeating fifteen-year cycle, commencing on September 1 and ending on August 31, thus dividing the Common Era year. Where indiction years are mentioned, it must often be assumed that the letter concerns actions to be taken in preparation for them, usually in the weeks or even months immediately preceding their commencement. Modern place names have been given wherever possible.

The letters have been translated from the volume produced by Theodor Mommsen, the great editor of late-antique texts, for the *Auctores Antiquissimi* series of the *Monumenta Germaniae Historica* (*MGH*) in 1894 (now accessible online, at www.dmgh.de). This has proven to be the most durable and frequently consulted Latin edition of the text. Åke Fridh's edition for the *Corpus Christianorum Series Latina* (1973) offers several lexical emendations and has been consulted throughout the translation, but I have preferred Mommsen's text for the simple reason that scholars and students will find it easier to consult his edition: it was reprinted by *MGH* in 1980 and is generally more available than Fridh's in academic libraries.

CHRONOLOGY OF KEY EVENTS

425–55	Reign of Valentinian III as emperor in the west
	Cassiodorus's grandfather appointed *tribunus et notarius,* leads embassy to Attila
453	Death of Attila
454	Defeat of Hunnic confederation at Nedao
	Theoderic born in Pannonia
473	Accession of Theoderic as king of federated Goths in Pannonia
476	Deposition of Romulus Augustus as western emperor
	Odoacer becomes king in Italy
	Vandals cede Sicily to Odoacer
	Cassiodorus's father named count of the sacred largesse (office held until 490)

Cassiodorus likely publishes his *Chronica* and begins work on the lost *Gothic History*

523 Hilderic's accession as Vandal king and rejection of alliance with Theoderic

Boethius deposed as master of offices; Cassiodorus assumes role (until 528)

524 Execution of Boethius for treason

525 Pope John I embassy to Constantinople for Theoderic

526 Death of Theoderic and accession of Athalaric under regency of Amalasuntha

527 Accession of Justinian as eastern emperor after death of Justin

533 Belisarius commences the campaign in Vandalic North Africa

Cassiodorus appointed praetorian prefect by Amalasuntha

534 Final annexation of the kingdom of Burgundians by the Franks

Carthage captured and end of Vandal rule in North Africa

Death of Athalaric and accession of Theodahad as Amalasuntha's colleague

535 Assassination of Amalasuntha by Theodahad

Belisarius crosses to Sicily, beginning the Gothic War

Unknown volcanic eruption disrupts agriculture in Italy and much of the Mediterranean

536 Theodahad sends Pope Agapetus as envoy to Constantinople

Belisarius captures Naples

Theodahad assassinated and accession of Witigis as king of Goths in Italy

Witigis marries Matasuntha (daughter of Amalasuntha), for which Cassiodorus performs a panegyric

Belisarius enters Rome

537 Witigis lays siege to Rome for a full year (until March 538)

Latest datable letter in the *Variae*

540 Ravenna captured by Belisarius and Gothic court sent to Constantinople

Cassiodorus in Constantinople

Cassiodorus composes the *De anima* and *Expositio Psalmorum* sometime after 540

541	Accession of Gothic King Totila extends war in Italy
	Arrival of the "Justinianic" plague in the Mediterranean
554	Justinian's "Pragmatic Sanction" signals the end of the Gothic War in Italy
	Cassiodorus's retirement at Vivarium in Calabria likely commences, as does his composition of the *Institutiones*
568	Invasion of Italy by Lombards
578	Cassiodorus composes *De orthographia* in his ninety-third year
580	Probable death of Cassiodorus at ninety-five

INDICTIONAL YEARS RELATIVE TO CASSIODORUS'S TENURE IN PUBLIC OFFICES

Quaestor *(c. 507–11)*

15th Indiction	September 1, 506–August 31, 507
1st Indiction	507–8
2nd Indiction	508–9
3rd Indiction	509–10
4th Indiction	510–11
5th Indiction	511–12

Master of Offices (c. 523–28)

1st Indiction	September 1, 522–August 31, 523
2nd Indiction	523–24
3rd Indiction	524–25
4th Indiction	525–26
5th Indiction	526–27
6th Indiction	527–28
7th Indiction	528–29

Praetorian Prefect (c. 533–40)

| 11th Indiction | September 1, 532–August 31, 533 |
| 12th Indiction | 533–34 |

Sixth-Century Italy in a Wider World

Diplomatic Letters from the Ostrogothic Court to the Eastern Imperial and Western "Barbarian" Courts

The dismemberment of a coherent provincial system in the western Mediterranean during the fifth century altered the flow and nature of political communication in the former Roman world. By the beginning of the sixth century, where a network of prefectures and provinces had previously reported to a central imperial court in Italy, now the mosaic of successor states in Gaul, Spain, North Africa, and Italy often engaged in competitive dialogue. As is evident in the *Variae*, diplomatic communication aimed to create stability in a regionalized landscape of newly emerging ruling dynasties, and although the eastern empire maintained its preeminence as a potential foreign partner, other powers (including those beyond the former Roman world) were increasingly important. The *Variae* present a view of the Ostrogothic court in Italy as the center of a still viable network inherited from the Roman Empire—doubtless to better portray the grandeur of the Amals as the stewards of the continuing Roman Empire.

LETTER 1.1 (C. 508)

Theoderic had been sent to Italy by the eastern emperor Zeno in 488, but tension and conflict defined his relationship with Zeno's successor, Anastasius. Here, Theoderic greets Anastasius with a request for peace. Mention of previous hostilities, perhaps a reference to the Amal annexation of Sirmium in Pannonia (504–5) and eastern reprisals along the Italian coast, provides a context for the elaboration of a political ideal envisioning the partnership of two Roman republics, eastern and western.

King Theoderic to Emperor Anastasius

1. It is fitting for us, most clement emperor, to seek peace, we who are known to have no reason for wrath: anytime someone is perceived to be ill-equipped for just things, that man is already considered at fault. Indeed, tranquility ought to be desired in every kingdom, where both the people profit and the weal of nations is preserved. For peace **is** the graceful mother of good arts: she increases resources, multiplying humanity in renewed generations, and she cultivates proper habits. Even one who is considered ignorant of such great matters knows at least to pursue peace. **2.** And therefore, most dutiful of *Principes,* it is becoming to your power and dignity that we ought to strive for harmony with you, the means by which we have thus far increased in love. For you are the most sublime dignity of every kingdom, you the beneficent defender of the whole world, whom other rulers rightly admire, since they recognize something special to dwell in you. We especially know this, who by divine providence have learned in your republic by what manner we are able to govern Romans equitably.[1] **3.** Our government is an imitation of yours, the exemplary form of the only good *imperium* set on display: however much we follow you, so much do we surpass other nations. Often you have encouraged me that I esteem the Senate, that I embrace gladly the laws of *Principes,* so that I might unite all parts of Italy. In what way would you be able to separate from imperial peace one whom you have not allowed to disagree with your own habits? Additionally, there is affection for the city of Rome which must be respected, from which those people who have conjoined themselves in the solidarity of its name cannot be separated. **4.** Consequently, we have determined that x and y must be appointed to your most sublime piety in the capacity of envoys, so that the integrity of peace, which is known to have been spoiled by causes now becoming evident, may endure thereafter firmly restored

1. Theoderic had been a political hostage at the court of Emperor Leo in Constantinople, subsequently being elevated to imperial dignities by Emperor Zeno.

with grounds for dispute erased. For we do not believe you will suffer any discord to persist between both republics, which had always been proclaimed to be a single entity under ancient *Principes*. **5.** It is not only fitting that these republics be conjoined one to the other with easy affection, but also it is seemly to be supported with shared strength. Let there always be one will, one mind in the Roman kingdom. And however we are able, may it attain your commendation. **6.** On which account, offering the dignity of a greeting, we ask with humble intention that you not suspend the ennobling affection of your goodwill, for which we ought to hope, even if it would not seem possible to grant to others. We have committed other matters to the bearers of this letter which must be brought to the attention of your piety by spoken word, as it could not be rendered more expansively in epistolary speech, nor would we be seen to have overlooked anything to our advantage.

LETTER 1.46 (C. 507)

Here Theoderic addresses a powerful neighboring king, Gundobad, who ruled the Burgundians and Romans settled in eastern Gaul from 473 to 516. Although Gundobad was quite familiar with Italy (he had served as the senior military commander, or *Magister Militum*, there from 472 to 473), Theoderic nonetheless attempts to use its cultural capital as leverage. Alliance with the Burgundians was essential to the security of northern Italy. This particular letter is preceded in the collection by a request to the Roman patrician Boethius to prepare clocks as gifts to the Burgundian court (see Section 12, *Variae* 1.45).

Theoderic to Gundobad, King of the Burgundians

1. Gifts that are proven entirely useful must surely be embraced, especially when what can fulfill a desire is not objectionable. For whatever price attaches to a thing, so much does the attention of the one desiring incline toward it, so that it should be fulfilled. Therefore, greeting your prudence with the usual kindness by carriers, x and y, we have determined these amusements must be dispatched—clocks with their own regulators. The one, in which human ingenuity seems to be gathered, is known to compass the extent of the entire day; the other knows the course of the sun without its presence and delimits the span of hours with drops of water. **2.** Possess in your country what you formerly have seen in Rome. It is fitting that your pleasure, which is conjoined to us also by marriage,[2] should enjoy our blessings. Let Burgundy learn under you to contemplate the most finely wrought things and to praise the inventions of the ancients. Through you, Burgundy sets aside the habit of a foreign nation, and when it reflects upon the foresight of its king it rightly yearns for the accomplishments of the wise. Let Burgundy mark off the span of the day according to its own determination; let her establish the most fitting passage of hours. **3.** A confused order of life is driven headlong, if its very divisions are not understood according to the actual nature of things. Indeed, it is the manner of beasts to feel the hours according to the hunger of their bellies and not to hold as certain what is well ordered in human practice.

LETTER 2.1 (C. 511)

This letter addresses the delicate issue of selecting a candidate for the annual consulship in Rome. By the sixth century, it had become tradition for two consuls to host annual celebrations, one in Rome and the other in Constantinople. Communications between rulers concerning consular appointments were diplomatic opportunities to negotiate other agendas. In this case, Theoderic has chosen Felix, a man from a leading Gallic family, illustrating one strategy to strengthen Amal authority in southern Gaul, which Theoderic annexed following the conflict with the Franks (507–11). Letters announcing the appointment to the candidate and to the Senate followed (*Variae* 2.2 and 2.3, not included in this volume).

King Theoderic to the Most Dutiful Emperor Anastasius

1. The custom of annual celebration reminds us to give a name to the calendar year, that adornment particular to Rome, the earthly distinction of the Senate, so that the grace of offices may continue according to the passage of years and so that the memory of the age is conse-

2. Gundobad's son Sigismund was married to Ostrogotho Areagni, Theoderic's eldest daughter.

crated by the generosity of the *Principes*. May a fortunate year take good omen from its consul,[3] and by such a name let the year named after him enter the gates of days, and let the good fortune of its beginning favor the remaining portion. **2.** For what could be better accepted by you than that Rome should gather back her own fosterlings to her bosom and that she should count the Gallic Senate among the assembly of her own venerated name? The curia knows well the distinction of Transalpine blood, which not just once has decorated its own crown with the blossom of that nobility. Among other offices, the curia knows to choose men from there as consuls. This man is a natural claimant to honors by right of antiquity, from which he is lead to the senatorial robe by a long pedigree. For who does not know Felix to be natively endowed with good qualities, a man who from the very first indications displayed that merit which is seen to hasten to the homeland of virtues?[4] Prosperity follows upon good judgment, and he increased in promotions with independence. We could not permit one to remain unglorified who has deserved to attain public office in the republic. **3.** He is plainly worthy of our generosity, who in the very flower of childhood curbed a perilous time of life with mature habits, and, because he is a man blessed with uncommon restraint, when deprived of a father he became a son to seriousness. He subjugated that cupidity so hostile to wisdom, he despised the allurements of vice, and he ground underfoot the vanities of pride. Thus with excesses overcome, he was already seen to hold the consulship with respect to his morals. **4.** Therefore, we would recompense that good moral foundation which tested probity confers and offer this candidate the curule fillets, so that we may be able to prompt the desire for excellence by rewards, since eagerness will not fail for an office which holds the most liberal reward. And therefore, you, who are delighted by blessings to both republics without preference, lend your support, attach your assent. A distinguished man who deserves to be raised to the very *fasces* is selected by the judgment of us both.

3. Here *felix annus* offers a play on "Felix," the name of the consul, after whom the year would be named.

4. *Ad patriam virtutum,* meaning Rome.

LETTER 2.41 (C. 507)

Demonstrating the familial interconnections of diplomatic partners in the post-Roman West, this letter invokes the ties of marriage that bound the Frankish and Ostrogothic kingdoms in order to make an appeal on behalf of Alamannic refugees who had fled to Italy from war in Frankish Gaul. The Frankish king Clovis defeated the Alamanni in 506, and refugees from that conflict may have sought asylum in Italy a year later.

King Theoderic to Clovis, King of the Franks

1. We take joy indeed in our splendid bond with your excellence because you have successfully roused the nation of the Franks, resting in its old age, to new battles and because you have subdued the Alamannic people, who, with their bravest cut down in heaps, have bent to your victorious right hand. But since the transgression is always seen in the authors of an execrable treachery, nor ought the fault of blameworthy leading citizens be the punishment of all, temper your intentions toward the exhausted remnant, since those whom you have seen fleeing to the protection of your parent deserve to escape by right of indulgence to us.[5] Consider these men forgiven, who have fled as fugitives to our borders. **2.** It is a memorable triumph to have belittled the bravest of the Alamanni, so much that you have witnessed him bend in supplication for the gift of life.[6] Let it suffice that their king has fallen, along with the arrogance of his nation. Let it suffice that an innumerable people has been subjugated, some by the sword, some by servitude. For when you continue to belabor the remaining people, you would not be believed to have overcome all of them. Listen to one often experienced in such cases: those wars have turned out successfully for me that achieved a moderate end. Indeed, he conquers continually who knows how to be moderate in everything, while a pleasant outcome favors those instead who do not become unyielding with excessive severity. And so, gracefully concede to our inclination what concern for family is accustomed to yield by well-known example. For thus it happens,

---

5. Theoderic was, in fact, Clovis's brother-in-law through marriage to his sister Audefleda.

6. A reference to the king of the Alamanni.

that you should be seen to give satisfaction to my requests, nor should you be overly concerned about that territory which you know pertains to us.[7] **3.** Wherefore, greeting you with respect and goodwill, as is due, we have sent to your excellence with the usual affection our legates x and y, through whom we would inquire after both the fulfillment of our requests and indication of your well-being. Indeed, we have entrusted to the bearers of this letter certain matters that have come to our attention on behalf of your advantage, which must be introduced to you by spoken word, so that, being made more cautious, you might steadily fulfill the desired victory. Indeed, your health is our glory and however much we know about your happiness, that much do we deem the kingdom of Italy to prosper. **4.** Moreover, just as you requested, we have sent a cithara player learned in his art, who should attract splendor to your power with his hands and his harmonious singing voice.[8] And therefore, we rather believe him to be pleasing to you, since you so ardently deemed he must be sent.

LETTER 3.1 (C. 507)

Theoderic initiated military action in Gaul shortly after the Frankish king Clovis defeated the Visigothic king Alaric II in 507. Book 3 of the *Variae* opens with a series of diplomatic exchanges that would have been preliminary to armed conflict. Here, a letter from Theoderic takes a paternalistic tone to restrain Alaric from involving the Visigoths in war with the Franks. Complicating matters was the fact that Theoderic was married to Audofleda, the sister of Clovis, and Alaric was married to Theodegotha, Theoderic's daughter by his first wife.

King Theoderic to Alaric, King of the Visigoths

1. Although the countless multitude of your family line grants confidence to your bravery, although you may recall that the might of Attila wavered before Visigothic strength, nonetheless, since the hearts of a fierce people have become tame in the course of long peace, beware

---

7. The phrase *ex illa parte* apparently refers to the region inside the Gothic boundary with the Franks to which the surviving Alamanni had fled.

8. This letter is preceded in the collection by a request to the Roman patrician Boethius to select a musician for the Frankish court (see Section 12, *Var.* 2.40).

sending into danger so suddenly those who have not had practice in war for such a very long time. **2.** Battle is dreadful for men if it is not frequently practiced, and unless it is adopted as a matter of habit, those entering the fray will immediately lose heart. Let it not happen that some blind indignation carry you away. Provident is the moderation that protects a people; rage, however, often precipitates recklessness; it is a practicable measure to rush to arms, then, only when justice is unable to find a place among adversaries. **3.** Therefore, restrain yourself, until we should direct our legates to the king of the Franks, so that the decisions of friends may remove your grievance. For we do not want anything to happen between two conjoined to us in marriage, whence it may be that one of you would be found weaker. The spilled blood of kinsfolk has not inflamed you, nor has an occupied province galled you grievously. Thus far, it is only a small contention of words.[9] You will settle this easily, if you do not incite your mind to arms. Although you are bound to us in kinship, we array before you distinguished nations, and justice, which the most powerful kings wield. One who perceives such things armed against him should quickly change heart. **4.** And therefore, we have decided that the aforementioned legates, x and y, must convey to you the honor of greetings. Let our admonitions influence you sufficiently through these men and let them hasten further, with our directive, to our brother Gundobad, and to the other kings as well, lest you be found laboring under the opportunity of those who malignly delight in the conflict of others. Indeed, may divine providence prevent this injustice from overcoming you. We deem your enemy to be a common threat. For that man who strives to be hostile to you will rightly endure me as an enemy.

LETTER 4.1 (C. 507–11)

This and the following letter (*Variae* 4.2, below) demonstrate a general policy of strengthening ties with peoples north of Italy. In this instance, alliance with the Thuringians was formed with a marriage between the Thuringian king and Theoderic's niece. This alliance would have

---

9. Gregory of Tours (*Decem libri historiarum* 2.37) claims that religious differences initiated the conflict (Alaric II was an Arian Christian and Clovis a Nicene Christian), but other sources (*Var.* 3.4.4, for example) suggest the influence of the eastern empire.

been pivotal to influencing Ostrogothic relations with the Franks, who neighbored Thuringian territory. Description of the union includes attention to the receipt at Theoderic's court of horses as a bride price.

King Theoderic to Hermanfrid, King of the Thuringians

1. Desiring to associate you with our family, we join you, with the blessing of divine authority, by the dear pledge of our niece,[10] so that you, who descend from royal stock, may now gleam even further with the brightness of Amal blood. We send to you the jewel of a royal home, the boon of a people, the comfort of faithful advice, a wife delightful and most pleasing, who, with you, should fittingly complete your dominion and join your nation to a sweeter manner of living. **2.** Fortunate Thuringia will have that which Italy has nourished, learned in letters, polished in behavior, charming not only in lineage, but even the extent of feminine dignity, so that your country may glitter in her very habits, no less than in its own triumphs. **3.** Therefore, greeting you with due pleasure, we confirm having received, with the arrival of your envoys, the agreed-upon gifts, indeed priceless, but according to the custom of nations, horses fitted with silver trappings, such as would befit nuptials. The breasts and legs of these horses are distinguished by appropriately rounded flesh; the ribs extend with that particular breadth; the waist is confined to a trim dimension; the head gives the impression of a doe, and they imitate the swiftness of those creatures they are seen to resemble. These creatures are mild from extremely abundant care, fleet from their great size, pleasant to look upon, and gratifying to ride. Indeed, they step with a light gait; those seated do not tire with senseless exertion; one reposes upon them rather than labors, and, having been trained with careful moderation, they know how to endure with continued agility. **4.** But you nonetheless acknowledge that this noble herd, these obedient beasts and other things that you have sent, are greatly inferior, considering that she who plentifully supplies charm to kingly power, by right, surpasses everything. Therefore, we have indeed sent what the rank of *Princeps* requires, but we have paid nothing more than what we gain by conjoining you with the distinction of such a woman. Let divine providence witness your

10. Amalaberga, Theoderic's niece by his sister Amalafrida, and the sister of Theodahad, later the third Ostrogothic king of Italy.

marriage, so that just as the cause of affection has bound us, so too may familial regard oblige our posterity.

LETTER 4.2 (C. 507–11)

Extending an alliance to the Herules, a people living north of Ostrogothic Pannonia and the Danube, this letter formalizes the relationship in terms strikingly different from those of *Variae* 4.1 (above). Rather than diplomatic marriage, it describes the bonds of martial virtue and loyalty. The Herules and other trans-Danubian peoples such as the Gepids contributed to Theoderic's campaigns in Gaul and probably also provided leverage with the eastern empire (cf. *Variae* 4.45 [not included in this volume] and 5.11 [in Section 6]).

King Theoderic to the King of the Herules

1. It is widely considered among nations to be commendable to become a son by virtue of arms, since one is not worthy of adoption unless he deserves to be considered the bravest. We are often disappointed in offspring; however, those whom judgment has brought forth are not known to be ignoble. For these men owe gratitude not to nature but only to their own merits when they become obligated to a stranger by a bond of affection. And there is such great strength in this impulse that they would prefer to die themselves before anything harsh should be inflicted upon their adopted fathers. **2.** And therefore, with this present gift, we adopt you as a son in the custom of the nations and in masculine bond,[11] so that you, who have become known for your warlike nature, are fittingly reared through arms. We therefore bestow upon you horses, swords, shields, and other gear of war; but what is in every way greater, we bestow our approval upon you. For you, who are accounted in the judgment of Theoderic, will be reckoned to be the greatest among nations. **3.** And so, take these arms for your benefit and for mine. That man who arranges to defend you the most seeks your devotion. Prove your bravery and you will not have a taxing obligation. Such a man adopts you, whose nation you otherwise would have dreaded. For the assistance of the Goths, with

11. The term *condicio* often refers to a marriage bond, hence the letter emphasizes the masculine character of the relationship with *condicio virilis*.

God's blessing, is known to the Herules. We have offered our arms to you; formerly, however, nations would only extend promises of courage to each other. **4.** Thence, greeting you with due pleasure, we entrust other matters to the native language[12] through our envoys, x and y, who may clearly explain our letters to you and may assist in strengthening that gratitude which must be spoken.

LETTER 5.1 (C. 523–26)

Like previous books in the collection, Book 5 commences with a diplomatic letter, in this case to a little-known Germanic people of northern or central Europe. The interest in a local commodity offered by the Warni (swords of native manufacture) pairs with the following letter to the Haesti (*Variae* 5.2, below). Interestingly, neither letter addresses a named individual. Both may owe to Cassiodorus's reading of Tacitus's *Germania,* which may offer the first mention of the Warni.[13]

King Theoderic to the King of the Warni

1. With the pitch-black furs and slave boys glowing with foreign fairness, your fraternity has sent us swords of iron, more precious than the cost of gold, that cleave even armor. On them, a polished brightness gleams, so that the face of the admirer reflects with true clarity; their edges taper to points so evenly that they may be reckoned not as fashioned with files, but as molded in fiery furnaces. Their mid-lengths seem to have been hollowed with a kind of elegant furrow, etched with curling patterns, where reflections of such great variety play that you would well believe clear metal has been blended with various colors. **2.** Your whetstone has carefully honed them and your finest sand has so meticulously polished them that it makes the steely light a kind of mirror for men. The sand has been bestowed by the native generosity of your country for the purpose that it would bring you special regard for this kind of work. The blades, by their very excellence, may be thought to be those of Vulcan, who was known to refine simple tools with such grace that whatever was fashioned from his hands was credited not to mortal but to divine craftsmanship. **3.** Thence, through our

---

12. The phrase *patrio sermone* seems to imply the Gothic language.
13. Tacitus, *Germania* 40, on the Varini.

envoys, x and y, who repay you the affection of an owed greeting, we declare that we have gladly accepted your arms, which have conveyed your concern for the blessings of peace. Our envoys offer a gift in exchange out of consideration for your expenses. Having arrived, may they grant as much satisfaction to you as yours were pleasing to us. Let divine providence bestow harmony, so that, achieving these things between us with goodwill, we may conjoin the wills of our peoples and, in turn, be roused to obligations of mutual advantage.

LETTER 5.2 (C. 523–26)

A curious diplomatic letter to the Haesti, a people presumably settled along the Baltic shore. Like *Variae* 5.1 (above), to the Warni, it seems indebted to Cassiodorus's reading of Tacitus, here explicitly so, and the basis of the exchange likewise appears to be a native commodity (in this case, amber).

King Theoderic to the Haesti

1. By the arrival of your legates, x and y, we have learned of your great eagerness to reach our attention, so that you, who are settled on the shores of the Ocean, have been conjoined to our intentions. Audience with them is both pleasing and quite flattering to us, in that our fame would have reached you, whom we have been unable to reach by any attempt. Enjoy the affection of one now known to you, whom unknown you sought by wandering course. For it is not an easy thing to arrange a route through so many nations. **2.** And therefore, being desirous of the amber that you have sent with carriers, we acknowledge you with affectionate greetings; your gifts have been received with a grateful disposition. And just as your report has maintained, the falling waves of the Ocean convey this lightest substance to you; but of whence it may come, which you have received in your country, offering it to all men, the bearers claim you to have no knowledge. It is read in the writing of a certain Cornelius[14] that, flowing from the sap of a tree, whence it is called *sucinum,* on the inmost islands of the Ocean, this substance gradually hardens in the heat of the sun. **3.** Indeed, it becomes a per-

14. Cornelius Tacitus, *Germania* 45, attributes the collection of amber along the seashore to the Aestii.

spired metal, with a transparent delicacy, sometimes glowing red with golden tincture, sometimes enriched with flaming brilliance, so that, by the time it has floated to the bounds of the sea, cleansed and deposited by alternating tides,[15] it is surrendered to your shores. On that account, we decided that this must be explained, lest you think that what you consider to be your secret has completely escaped our notice. Thence, seek us more often along that route that your desire has opened, since the search for riches always procures harmony among kings, who, while they are comforted by small gifts, always provide greater things in compensation. Moreover, we have committed certain matters to words for you through your envoys. These things that we have sent ought to be pleasing.

LETTER 5.43 (C. 511)

This letter provides a glimpse into the interconnection of family and diplomatic affairs in the western Mediterranean and the continued consequences of Alaric II's death in his confrontation with the Franks. Because Gesalic, Alaric's eldest son, was not related to Theoderic, as his younger brother was, he proved unsuitable to Ostrogothic interests as a prospective ruler of the Visigoths. The assistance that Gesalic received from the Vandal king Thrasamund threatened to destabilize the relations between North Africa and Italy that had been tentatively secured by the marriage of Theoderic's sister (Amalafrida) to Thrasamund.

King Theoderic to Thrasamund, King of the Vandals

1. Although, with God's guidance, we have given both our daughters and granddaughters in marriage, as they are sought out by diverse kings for the sake of confirming peace, we have nonetheless reckoned to confer nothing upon any other man equal to our sister, that unprecedented distinction of the Amal family, whom we have made your wife. A woman equal to your wisdom, who not only deserves respect from the kingdom, but is also wondrous in her advice. 2. But I am dumbfounded that you have become bound by these favors to Gesalic,

---

15. The *aestu* of *aestu alternante purata* refers to both the heat of the amber's appearance and the tumult of its supposed conveyance on the Ocean.

a man who, even while he was associated with us and supported by us, was hostile to us. This man has thus been taken into your protection, so that, while he had come to you deprived of property and destitute of means, he suddenly appeared having been sent to foreign nations and endowed with a wealth of money. And while this, with God's blessing, is able to cause no harm, nonetheless, it has uncovered the nature of your intentions. **3.** What could laws expect of strangers, if kinship merits this? For if he was received in your kingdom for the sake of pity, he ought to have been held there. If he had been expelled by us, it was not fitting that he should be sent with riches to foreign nations, which would unreservedly wage battle against us, lest they gain your hostility. Where is your habit, nourished with such great reading, of teaching others good character? If you had wanted to accomplish this with our sister, she certainly could not have assisted you, since she would neither permit her brother to be harmed, nor cause her husband to be discovered in such affairs. **4.** And therefore, we send duly respectable salutations through our envoys, x and y, so that your deliberation may study this injustice, lest the disposition of your kinsman, agitated for obvious reasons, be compelled to attempt something that would see peace destroyed. Indeed, that insult wounds grievously which happens unexpectedly and if deceit should appear there where assistance was expected. We have committed to the bearers of these letters further things that truly must be imparted to you by spoken word, so that considering everything, your foresight may reckon whatever would be fitting to happen in such circumstances, since it is not lightly that wise men sin against the foundations of peace.

LETTER 8.1 (C. 526)

The death of Theoderic in August 526 found Cassiodorus serving in the Amal court as master of offices. In that capacity he wrote a series of letters, beginning with the present address to the eastern emperor Justin, announcing the elevation of Athalaric, Theoderic's grandson, as ruler of Italy and the western provinces under Ostrogothic control.

King Athalaric to Emperor Justin

1. I would be justly reproved, most clement of *Principes,* if without enthusiasm I should ask for your approval, which it happens my kin sought so ardently;[16] in what sense would I be a suitable heir if I should be found unequal to my predecessors in such a matter of reputation? The purple rank of my forebears ennobles, and thus the royal seat elevates, only to the extent that your open affection celebrates us. For if we feel this has been withheld from us in no way, we shall believe everything in our kingdom is in perfect harmony. **2.** But as it concerns the reputation of your duty to cherish those whose fathers you have loved— for nobody is believed to have devoted pure kindness to the elders of a family unless he is shown to regard the offspring as his own—let animosity be buried with the deceased. Let wrath perish with the impudent. Friendship should not die with the dearly beloved, but who is found innocent in the quarrels of ruling must be treated more favorably. Consider what a successor to good men should deserve from you. **3.** In your city, you elevated our grandfather to the lofty curule seat; in Italy, you decorated my father with palmate distinction.[17] Through a desire for concord, one who was almost equal to you in years was also made your son-in-arms.[18] This honor, which you bestowed upon our elders, you would give more fittingly to a youth. Your affection should transfer the parental role now, for by the laws of nature the offspring of your son should not be considered unrelated to you. **4.** And therefore, I seek peace, not as a distant relation, but as nearest kin, since you showed me the favor of a grandson then, when you bestowed the joy of adoption on my father. We have arrived at a royal inheritance; let us also be admitted into your heart. To have the regard of such a great ruler is more important to me than ruling. And so, let our commencement deserve to have the support of an elderly *Princeps;* let the tutelage of friendship attend my youth, and we who are propped by such protection will not be totally bereft of family. **5.** Let our kingdom be bound to you by cords of gratitude. You will rule more in a realm where you

16. This may be said of *Var.* 1.1, to Anastasius, but no communication between Theoderic and Justin survives; if Justin began imperial service among the palace guard under Emperor Zeno around 470, he may have known Theoderic, who was a diplomatic hostage at Zeno's court until approximately 472.

17. This is not precisely true: Theoderic was appointed consul in the east by Zeno in 484, although Justin did appoint Athalaric's father, Eutharic, to the consulship in 519.

18. Cassiodorus may be conflating the facts here: Theoderic was nearly as old as Justin, but had been formerly adopted in arms by Zeno; Eutharic, whom Justin did adopt in arms, was thirty years junior to the emperor.

order all things with affection. Therefore, we have determined that our legates, x and y, must be sent to your serenity, so that you may grant us your friendship in these arrangements, and by those conditions which your celebrated predecessors are known to have had with our lord grandfather of divine memory. Perhaps I merit something even more from sincerity, because my age is not experienced and my origin is already proven not to be foreign. We have, in fact, entrusted certain matters to the above-mentioned legates that must be revealed verbally to your most serene hearing. May you cause these matters to reach completion after the habit of your clemency.

LETTER 9.1 (C. 526)

In 523, the Vandal king Thrasamund died and was succeeded by Hilderic. Amalafrida, Thrasamund's wife and Theoderic's sister, led a revolt against Hilderic's rise to power. Her party was defeated and she subsequently died in prison, hence breaking the alliance between Vandals and Ostrogoths. Her death may have coincided with Athalaric's accession in Italy (526), although this letter may simply have served to apprise Hilderic's court of the new Ostrogothic king's position on the earlier death of his great-aunt.

King Athalaric to Hilderic, King of the Vandals

1. We are constrained by a grievously bitter lot, that we, who are known to value tokens of devotion, would now attribute the bitterest circumstance to those whom we had formerly called sweet kin. For who does not know that Amalafrida of divine memory, that rare grace of our family, came to a violent fall from splendor by you, and that one whom you formerly held as a matron you could not even allow to live a private life? If this woman seemed to be at odds with the dignified comportment of a kinswoman, a respectable man ought to have returned to us the woman whom he had sought with great entreaties.[19] 2. It is a kind of parricide that after the king's death you would involve his wife, a kinswoman to you, in unmentionable intrigues. How could a woman deprived of her own husband have merited such a great evil? If the succession of another had been required, how could a woman possibly

19. Hilderic had not sought Amalafrida, but rather the Vandal court had.

be involved in this course of action? Rather, she ought to be considered as the mother who transferred the kingdom to you. For this, too, would have been advantageous to your nobility, if you would have retained within the line of the Hasdings the purple dignity of Amal blood.[20] Our Goths more correctly understand this to be an insult against them. For one who precipitates the murder of a foreign matron is seen to have wholly despised the honor of her family, when no man would suppose to be unavoidable what he knows must be avoided. **3.** And therefore, admonished by moral reason, for now, we await redress from your words through our legates, x and y, anticipating what kind of excuse may be brought to bear for so great a calamity. For no matter what kind of scandal had risen against a woman of such standing, it ought to be intimated to us, so that how she had involved herself in the worst kind of affairs should pass to our judgment. It may be that her death was fashioned from natural causes. We do not say it was impossible, we do not claim that she was young; relate it to x and y, through whom the fact of the matter ought to come to light. Let final judgment over the entire affair be theirs, without war, without slaughter, whether it would satisfy us or render you hated. **4.** If you believe this should be disregarded, or if you do not prepare a reasonable response, being injured, we, who were not held by a bond of alliance, are absolved of the condition of temporary peace. However artfully it was committed, the crime will be punished by supernal majesty, which calls upon the impious slaughter of fraternal blood to reveal itself.[21]

LETTER 10.1 (C. 534)

King Athalaric died in 534, leaving his mother, Amalasuntha, as the closest direct link to the line of Theoderic. In order to secure her position, Amalasuntha appointed her cousin Theodahad as her ruling colleague. This letter announces his elevation to the eastern emperor. In comparison to other letters to emperors, this is a curious specimen, both for its brevity concerning such a sensitive topic and because it never actually names Theodahad.

20. The Hasdings were the line of Vandal royalty, as the Amals were of Ostrogothic royalty.

21. Perhaps a reference to the death of Thrasamund?

Queen Amalasuntha to Emperor Justinian

1. Until now, we have delayed relating to you, most clement *Princeps,* the death of our son of glorious memory, lest we wound the sensitivity of one who loves him through the grief of those bearing the news; but now, by the blessing of God, who is accustomed to commute harsh accidents into something prosperous, we have decided to bring better news to your attention, concerning which you will be able to rejoice with us in shared celebration. **2.** We have brought to the throne a man bound to us in fraternal relation, who with the strength of shared counsel would bear the royal office with us, so that he should shine in the purple grace of his own ancestors and so that the comfort of a wise man would support our resolve. Lend your assent now to these felicitous designs, so that, just as we eagerly desire all things to be prosperous in your piety's *imperium,* thus would we wholly appreciate your benevolence to be well-disposed to us. And so with this announcement made, which we believe to be desirable for you for the sake of natural courtesy, we furthermore add the service of a most pleasing legate, so that you would advance the peace, which always occupies your mind and which you already retain for me especially, to be confirmed by the addition to my household. For given that the concord of *Principes* would always be preferred, harmony with you ennobles me absolutely, when a man committed to your glory without reservation is elevated so greatly.[22] **3.** But since the brevity of a letter would fail to explain everything sufficiently, we have entrusted those things that must be related to you verbally to our legate, bearing duly reverent greetings, which you should receive in the accustomed manner of your serenity, so that it would be possible to clearly recognize everything that we have shown to be justly promised to us from your generosity. For it is doubtless appropriate for you to agree, when we have even sent on this errand those whom you have approved, for the purpose of gaining your support for the kind of matters we know you desire.[23]

22. Theodahad.

23. Justinian was apparently familiar with the legates whom Amalasuntha sent to Constantinople.

LETTER 10.22 (C. 535)

A continuation of attempts to reach a diplomatic solution to the Gothic War with the eastern emperor, this letter has an urgent tone suggesting that the conflict had begun in Italy.

King Theodahad to Emperor Justinian

1. Our legate and that most learned man Peter, whom your piety recently dispatched to us, both remind you, wisest of *Principes,* with what zeal we desire concord with your august serenity. And now we believe the same attempt must be renewed again through that most blessed man x, so that you would judge as true and good-natured what you recognize has been sought repeatedly. Indeed, we, who have no cause for conflict, seek peace with all sincerity. Therefore, let this great thing come to us, so arranged, so glorious, that we may seem justified in seeking it with such great entreaties. But it would be a failure if what has been conjoined on our behalf should weigh heavily. **2.** Act, rather, that it would be agreeable to us. One who must settle a cause according to reason is not able to show preference for his own advantage; it is to his greater glory to take responsibility for future affairs. Consider too, learned *Princeps,* and recall from the historical testimonials of your books, how much your predecessors strove to depart from their own lawful advantage, so that they could create alliances with our ancestors. Estimate with what gratitude the concessions which were customarily demanded ought to be received. We, who depend upon the truth, do not speak arrogantly. What we strive to demonstrate profits your glory instead, when those who recognize that they are more fortunate than their forebears now seek your favor in addition. Let those whom you formerly bound to yourself for the sake of generosity be tied to your heart in voluntary friendship; let those blessings, which you surpass with abundant kindness and flowing rewards, not be credited only to former times. **3.** And therefore, extending the honor of greeting, we have caused the venerable x, distinguished by priesthood and conspicuous for the fame of his learning, to bear the desires of our embassy to your piety. For trusting in divine virtue, that he will please you abundantly with his merits and obtain the object of an honest petition, we believe that we ought to receive him quickly with the object of these exchanges attained. But since it is not possible to include everything in epistolary correspondence, we have entrusted certain matters to him which must be disclosed to your sacred attention by mouth, lest the extended reading of documents be distasteful to you.

LETTER 10.23 (C. 535)

This letter has a tone that is decidedly more optimistic than those of previous letters to the eastern court, although it is not clear what may have transpired that could have emboldened Theodahad's assessment of the state of affairs. Nonetheless, it seems apparent that the ratification of a treaty was entrusted to the intervention of the empress, who was expected to advocate for terms that would not be overly harsh.

King Theodahad to Empress Theodora

1. Having received your most eloquent legate Peter and, what is more honorable than any distinctions, complying with your requests, those things desired by us have shone like monuments to your august favor, so that we learn through him that what has occurred in this republic is acceptable to you. You have shown that you esteem whatever obviously pertains to justice, when the desired concord, having been cleansed of any suspicion through divine providence, is able to endure. It is rather now that a firm oath and prayed-for harmony may conjoin our kingdoms. 2. And therefore, we believed our legate, the venerable x, must be sent in particular to you, for he is truly worthy of your audience, so that, by your careful attention, the grace of peace should be confirmed by your most serene husband, to the extent that the public may clearly know that we have duly attained the blessing of an alliance through the great bond of love. 3. And since nothing begun well ought to be interrupted by mishap, if there is anything so harsh that should not be imposed upon us, let it be mitigated by the moderation of your wisdom, so that we may increase with perpetual zeal the affection that we have begun to hold for your kingdom. 4. Therefore, erect the strength of your wisdom and claim this as your particular laurel of peace, so that, just as the glorious fame of a forgiving emperor is proclaimed on the battlefield, thus your reputation will be praised for the practice of peace, to the admiration of all. Let the bearer of these

letters whom I have sent have audience with you regularly and in private, to the extent that one who is clearly sent on the presumption of favor should be able to attain immediate effect. For we hope for things that are just, not onerous, although we know that nothing we entrust to such a glorious patron may seem impossible.

Section II

The Senate in Public Life and Public Office

Letters to the Senate, Letters to Individual Senators, and Letters Announcing the Appointment of Senators to Office

By the sixth century, the Senate at Rome had a storied history of participation in the growth and decline of the Roman Empire that was more than twelve centuries long. Under the Amals of the Ostrogothic kingdom, the Senate (consisting primarily of *illustres,* drawn from the hereditary ranks of *clarissimi* and *spectabiles*) still presided over civil and legal affairs at Rome. Although its responsibilities were greatly reduced from earlier imperial days, it maintained immense political capital, which the Amal rulers prized. Senators from prominent families such as the Symmachi and the Anicii had familial and political connections with the governing circles of the eastern empire, especially at Constantinople. Additionally, the Senate was crucial to maintaining relations with the Church of Rome under the pope, itself a conduit to diplomatic communication with the wider Mediterranean world. Furthermore, the educated sons of senatorial families such as the Decii and Cassiodori frequently served as a talent pool for the upper tiers of state service under the Amals. For all of the above reasons, relations between the Amal court and the Senate were carefully choreographed to demonstrate deference to a tradition of senatorial distinction. This facade shattered during the Gothic War, when prominent senators allied with Justinian, and although he eventually succeeded in extinguishing Gothic rule in Italy, the Senate as a functioning body at Rome never recovered.

THE SENATE IN PUBLIC LIFE AND PUBLIC OFFICE   45

LETTER 1.3 (C. 507)

The first of many elaborate letters of appointment, this one advances Cassiodorus's father to the rank of patrician, describing his merits and previous services to the state, especially as praetorian prefect. This letter should be considered a companion to *Variae* 1.4 (see below), which announces the senior Cassiodorus's prestigious elevation to the Senate at Rome.

King Theoderic to Cassiodorus, Illustris *and Patrician*

1. Although what is laudable by nature enjoys its own particular nobility, lest the rewards of outstanding character be wanting, when it begets distinction for the soul—for indeed, everything good is conjoined to its own benefits, nor is it possible for virtue to be acknowledged which is detached from its reward—nonetheless, the summit of our judgment brings eminence, since he who is promoted by us is deemed abundant in outstanding merits. **2.** For if one whom a just man would appoint must be regarded as fair, if one whom the temperate man would adopt must be regarded as endowed with moderation, then clearly the one who earns the opinion of the judge of all virtues is capable of every merit. For what is wanted more than to have found a witness to praises where partiality cannot be suspected? Indeed, the decision of the king obtains its judgment by virtue of deeds alone, nor does the mind of the ruler deign to be flattered by the influence of gifts. **3.** Certainly, what brought you to my attention should be recollected, so that you might enjoy the fruit of your labor, when you know each merit to have pleasingly ingrained itself in my mind. Already devoted at the very first of my *imperium,* when the inclination of the provinces wavered with the tide of events and novelty itself permitted an untried ruler to be disregarded, you diverted the minds of mistrustful Sicilians from a hasty resistance, directing them away from fault, and removing from us the necessity of punishment. **4.** Edifying persuasion accomplished what impetuous severity would have been able to correct. You gained for a province reprieve from a condemnation that it did not deserve to experience by reason of its devotion. There, protecting civil law in military dress, uncorrupted as a judge you weighed private and public interest, and while neglecting your own property and avoiding the stain of personal profit, you restored the wealth of high character. You denied an entrance to accusers and a place for detractors. And there, where it is hardly the custom for silent forbearance to be practiced, the voices of praise took up arms for you. For we know, from the testimony of Tullius,[1] how the nature of Sicilians is suited to quarrels, so that from habitual practice they would accuse their governors even on mere suspicion. **5.** Not for the extent of your praises did I grant the privilege of governing Bruttium and Lucania,[2] but lest the fortune of your native country alone not know that good which a foreign province had earned. But you, rendering your accustomed devotion, have placed us under obligation by affectionate service, where we had thought to discharge all obligation to you; hence, you have increased the debt where we had thought it to be absolved. You have acted, in every matter, the part of the judge exempt from error, neither oppressing any man out of jealousy, nor elevating another in gratitude for blandishments. Since this conduct would be difficult anywhere, it becomes glorious in one's own country, where it is the case that either relations call out for favors or long-standing animosities provoke hatred. **6.** It therefore pleases us to revisit the deeds of your prefecture. A most celebrated blessing to all Italy, you demonstrated, by accomplishing matters with every provident arrangement, how easy it could be to pay taxes under a magistrate of integrity. No man reluctantly proffers what is distributed with equity, since nothing contributed according to proper arrangements is considered a loss. **7.** Enjoy now your blessings and receive multiplied those benefits which you despised out of concern for public regard. For this is a glorious model of life, for rulers to be witnesses and for citizens to bear praise. **8.** Therefore, urged on by such abundant praise, we confer upon you in just remuneration the distinction of the patriciate, so that what is payment to others for you would be the return of good deeds. Congratulations, honored man, for your praiseworthy fortune. You have compelled the mind of your lord to this declaration, that we confess we believe these benefits to be more correctly your own. May these blessings be providently lasting, so that, while we pay this as remuneration, we may next time demand better accomplishments from your talents.

1. Cicero.
2. This was regarded as a single province in southern Italy.

LETTER 1.4 (C. 507)

A more detailed companion to *Variae* 1.3 (see above), announcing to the Roman Senate the elevation of Cassiodorus's father to the rank of patrician. This letter reads like a panegyric, extolling the senior Cassiodorus's virtues and digressing into his family's interesting fifth-century background. Both *Variae* 1.3 and 1.4 serve to frame the family's commitment to an extended tradition of service to the Roman state that continued under the Amal Goths.

King Theoderic to the Senate of Rome

1. We truly desire, conscript fathers, that your garland be painted with the blossom of diverse distinctions. We desire that the spirit of liberty should see a Senate favored and thronged. Indeed, such a gathering is the honor of those ruling, and whatever reflects upon you with joyful thanksgiving likewise applies to our praise. **2.** For all that, we have been especially desirous that ornaments of worth should adorn your assembly, when those who have increased in palatine influence rightly confer benefits on the homeland. Our attention scrutinizes these men, and we rejoice in those found with the treasure of good habits, in whom the grace of our countenance is imprinted, just as in the modeled likenesses given for an office. **3.** Hence it is that we have bestowed the patriciate upon the grand *illustris* Cassiodorus, upon a man esteemed for his most noted distinction on behalf of the republic, elevated in recompense so that the merits of one serving are proclaimed with the mark of a great title. He is not one who hurtles to the peak of offices with unexpected succession through the ranks, projected to a tenuous fortune by a game of fate; rather, just as virtues are accustomed to increase, so has he ascended to a position of great renown through deserved ranks. **4.** For as you know, his first entry into administration was set in the toil of the count of private properties, where, neither faltering with the weakness of inexperience nor wandering unknowingly into the errors of novelty, he instead lived by an example to be imitated, along the firm path of restraint. Soon after, he rose to accept the honor of count of the sacred largesse, with common praise for how much he had deservedly accomplished. **5.** Why mention the discipline restored to the provinces, or the edifices of justice administered for men of diverse condition? He has lived with such self-control that he could instruct equanimity with firmness as well as teach by example. For a blameless magistrate is the advocate of probity. It would be a shame not to possess correct habits under one with such a praiseworthy reputation. For who would avoid crime, who observes it implicated in the heart of the elevated? He adopts a hollow demeanor of feigned severity when the man tainted by money opposes bribery, when the unjust man decrees in law what must be obeyed. He who does not administer authority with an unimpaired conscience does not possess the spirit of fairness, since excesses are held in dread only when they are believed to displease the magistrates. **6.** And so, trained in these practices under the preceding king,[3] he succeeded to our court with a veteran's commendations. For you will recall, and in this the memory of recent events assists you, with what moderation he took his seat on the praetorian summit, and thus, born aloft on high, he spurned the faults of good fortune all the more. **7.** Indeed, in no way did he raise himself up in the pretensions of great power, elevated by the favor of fortune, as is the habit of many, but having conducted everything with equity he reflected nothing hated back upon our favor to him. He caused greater things to be bestowed upon him, while within the bounds of modesty he restrained greatness. For here is the most pleasing benefit of an upright conscience, that although he was able to obtain heights, nonetheless he is judged by all to merit more. He aptly joined our revenues to a communal happiness, being liberal with the public treasury and justly meritorious in expenditures. **8.** The republic then experienced a man from the assembly of Romulus who was free of blame, who was permitted to make himself glorious by self-restraint; he nonetheless conferred something greater, in that he left behind, to those who would follow, an example of good works. For it disgraces one to sin who is able to follow after such praiseworthy deeds. He has been, as you know, fear-inspiring to public servants, gentle with the provincials, greedy for giving, full of loathing for receiving, a hater of accusations, and a friend to justice. It was not difficult for him to act as a guardian, who demanded himself to refrain from the property of others. For it is the mark of an unconquered spirit to esteem the advantage of reputation and to instead despise profit from litigation. **9.** But those who are not familiar with the lofty characters of his father and

3. Odoacer, king of Italy, 476–93.

grandfather rightly marvel at him. Indeed, fame celebrates these former Cassiodori. Even if the name may be known among others, nonetheless it remains peculiar to his family. An ancient line, a praised stock, honored among citizens, exceptional among courageous men, since they flourished in both vigor of limbs and height of body. **10.** For the father of this candidate bore the praiseworthy dignity of *tribunus et notarius* under the *Princeps* Valentinian,[4] an office which was then given to the outstanding. At that time, such men in whom it was not possible to find the blemish of recrimination stood for selection to the most privy of imperial affairs. **11.** But as kindred spirits are always accustomed to prefer each other, he was the greatly cherished associate of the patrician Aetius in the governance of the republic, that Aetius whom the ruler of state at that time followed in every matter of advice, on account of his wisdom and the glorious labors undertaken on behalf of the republic. Therefore, not in vain was he sent with Carpilio, the son of Aetius, in the capacity of legate to the formidable warrior Attila.[5] He beheld without fear one whom *imperium* feared, and, relying on truth, he remained above those terrible glares and threats, nor did he hesitate to stand in the path of argument with that man, who, overcome with I know not what fury, seemed to expect mastery of the entire world. **12.** He found a proud king but left him pacified, and he overturned the king's false accusations with such honesty that the king sought to ask for clemency, when it was advantageous not to have peace with such a wealthy kingdom. He encouraged those fearing Attila with his own steadfastness; nor were those known to be armed with such legates[6] believed to be unwarlike. He brought back a peace thought untenable. What his delegation produced is commonly known; it was accepted as gratefully as it was sought after. **13.** Already decorated, the fair ruler first offered him office, then gifts of revenue. But this richly blessed man, with his native restraint, instead accepted a leisured dignity in place of remuneration and sought out the pleasantries of Bruttium. It was not possible to deny that preferred solitude to one who had brought safety from a hostile enemy. With sadness, he released from his employ one whom he knew had been essential. **14.**

4. Valentinian III, western Roman emperor, 425–55.
5. Attila, king of the Huns, 434–53.
6. That is, Valentinian III.

Now, the grandfather, a Cassiodorus girt with the honors of gleaming rank, which it was not possible to withhold from that family, freed Bruttium and Sicily from the incursion of the Vandals by armed resistance, so that he deservedly held the first place of honor in these provinces, which he defended from so cruel and unexpected an enemy. And thus the republic owed it to his strength that Gaiseric did not so devastate those neighboring provinces with the rage that Rome afterward endured.[7] **15.** These Cassiodori, moreover, also waxed in the praise of relations in regions of the East. For Heliodorus, whom we saw administrating the prefecture with distinction in that republic for eighteen years, was known to be related to them by blood. A family elevated on both sides of the world, it is aptly fixed to twin Senates as though conspicuous with two lamps; it shines with the purest brilliance. For where do you find nobility extended further than this, which merits being exalted on both sides of the world? **16.** And this Cassiodorus has lived in his province with the esteem of a governor and with the peace of mind belonging to a private citizen. Superior to all men by his nobility, he drew the hearts of all to himself, so that those who by right of their privilege were unable to be subdued instead became pleasantly bound to him more by the increasing advantages of his association. **17.** Moreover, he is so endowed with the abundance of his own patrimony that, among other good deeds, he surpasses *Principes* in herds of horses, and by often making gifts of these, incurs no jealousy. Hence it is that our candidate always equips the Gothic army, and, improving on the beneficial arrangements that he received from his forebears, he preserves the hereditary bounty. **18.** For which reason we have conveyed everything in order, so that anyone may understand that one who chooses to live according to an elevated rule of life may be able to recover the reputation of their family through our praise. And therefore, conscript fathers, since the honor of good men is advantageous to you and your assent attends our judgment, let the elevation of one who has sought to take upon himself the service of all be supported by good fortune. For it is rather by remuneration than by gift that those who have honored you with worthy deeds should be thanked with reciprocal favor.

---

7. Geiseric, king of the Vandals from 428 to 477, sacked Rome in 455.

LETTER 1.12 (C. 507-11)

This letter elevates a former *Quaestor* to the role of master of offices.

King Theoderic to Eugenitus, Illustris
and Master of Offices

1. The solemn celebration of the deserving is a royal prerogative, since we know not how to dispense anything except to the worthy. And although we want, with God's favor, everything to be associated with our authority, nonetheless our desire is measured by reason, so that we value it more to choose what is worthy of the approbation of all. **2.** Hence it is that we have found you, long since attaining the height of *Quaestor,* commendably pursuing the study of learned philosophical principles, such that the distinction of letters, for you, has become the reward for noble service. For what is more adorning than duty in legal service which, if it is conducted honestly, attracts the legal affairs of others to its own inconvenience, so that it may provide relief to the labor of others? In this field of exercise, you graduated through a course of services to the honor of our notice. **3.** However, not content with one reward, our generosity doubled; it extended increased gifts and in its zeal prepared yet more, as if to bestow everything that it ought. Take, therefore, the badges of distinction of master of offices, enjoying every legal privilege that it was proper for your predecessors to hold. And therefore, with such a judgment joyfully rendered, you who earned honor on behalf of your worthy labors, now accept another. For what we have perceived concerning the earlier reward, we declare increased by the second dignity. Branches properly culti-vated retain the nature of the tree and shoot forth again; thus *fasces* are sprung from *fasces.* **4.** Indeed, may this compensation not satiate you, lest the praise created by our judgment give rest to your labors. Nay, on the contrary, let respectability be more desirable when it attains a reward, and then anxious labors become more pleasing to have been perpetual when you know their reward to have found you. Therefore, what honors you take from legal writ, give back from your merits. Know well with what eagerness it pleases us, you who arrive from the inner chambers of our very council. Remember that however much the blameless are praised in our presence, so much do we bestow good acts in turn. By your speech, we shall pronounce our judgments; by your mouth, we speak to rouse with distinguished examples. Be a temple of innocence, the sanctuary of restraint, and the hall of justice. Anything profane should be absent from the mind of the judge. Let a pious *Princeps* be served by a kind of priesthood.

LETTER 1.13 (C. 507–11)

An address to the Roman Senate confirming the elevation of Eugenitus to master of offices (see *Variae* 1.12, above).

King Theoderic to the Senate of Rome

1. The distinction of office, conscript fathers, when it comes to an unknown man is a gift; when it comes to the experienced man, it is as payment for just desert. Of these, the one is dependent upon judgment, while the other is obliged to partiality. For we elevate some in estimation, to others we show gratitude, and to all our kindness extends itself as a path to blessings. But we recall by beholding your affection how much is said in your assembly that is appraised on the basis of the celebrated virtues. For if anything is the flower of the human race, it deserves to be the curia, which, just as the citadel is the prominence of a city, thus is the jewel of other ranks. 2. And therefore, we have elevated the *illustris* Eugenitus, shining with the reputation of learned philosophical principles, to the honor of master of offices, so that he might bear in title that dignity which he claimed by desert. For who could be so ignorant of his public service, which he accomplished not with meanness of spirit, but which he attended to with the respect of an obligation? And so we grant a role equal to such high distinctions, so that shining with the grace of both, each might adorn the other with the pleasantness of its nature. Here he is who long ago as *Quaestor* and jurist clung to our side, whom no cloud of jealousy ever darkened, nor did he with venomous feelings seek devices for harming others out of devotion to malevolence: he obeyed us honestly with a hidden purity of heart, and he offered his own faultlessness to devotion to commands. For a troubled mind does not follow the decision of one ruling, but it would rather pursue its own inclination. 3. You clearly know our opinion on this account, that after the highest honors of this office, he would climb to yet another dignity. Nor would we allow one to be at leisure whose merits do not permit him to remain a

private citizen: it is appropriate that he should be considered with regard to the nature of the bright sun, which, having completed an undertaken day, nonetheless illuminates another with the same pleasant brilliance. Here then, conscript fathers, let your approbation welcome one shining so completely with merits. For you are thoroughly indebted to those serving, just as the approval of your praise accompanies them. For if the pace of horses is hastened by the acclamation of spectators and driven by the clapping of their hands, and thus speed is drawn from dumb animals, so much do we believe it possible to stimulate men, whom we find particularly fitted by nature to an eagerness for praise.

LETTER 1.15 (C. 507–11)

This letter orders a patrician senator to provide *tuitio,* or legal patronage, to the household of a fellow patrician acting on Theoderic's behalf at the Vandal court in North Africa. The letter's recipient was the former consul of 492.

King Theoderic to Festus, Illustris *and Patrician*

1. It is pleasing to us that, however so much an appraisal of the extent of your merits increases, thus too should you be entrusted as the guardian of the absent and the patron of the weak. For, on that account, you formerly deserved to be in the Senate, so that you would illustrate the consideration of justice to those following. Thence it happened that good opinion of you increased from the example of glorious legal acts. For never was your own advantage increased by abandoning another, except that it was decided properly from good conscience. **2.** For that reason, we have decided on the present injunction concerning the household of the patrician Agnellus, who, departing for Africa, will serve our advantages by petitioning the kingdom of another. This household would do well with your guardianship in respect of sound legal matters, lest, lacking the protection of a master, it endure any violent attack. For there are always opportunities for harm to the resources of the absent, and the occasion appears by whatever means to drag into litigation what the attention of the traveler is not able to deter by resistance. **3.** And therefore, let your exalted status, which is a blessing to have nearby, uplift the humble, rescue those otherwise oppressed, and, what is rare among the influential, benefit everyone, because you are more eminent than all.

LETTER 1.27 (C. 509)

This letter responds to a petition from the Green Faction at Rome claiming that two senior senators harassed its members. Like *Variae* 1.23 (see Section 11), this injunction takes into account the esteem of those accused by delegating the inquiry to men of equal rank. It also offers thoughts on the appropriateness of senatorial involvement in public spectacles. The addressee of this letter is described as an official of the praetorian prefect's staff (*comitiacus*) in *Variae* 2.10 (see Section 10).

King Theoderic to Speciosus

1. If we moderate the conduct of foreign nations under law, if everything connected to Italy observes Roman statutes, how much more fitting is it that the very seat of civil harmony possess more deference for the laws, so that the grace of dignified appearance should shine through the example of moderation? For where may a restrained disposition be sought, if violent acts would bring shame upon patricians? **2.** And so it has been brought forward to us in a petition from people of the Green Faction, since they have arranged to come to our *comitatus* seeking the accustomed redress, that savage attacks have been committed against them by the patrician Theodorus and the *illustris* consul Inportunus,[8] so that one among them is mourned as dead. **3.** This, if it is true, moves us by the very savagery committed, that armed fury should persecute harmless citizens whom civic affection ought to cherish. But since the condition of lesser people justly implores the assistance of one who rules, we have decided that the above-mentioned *illustres* are to be advised by the present command that, by your urging, they should not delay to send informed representatives to the court of Caelianus and Agapitus, likewise *illustres,* to the effect that the familiarity of these men with the laws may bring closure with a weighed sentence. **4.** But lest the gossip of the people perhaps offend these great men, an end to such presumption must be had. Let whoever impudently brings insult upon a passing reverend senator be held at fault, if he intended evil,

---

8. Inportunus and Theodorus were brothers.

when he ought to speak well. **5.** Nevertheless, who expects serious conduct at the games? The Catos knew not to gather at the circus.[9] Whatever is said there by a celebrating people should not be deemed an insult. It is a place that excuses the excess of those for whom, if chatter is patiently indulged, it is shown even to adorn *Principes.* Let those who are occupied by such pursuits answer us without ambiguity: If the senators desire their opponents to be peaceful, clearly the senators want their opponents to be the victors, since the senators leap to insults then, when they blush to see themselves bested to their own disgrace. Why, therefore, do they choose to become enraged at what they know themselves without a doubt to have desired?

LETTER 1.39 (C. 507–11)

A curious letter refusing the request of a man serving at court that the sons of his brother be restored to their hometown of Syracuse. The children were living in Rome ostensibly for the purpose of obtaining an education, but in reality as political hostages. The letter orders an *illustris* senator and patrician, the same Festus as the recipient of *Variae* 1.15 (see above), to maintain their custody at Rome.

King Theoderic to Festus, Illustris *and Patrician*

1. We gladly embrace the reasonable requests of supplicants, we who consider not only the rights of the petitioner. For what is more worthy than that we are wrapped in constant deliberations both day and night, so that just as arms protect our republic, equity too would preserve the state inviolate? And so the *spectabilis* Philagrius, abiding in the city of Syracuse, being long detained by the duties of our court, entreats that those sons of his brother whom he presented at Rome in order to study should be returned to him at their home. **2.** Let your *illustris* magnificence situate these sons, retaining them by our order in the above-mentioned city; nor should it be permitted for them to depart until such time as we have decided upon the matter with a second order. For thus is advancement of character acquired by them, and for us a measure of advantage is preserved, by which a delay can be beneficial, when

9. Cato the Elder (234–149 BCE) and Cato the Younger (95–46 BCE) were iconic in the Roman imagination as exemplars of discipline and restraint.

one who is able to acquire wisdom occasionally seeks to avoid his homeland. Only by chance had Ithaca concealed in his own home that Ulysses whose wisdom the noble song of Homer especially claims, because he wandered among many cities and peoples, where those men wiser than himself always dwelled who were considered learned from their frequent dealings with many men. For indeed, just as human nature is instructed by hard work, thus lethargy is inspired by leisure.

LETTER 1.41 (C. 507–9)

This letter announces to Rome's urban prefect the award of senatorial membership to a young man, with interesting commentary on the heritable nature of positions in the senatorial order and an oblique comparison to the eastern Senate of Constantinople.

King Theoderic to Agapitus, Illustris and Urban Prefect

1. An especially protective concern for your order leads me to prefer deliberation, and the Senate's accustomed state of honor compels me to investigate whoever must be admitted to an assembly requiring such deference. We want the Senate not only to increase by the number of its members, but to be especially adorned with the brilliance of those deserving membership. Let another order accept mediocrities by mistake;[10] this Senate rejects those not proven to be exceptional. Therefore, we seek in a colleague that nobility which is better than nobility of the blood, which may produce morals inconsistent with itself, some worthlessness that hides in the blood. And therefore, concerning Faustus, the adult son of the *illustris* Faustus, let your *illustris* magnificence determine what the venerable order has dictated to be allotted concerning those who would be brought into the curia. For in this request, we diminish no precepts concerning the customary authority of the sacred order, since it is a greater glory to behold the decision of leading men after a royal decree. Indeed, it is an honor for those very same men, if we bid what they are accustomed to choose for themselves, and if we should grandly demand what is sought from them daily.

10. That is, the Senate at Constantinople.

LETTER 1.44 (C. 509–10)

Following previous announcements of Artemidorus's appointment as urban prefect (*Variae* 1.42 and 1.43, not included in this volume), this letter states rather forcefully the direct authority that he will have over civil disturbances at Rome.

King Theoderic to the Senate of Rome

1. You will be able to recognize the special esteem that we have for you by the very same cares by which we are seen to be so disturbed, that we should permit no admonition to be disregarded. Affection promotes caution, and what we prize most eagerly we watch over with greater regard. **2.** Hence it is that we gave the ruling *fasces* of the urban prefecture to the *illustris* Artemidorus, who has been long educated in our service, so that, since civic harmony has been overturned by the lawless rioting of certain persons, the innocent should have a witness of pure conscience and the errant should be subject to a just punisher. We, who are delighted by the guiltless, have decided what must be given preference for the reputation of all concerned, lest anyone presume unexpectedly to exceed accustomed punishment. **3.** On which account, you will want to transfer such matters to us through the aforementioned man, so that, if any disorderly person comes forth, he would meet with the impediment of our mandates on the spot. And although the laws have conceded this authority to the urban prefect, we have nonetheless transferred that authority to him in particular, so that he would be able to accomplish more confidently what had been permitted to two. **4.** He will, therefore, stand bold before the most outrageous persons and by our authority overthrow the unreasonable with public punishment. Let the rage of the most disruptive minds be at rest. Why should the blessings of peace, which by the grace of God you have earned through our labor, be spoiled by lawless rioting? The traditions of your forebears have never been more in danger of harm than when Roman seriousness is at fault. And so let an honorable city restore its restraint. It is shameful for the most prominent citizens to have degenerated, especially at a time when you know yourselves to have the kind of *Princeps* who confers rewards on the well deserving and punishment on the disruptive.

LETTER 2.6 (C. 509–11)

This letter appoints a former urban prefect to a delegation being sent to Constantinople. The skill needed to negotiate with highly educated officials at the eastern capital receives emphasis.

King Theoderic to Agapitus, Illustris *and Patrician*

1. Our deliberative council requires the service of discerning men, so that the administration of what is useful to the public may be fulfilled with the assistance of wisdom. And therefore, your *illustris* greatness, let it be known that, God willing, we have determined to send a delegation to the east, for which, judging you to be suitable, we nominate you by this present dictate, so that thus equipped you should increase our estimation of you and through you the business required by us should be advanced. **2.** And granted that any delegation would require a wise man who would be wholly committed to protecting the standing of the kingdom and the advantage of the provinces, it is nevertheless now necessary to choose the most prudent man possible, who is able to dispute with the most sophisticated men and thus maneuver in the company of the learned, lest some invention of clever learning prevail over the undertaken cause. It is a great skill to speak against clever men and to plead any case in the presence of those who consider themselves to have anticipated every argument. Therefore, take cheer in such high estimation, that you had been able to prove your native character even before you accepted the gift of this delegation.

LETTER 2.24 (C. 507–11)

In tenor quite different from the carefully crafted deference shown to the Senate elsewhere in the collection, this letter offers a scathing rebuke of senators who have avoided paying taxes, for which citizens of lesser means are burdened instead.[11] The letter also alerts the Senate that the court has informed the public about its resolution in an edict (*Variae* 2.25, below).

---

11. Agents assigned to collect revenues from a particular area were concerned only with the total amount assessed for that municipality; withholding tax payments could force the agent or local curia to exact the difference owed from poor landowners with less ability to resist.

King Theoderic to the Senate of Rome

1. It stands that the Senate has projected for the people a standard by which one must live, for the name Roman adorns what is chosen by you as established practice. For this reason were the fathers so named in the beginning, since a way of life was arranged by you as though for children. For you decreed the devotion owed from the provinces and you decreed rights for private persons. And you have taught your subjects to gladly obey every aspect of justice. And it is therefore not fitting to bear the mark of contrariness, where once an example of moderation was able to blaze forth. Our kindness, for which it is a passion to assay the measure of every affair, entrusts to your attention what must be accomplished, lest a transgression be nourished more from ignorance in those for whom good conscience is not permitted to be perpetually in error. **2.** Accordingly, we have learned from a report of the provincial governors sent to his magnificence the praetorian prefect, thus some time removed from the first occurrence, that nothing or very little may be collected from the senatorial houses, alleging that the weak, whom it would be better to relieve, are oppressed by this difficulty, for it happens that the balance owed to the revenue officials, when it is despised by the influential, weighs instead against those of slender means, and that man who is devoted to his own obligation instead pays for another person. Moreover, they add what is more bitter, that each according to his own will deems it proper to cast forth anything to the collectors, which loss they nonetheless claim to be entirely inflicted upon the town counsellors, and those who had been restored to public service by our own provision have been torn to pieces by this contumacious disregard. **3.** And therefore, conscript fathers, you who ought to strive for the republic equally with us, arrange it thus fairly, that whatever each senatorial house should be assessed, let it be paid in three installments to the revenue agents sent to the provinces. **4.** Or certainly, what you have become accustomed to ask in place of a favor, if you choose, send the complete amount to the treasury of the vicar's office, lest it become necessary for the town counsellors to assume, in place of your own slender obligations, a loss to themselves through complicated and inefficient labor of the assembly, and lest it bring forth a detestable situation, so that a loyal man who had barely been able to bear his own taxes then becomes feeble, squeezed by the burden of another. **5.** We are unable to conceal this, for the sake of sound civil harmony, that even without the bitterness of war the oppressed are stripped of their own property and those who hasten to obey the republic perish more. Moreover, you will know that we have sent notice by the proclamation of an edict to all provinces, to the effect that whoever knows himself to be oppressed by the weight of another's taxes may freely come forth and make an accusation in public. The fruit of justice will soon return to us, we who know to offer protection to the weak.

LETTER 2.25 (C. 507–11)

This general edict declares the intent to correct abuses of elite citizens in the payment of taxes. Town counsellors and landowners are invited to report abuses, as announced in the previous letter (*Variae* 2.24, above), addressed to the Senate. Senators are not specifically indicted here.

Edict of King Theoderic

1. Although the voice of grief may be contentious, although the threatened may not restrain themselves and a wounded soul may be fed on shouting, nonetheless, the voice that is relieved under our authority calls forth more freely. For we despise that the lowly should be degraded. We are even stirred by the afflictions of those not complaining, and what the shame of the suffering conceals comes to our attention more quickly. When the injuries of everyone reflect upon us, rightly do we then feel as a loss to ourselves any cause for the middling person which we know has escaped our devotion. **2.** And so, we recently learned by report from the provincial governors that certain houses of the very powerful have not fulfilled their own obligations to regular taxes. Hence it happens that, when the amount of payment due is sought, typically the greater portion is exacted from people of slender means. Then, with arrogance of landlords, the imminent hand over the scheduled *solidi,* not in due manner, but cast forth coin of substandard weight; nor do they yield according to standard practice the common *siliqua,* which they had been accustomed to pay. Consequently, it is the case that the town counsellors, for whom we have wanted to act as guardian, experience severe loss from the coercion of the collecting agent, and, if it is even proper to admit, since they are compelled by harsh collection agents on account of the debts of others, they are impoverished by the loss of their own properties. **3.** Because this offense must be amputated, we have sent instructions to the most reverend Senate and we have now determined by this proclaimed edict that whoever, whether of the town counsellors or of the landowners, feels himself to be weighed down by the payment of another's taxes may hasten to approach the court of our serenity, where he will learn that former excesses have wholly displeased us when he sees the benefits that follow. Therefore, the arbitration of a just *Princeps* is open to you, even though it would ever be declared by many signs. Now either conceal your resignation to grief in silence or lay bare a just path with a voice. Now the focus of this counsel, which is at hand to learn what you believe will disentangle you, will be on you.

LETTER 3.21 (C. 507–11)

This letter is addressed to the praetorian prefect and may be a politically polite way of removing him from office. It responds to a request for a sabbatical from Rome in a tone that verges on the ironic. Terms such as "armistice" (*indutiae*) and "retreat" (*regressio*) suggest failure in a military enterprise, a not uncommon metaphor for public life.

King Theoderic to Faustus, Illustris

1. It is the way of human custom that adornment would attract more, and although distinctions may be held in legal right, anything that satiates desire may introduce aversion. Thence, you claim that you ought to be granted a hiatus from constant residence within the sacred walls[12] for the sake of arranging affairs to your own advantage, not because such a lofty dwelling would be wearisome, but by which a renewed return might become all the more sweet. And therefore, your *illustris* greatness, our devotion bestows a leave of four months for the purpose of withdrawing to your province, on the condition that you hasten to return to your hearth within the same amount of time, so that your home of Rome, that most prized of lands, which we want to be frequented by numerous assemblies, should not become thinned by loss of inhabitants. And, moreover, we deem it most agreeable to

---

12. The phrase *sacris moenibus* more than likely means "at Rome."

you, when it would be possible for a Roman senator to be delayed elsewhere only with resentment. For where else is there that charm of kindred? Where else is such great beauty to be observed within city walls? It is a kind of sacrilege that those who are able to dwell in familial homes in Rome would make it overly distant from themselves.[13]

LETTER 3.39 (C. 512)

This letter responds to a claim that charioteers hired for recent consular games in Milan had not been paid by the sponsoring consul. The consul is reminded that debts acquired in public munificence are their own kind of reward. The recipient had been appointed consul for 511 (see *Variae* 2.1, in Section 1, and 2.2 and 2.3, not included in this volume).

King Theoderic to Felix, Illustris *and Consul*

1. The rationale of equity persuades that we should preserve the customs of antiquity by the observance of public celebrations, particularly celebration initiated by the consul, for whom it is the established purpose that he ought to be praised for liberality, nor should the office seem to promise one thing and a senator want to accomplish something else. Concerning which, it is not fitting to be found sparing in generosity in public opinion, since the shadow of stinginess darkens public fame for a consul. **2.** Therefore, your *illustris* greatness should know that we have been approached by the charioteers from Milan. That munificence which ancient custom concedes, while in the present day it would be as though law, was withdrawn from them during your tenure. Thence, if these assertions are spoiled by no dishonesty, bring your loftiness to follow antiquity, which, as though a special kind of privilege, openly displayed for itself the debts that were acquired. It is not permitted that what you know has been granted since antiquity should be denied by you.

LETTER 4.16 (C. 509-11)

An announcement appointing a count to manage the affairs of the Roman Senate. Although this responsibility had previously fallen to

---

13. The use of terms such as *lares* and *penates* for "home" intensifies the sentiment in this last statement of sacrilege against family.

the urban prefect, it seems that corruption had not abated on his watch. Somewhat ominously, the letter emphasizes the candidate's military discipline during his previous assignment in Gaul.

King Theoderic to the Senate of Rome

1. For the sake of public weal, to which our attention always gives consideration, we had thought some time ago that your citizen the *illustris* Count Arigernus must be sent to Gaul, so that the hearts of the wavering might be fortified by the maturity of his counsels. Indeed, he caused the nervous inexperience of the province to embrace wise governors, so that, just as order will fashion every manner of life, thus may devotion hasten instruction. With these affairs arranged to our satisfaction, he both restored the glory of civic harmony and, displaying what he learned in your presence, brought back the trophies of battles. **2.** We have returned this man to your assembly, as we judged this to be your desire, so that one who had already pleased you for a long time would now become even more pleasing, since additional blessings now commend him. For this reason, let the Roman Senate restore itself to the discipline of the aforementioned man and let what is instructed by an affection for peace be fulfilled in a dutiful spirit, to the extent that leave for corruption is abolished and, what is especially important, no place should be found for feuding. **3.** And so, if anything blameworthy advanced during his absence, correct it among yourselves with consideration for justice, so that one for whom probity is always pleasing may come to work with your nobility. Know him to be intimately bound to us, so that any erring behavior that has not been emended by its own authors will be cut short by the punishment of the laws. Therefore, conscript fathers, let him be obeyed, a man already approved for such a long time, for whom it is a necessity to pursue anything requiring admonishment. This man thus far has conducted himself in your company with the praise of all, and, in so great an assembly, he has encountered a hostile opinion from none.

LETTER 4.22 (C. 510–11)

This letter addresses charges of sorcery against two prominent senators by appointing the urban prefect to judge the case in consultation with a traditional panel of five senatorial colleagues. The prefect is furthermore notified that the count assigned to Rome will be at hand to ensure civil order.[14]

King Theoderic to Argolicus, Illustris and Urban Prefect

1. That transgression is intolerable which effects injury against supernal majesty and, forgetful of piety, repeatedly follows the barbarism of error. For what chance of pardon will he hope, who despises that author deserving reverence? Let profane rites now depart from our midst; let the punishable murmuring to the spirits fall silent. It is not permitted in Christian times to be entangled in magic arts.[15] **2.** And so, we have learned from the report of your greatness that Basilius and Praetextatus, already long polluted by contact with perverse arts, have been brought to indictment under your examination by the accusation of certain persons. You claim to observe our decision over this matter, so that what the authority of our piety recommends may happen more confidently. **3.** But we, who know not how to differ from the laws and whose intention it is to hold moderated justice in every way, have decided in the present dictate that you should consider this case by lawful examination with five senators, that is, with the honored patricians Symmachus, Decius, Volusianus, and Caelianus, as well as the *illustris* Maximianus. And with procedure of law observed in everything, if the crime that is maintained has been found substantiated, let it also be punished according to the stricture of the very same laws, so that hidden and secret members of this art, those whom uncertain information cannot drag before the laws, may be restrained from such crimes by the nature of their punishment. **4.** We have sent instructions to the *illustris* Count Arigernus concerning this affair, so that, with the violent reaction of any person restrained, he may drag the accused to court, if they should conceal themselves, and sitting with you in this trial, he may give assurance that the innocent have not been oppressed and that the guilty may not evade the law.[16]

14. The trial is later mentioned by Gregory the Great in *Dialogues* 1.4.

15. This could be a reference either to the continued (and at that time illicit) practice of rites associated with former public "pagan" religion or to the less formal substratum of common, non-Christian ritualistic practices thought of as "magic."

16. Given that a military count was alerted to maintain order in Rome, it is safe to assume that this was a high-profile case with active partisans.

LETTER 8.2 (C. 526)

Theoderic died in 526, and this letter declares the accession to the throne of his grandson Athalaric. The announcement is striking for requiring an oath (*sacramentum*) of loyalty to the new king.

King Athalaric to the Senate of Rome

1. Acknowledging the rise of a ruler, conscript fathers, is known to be the greatest cause for celebration, so that one who is known to protect everything may be proclaimed for having attained the eminence of the kingdom. The scale of rejoicing comes from the grandeur of the announcement, and however eager the spirit is for this, thus will there be reflection upon its importance. **2.** For if the promised delights of companionship stir wise men, if news of the well-being of friends comforts them, with what exaltation ought news be received that a ruler of all territories has happily come forth, whom chaotic sedition did not produce, whom seething wars did not beget, whose gain was not a loss to the republic, but who was thus elevated through peace, just as would befit the arrival of a founder of civic harmony! It is truly a great species of good fortune to become *Princeps* without conflict and for a youth to become master in that republic where it happens that many are found with seasoned character. For it is not by any means possible to lack the counsel of years where it is known that so many parents to the republic may be found. **3.** Hope for our reign, therefore, has been carried on the good intentions of all men, and that should be more readily believed concerning us than what has been assumed concerning others.[17] Since the distinction of the Amal family permits no insult whatever, and just as those who are born to you become nominated as heirs in the senatorial order, thus one who advances from this family should be approved the most worthy for the kingdom. The things of which we speak are proven by the facts at hand. **4.** For when the sweet memory of our lord grandfather severely grieved you on account of the quantity of his kindnesses, it transferred the grandeur of his lordship to us with such swiftness that you would

17. Although vague, following from the earlier statements concerning rulers coming to power through strife and warfare, the letter should be assumed to be making a similar comparison here.

have thought a garment had been changed rather than the kingdom. So many leading men, renowned for their advice and strong arms, fostered no murmuring, as would be expected; but with great rejoicing they followed the decision of their *Princeps,* so that you would instead admit that divine will had converged there. Therefore, by the grace of God, we have introduced the need to make you more certain concerning the commencement of our reign, since *imperium* should appear continued rather than altered when it passes to heirs; for in whatever manner that same man[18] is thought to live on, his offspring is recognized to rule over you. **5.** Your prayers had tended toward this, what was doubtless his decision, that he should leave an heir of his own good family who would be able to increase his kindnesses to you. It is proper to be formed in the affection of *Principes,* as though the fidelity to his likeness had been preserved in a bronze sculpture, to the extent that the incumbent offspring would resemble the author who had obligated the republic to himself with many kindnesses. But how much more authentic is one who lives as his posterity, through whom in a large part both the form of the body is returned and the vigor of the soul is prolonged. **6.** And therefore, you now ought to extend the fidelity of your noble order with greater enthusiasm, such that it would appear former gifts had been conferred upon the deserving and that without hesitation we may bestow future gifts on those whom we feel to be the most mindful of past events. **7.** Moreover, we know this was arranged by divine providence, just as the common consent of Goths and Romans receives us and they have also confirmed their inclination, which they offered with pure intention, with the bond of a sworn oath.[19] **8.** We doubt not that you would follow this example at a distance, but not by affection; for you are able to commence what we would anticipate from a distance. Indeed, it is fitting that the most outstanding senators can show so much more respect, because they are known to have received distinction greater than other ranks. **9.** But so that you would be able to acknowledge the commencement of our benevolence toward you, since it is fitting to enter your curia with favors, we have sent our *illustris* Count Sigismer to you, with those who are directed to administer the oath, since we desire to preserve as

18. Theoderic.
19. For this, see *Var.* 8.3, 8.4, and 8.5 (the last in Section 6).

inviolate what we have promised by public authority. **10.** If, however, you believe anything must be required of us by which your peace of mind would be increased, let those whose entreaties we are clearly known to encourage to be poured forth seek us unhesitatingly to be advised. Indeed, such a thing is more a promise than advice: for one who takes it upon himself to entreat such a venerable Senate can nonetheless obtain what he had set before them. It is now yours to hope for whatever would increase the common weal of the republic.

LETTER 11.13 (C. 535)

This letter serves as the Senate's formal request that Justinian recognize the kingship of Theodahad, Athalaric's successor. The reference to Libya's liberty indicates that it should be placed after the Vandalic War (c. 534), and the plea from the personification of Rome suggests that it was written after the death of Athalaric's mother, Amalasuntha (c. 535), when Belisarius's actions threatened stability in Italy.

The Senate of Rome to Emperor Justinian

1. It seems a quite honorable and important charge to beseech a dutiful *Princeps* on behalf of the safety of the Roman republic, since it is proper to seek from you what is able to advance our liberty. For among the other blessings that divine providence has conferred upon you especially, nothing more glorious is manifest than that you are everywhere recognized as preeminent. Therefore, we entreat you, most clement emperor, and we extend hopeful hands from the breast of the curia, so that you may offer your most enduring peace to our king, lest we, who have ever been known to be the recipients of your concord, be allowed to become deserving of your hostility. **2.** If you truly have regard for the Roman name, thus will you concede this kindness to our masters. Your favor exalts and protects us, and we know that what appeals to your disposition is deserved. Therefore, let your agreement bind tranquility for Italy, since we are then loved, if promised affection is conjoined through you. If our prayers still do not seem sufficient for this goal, imagine our country bursting into this pleading speech: **3.** "If at any time I have been pleasing to you, most dutiful of *Principes*, love my protectors. Those who rule me ought to have concord with you, lest such things begin to happen in my realm as they know would depart from your wishes. For you, who have always bestowed the joys of life, would not be the cause of my cruel destruction. Behold how I have united my fosterlings to your peace; behold how I have radiated honors to my citizens.[20] If you suffer me to be injured, where then would you extend the reputation of your devotion? For what would you attempt to accomplish more grandly for me, whose religion is yours and which is known to flourish thus? My Senate grows in honors; it ceaselessly increases in resources. **4.** Do not allow what you ought to defend in war to be dismantled in discord. I have had many kings, but none of such literary talent; I have had prudent men, but none so vigorous in learning and piety. I prize the Amal nourished at my breast, a brave man formed in my association, dear to Romans for wisdom, respected among other nations for virtue. Indeed, truly unite your intentions, share your counsels, so that your glory may increase if we attain any prosperity. Do not intend to call upon me in such a way that you would not be able to find me. I am no less in your affection if you cause none to rend my limbs. **5.** For if Libya deserved to receive liberty through you, it is cruel that I lose what I have always been seen to possess. Peerlessly triumphant, control the tumult of your wrath. What the public voice seeks is greater than your temperament's being conquered by the wound of some ingratitude." **6.** Rome utters these words while she implores you through her senators. But if this is as yet of minor importance, consider the most holy petition of the blessed apostles Peter and Paul. What will you, a *Princeps,* not offer on behalf of the merits of those who have often been proven to defend the security of Rome from enemies? But so that all these things may be found agreeable to your reverence, we have decided that our entreaties must be poured forth through the venerable bishop x, the legate of our most devoted king, sent to your clemency so that many things may be accomplished which individually would be possible to obtain in the presence of pious souls.

20. Here "fosterlings" (*alumni*) and "citizens" (*cives*) are analogous to Goths and Romans, respectively.

Civil Bureaucracy
and Administration in Italy

*Letters Describing Activities of the Court
Bureaucracy and Letters of Appointment to
Bureaucratic Posts*

Nowhere is a civil bureaucracy in greater evidence in the western Mediterranean at this period than in the *Variae*. In many ways, the tiers of civil administration (municipal, provincial, and prefectural) in Italy appear to mirror those in Constantinople and the rest of the eastern empire, although profound differences certainly existed. The scale of the administrative structure was small in comparison to the sheer number of personnel at Constantinople, which doubtless impacted the efficacy of essential functions, such as tax collection. More important, however, sustaining a civil administration focused on Ravenna allowed the Amal government to maintain the ideological fiction of a Gothic military in support of Roman civil institutions and the more concrete benefit of cultivating relations with prominent families across Italy, who contributed to the project of a Roman republic under the Amals.

LETTER 1.22 (C. 507–11)

This letter appoints a man as a legal representative of the treasury. The appointee's legal training receives due attention, alongside interesting public-relations advice concerning the desirability of an acceptable amount of loss to the fisc.

King Theoderic to Marcellus, Spectabilis *and Legal Aid*

1. Praise is the gold standard of regal generosity, however much indulgences combine with good judgment, nor does the balance of good administration dare to make a faulty appointment, since where offices are affixed to merits, nothing ought to be uncertain. For we bear no regard for the uncultivated, but rather we approve of the most upstanding. **2.** Indeed, as a man of reputation you have polished your talent with the whetstone of a richly varied legal career, and you have nurtured eloquence in the exercise of legal cases. You have become skilled, in the way that devotion bears sweet fruit, just as that very devotion also would win over the hearts of those ruling. Our intuition, that spy of virtues, sees this quality in you. You have succeeded in pleasing those among us possessing discernment, so that you, who heretofore have managed private cases with integrity, stand out as worthy to take up cases for the state. **3.** Take, therefore, those cases that must be handled for our fisc, following the example of your predecessors in enjoying the advantages of your post. And so, thus as a man of moderation, walk the middle path of justice, so that you neither load false accusations on the innocent nor unburden those restrained by just complaints. For this we deem to be true wealth, which we discern with the support of integrity. Therefore, we shall not inquire after how often you succeed, but rather by what means you prevail. **4.** Favoring impartiality will please us. Let it be that you seek victories not from our influence but rather from the law, since that most praiseworthy aspect of the fisc is lost when justice is lost. For if the master should win, it is begrudged as oppression. Equity is truly credited if it should happen that the suppliant prevails. Thus, we do not pursue cases with small losses, where our reputation then gains when the unfair advantage is restrained. For that reason, occasionally allow a case to go poorly for the fisc, so that the *Princeps* may be seen to be good. Indeed, we lose a greater advantage if victory should favor us without loss.

LETTER 1.34 (C. 507–11)

This letter directs the praetorian prefect to regulate the amount of grain being shipped from each province in order to ensure that local inhabitants have proper provisions.

King Theoderic to Faustus, Praetorian Prefect

1. The harvest of grain first ought to supply the province in which it was sown, so that the local inhabitants would be sustained by their own fruitfulness, which is drained dry by the eager greed of foreign merchants. Indeed, that which is surplus ought to be assigned for other regions and should be intended for foreign lands then, when the amount for local needs has been satisfied. **2.** And therefore, your distinguished *illustris,* let those who are known to have the administration of the shores in each port be advised that nobody should load grain onto merchant ships bound for foreign shores before they determine the amount most suitable for public distribution.

LETTER 1.36 (C. 507–11)

This letter grants a man of senatorial rank a public post of undisclosed title. More attention is given to the recipient's first duty, which is to provide legal guardianship to the surviving sons of the man who previously held the position.

King Theoderic to Ferriolus, Spectabilis

1. The utility of good men in leading roles ought to be to renewed by their successor, lest any interrupted office suffer a loss through the inability of its ministers. And therefore, we bid you to undertake the place, by our authority, once held by Benedictus in the city of Pedona,[1] so that, setting forth everything with diligent care, you should merit the increase of our gratitude. You should also direct your attention to those surviving Benedictus, since we are eager to recompense the relations of the deceased, whose good faith we are unable to forget. **2.** Moreover, we recall this out of the habit of our duty, because the good memory of loyal servants does not flee from us. Thus, should you bring those sons of the aforementioned Benedictus, who was known to obey us with sincere devotion, to be protected by legal guardianship, to the extent that, fittingly alleviated of cares by your protection, they would rejoice to have been conferred security from their father's servitude. What was able to stand out by the devotion of one man

1. Located on the Ligurian border with Gaul.

would, therefore, profit the sons, since it is fitting that we contribute more than we are seen to receive from our servants. Here fairness is not equal, but our portion is weighed most justly when it is burdened more by making recompense.

LETTER 2.26 (C. 507–11)

This letter responds to the corruption of agents in charge of the public grain (collected as taxes), who have charged merchants unregulated commissions. It also addresses other issues related to the taxation of sales. The problems described could have deleterious effects on local municipal finances by discouraging merchants from purchasing grain (whose public sale was the means by which taxes collected in kind were commuted to coin revenue).

King Theoderic to Faustus, Praetorian Prefect

1. We are pleased by no kind of unjust profits, nor should what departs from the grace of probity be associated with the spirit of our devotion. Indeed, the republic has ever increased by right of equitability, and when moderation is prized, benefits swiftly follow. 2. And therefore, your *illustris* magnificence, being greatly stirred by a petition of the merchants of Apulia and Calabria, we decree what must be done so that, concerning the grain that the above-mentioned merchants have bought on the public market, no amount of *solidi* should again be required from them in the name of a commission. For if you should not maintain a reasonably legitimate appearance with respect to public expenses, then the measurement of grain charged may be appropriately drawn from your office. The accounting of fiscal affairs has a record that is known to reject what has been unjustly imposed. Indeed, it is especially unseemly that one who serves the other *imperium* should endure this expense.[2] 3. And those assessing a measure of grain in the same manner, whose merchant is seen to come from the same province, let no impudent person dare to exact a continually condemned price. And so that we may check such abuse more vigorously, we have imposed a penalty of thirty pounds of gold on the office of

2. The merchants from whom commissions were extorted apparently were from the eastern empire.

your prefecture if anyone attempts to move against this most healthful edict with dishonorable daring. Moreover, the staff of the office will find itself bearing a loss in the amount of ten pounds of gold if it presumes to maintain prohibited practices. **4.** And in this way our clemency extends to the weak, so that if the merchant should offer payment to the tax agent for the proper entitlement, he too should enjoy use of the grain monopoly. If the tax agent truly deems this entitlement must be removed from merchants, he may exact no payment from them, since it is thoroughly absurd that one who does not have the remuneration of a legal right should be afflicted with an expense. **5.** Henceforth, let the ancient usage be observed by the import officials and let its observance apply only to those whom the authority of antiquity wanted to practice this entitlement. Therefore, our favor extends protection in every way to those merchants who are properly confirmed with contracts from your office, lest the kind of man who lives by profit be able to catch his death from loss.

LETTER 2.28 (C. 507–11)

A classic example of the ideology of public service, this letter elevates a former *princeps,* or head of a governmental bureau, to senatorial rank. Given the legal nature of the duties described, the recipient was likely a chief within the departments of legal secretaries. Remuneration includes exemptions from fiscal obligations.

King Theoderic to Stephanus, Count of the
First Grade and Former Chief of Our Bureau

1. Compensation of the first order must be paid for work performed well, since service that passes unremunerated is looked upon as having been reproached. The palm designates the athlete as a victor before the people. The civic crown bears witness to exertions in war. Even horses await their own reward, and such is the strength of justice that a fee should be given unhesitatingly for those services that are not found wanting. **2.** Because, if these things are true, it is worthwhile to return something to a man who is recognized for pleasing with honorable obedience. For you have held a firm course of upright service among so many dangerous uncertainties of the courts, and, what appears rarely among those serving, the alternation of judges around you never altered your course. Nor was there in you any jealousy for the judgment received by another, even when an opponent restored the verdicts of your predecessors in office. Indeed, you have managed to please all, since you have ever been a watchman to what is most cherished, a confidant in secrets, effective in legal cases, and constantly at the work of public office. And what the frequent vices of men have made a blessing of rare self-control, while you offer dutiful respect to many, to none would you sell your service. **3.** You have smeared the name *princeps* with no filth, protecting the dignity of the title with the application of virtue.[3] Hence it is that, in the present dictate, we confer upon you the dignity of *spectabilis* rank, which antiquity rightly designated for those scrubbed clean by the sweat of public service. So that you may at length end the vigils of your labors, know yourself now secure in remuneration as a count of the first grade. **4.** And because a dignity should not be joined to the gratitude of a *Princeps* as though naked, nor something experienced with no utility be called a favor, we have also added to that generosity the same privileges which the divine constitutions had intended to be granted to former heads of your corps. Nor should you fear anything in these benefits which would perhaps be attempted in a novel usage. Thus, ancient mandate has discharged you from every exaction and base labor. **5.** But although we rightly free you from any obligation with this present remuneration, we nonetheless promise to have greater hope for future service. But since favors are cheap that do not offer something for the future, the foresight of a *Princeps* will add to it, so that those whom we have found worthy of our goodwill we should also heap with the greatest distinction. Since the blessing of kings truly ought not to be concealed, let the present elevation come to the attention of the provincial governor, with the effect that the intentions of all may recognize your proper elevation to the rank of *spectabilis* by our testimony, and that respectful observance of your discharge from the duties of public service be preserved inasmuch as it agrees with praise for our reign.

3. Note that the letter here describes how Stephanus preserved the dignity of his rank as *princeps* of an *officium*, not that of the king as *Princeps*; elsewhere in the letter, *Princeps* refers to Theoderic.

LETTER 2.31 (C. 507–11)

The oarsmen of state vessels (*dromonarii*) on the Po River are ordered to assemble and transport the couriers of the public post (*veredarii*) in order that the couriers may receive their salaries. It is not clear how often this may have taken place; by comparison, Gothic soldiers assembled once per year for the distribution of the donative, a bonus cash payment.

King Theoderic to the Dromonarii

1. Those who claim the name of civil servants ought to toil on behalf of the public. For what may a man accomplish if he should fail his avowed obedience, so that he neither finds private profit nor acquires glory from vigorous application? And therefore, our authority has prevailed upon the count of the sacred largesse, so that you ought to be gathered in place at Ostiglia, to the end that you would make an expedition along the Po River, in customary fashion with the state couriers, in order to be refreshed by the treasury's kindness. Thus, by a division of labor, it ought to assist the public couriers, since your path does not wear away, you who set out upon a watery course. For it does not happen that you, who travel by means of the strong arm, would become lame with excessive toil. Your conveyance feels no injury, nor does that which is carried instead by flowing waves suffer failure.

LETTER 3.19 (C. 507–11)

This letter appoints a craftsman to superintend the production, sale, and disposition of marble sarcophagi at Ravenna. The appointee's obligation to prevent corruption is couched in terms of duty to the bereaved.

King Theoderic, a Notice to Daniel

1. It is fitting that we reflect upon just deserts for those serving in our palace, since public duty ought to be most advantageous, so that, although willing obedience should rightly be owed to us, nonetheless, we provide enticement for service by means of moderate payment. And therefore, having been delighted by the skill of your craftsmanship, which you practice so carefully by carving and adorning marble, we grant in the present dictate that the sarcophagi which are arranged for the disposition of burial remains in the city of Ravenna should be administered according to your own reasonable management, by which benefit corpses are interred above ground, no small consolation for the bereaved when so many souls depart from worldly association, but the survivors may not abandon once sweet countenances. **2.** Hence, the grieving agree to any price, and profit from commerce in human dead increases with the wretched lot of the devoted. Nevertheless, let the appraisal not be unjust under this circumstance, lest the wretched be compelled to bemoan the loss of their means in the midst of the bitterness of painful grief and be forced to acts contrary to devotion, with the grieving being pressed upon either to lose patrimony on behalf of the dead or, instead, to cast a beloved body into some base pit. Let the cost be at the inclination of those requesting, when lamentation itself reveals those counterfeiting grief. For he ought to be outraged less, who is known to be cheated more on account of duty to piety.

LETTER 4.47 (C. 507–11)

A lengthy letter to a *saio* charged with regulating the usage of the public transport system. The letter seeks to remedy a number of abuses that had been common since the high empire.

King Theoderic to Gudisal, Saio

1. Those things known to be placed in constant use must be revived with careful attention. Given that, how might the conveyance of the post-horses suffice for the necessary task if they are permitted to be used beyond measure? Truly, a neglected stewardship is an inducement to wrongful presumptions. **2.** And so, we have learned from the report of our envoys that the post-horses are weakened by frequent misuse,[4] and that which we wish to preserve for public necessity we know has been taken for use by private inclination. And therefore, we order you to reside in Rome in the command of the praetorian prefect and the master of offices, whom public need will advise, so that you should permit neither Goth nor Roman, except those whom the deputy assistants of the aforementioned offices will have sent forth, to set

4. Envoys regularly used the public transport network.

out thence on public mounts. **3.** And, because it is reported to us that this misappropriation occurs frequently, if anyone has perhaps attempted to claim post-horses from those unwilling agents to whom this care has been entrusted, whether it would be on account of his birth or his rank, let him be compelled to bear the fine of one hundred *solidi* per horse, not because the harm to a single beast of burden is deemed so great, but because insolent abuse must be reprimanded by considerable loss. **4.** Henceforth, you should permit none of the *saiones* to make excursions except for a purpose that has been ordered. They are permitted to travel and return only by one route. On much longer routes, let frequent changes of horse occur. **5.** Moreover, let none of the packhorses exceed a load of one hundred pounds. For we want those who must be dispatched to hasten unimpeded; we do not expect them to travel widely. Whoever carries many things with himself produces his own slothfulness, nor does one who prefers to haul himself about in luxuriously outfitted travel understand anything of speed. When storks are about to cross the ocean, they clutch small pebbles in the claws of their feet, so that their lightness may not be snatched at by excessive winds, nor is their native swiftness overburdened by unsuitable weight. Should not one who knows he has been chosen for public needs imitate this? And so, let anyone who supposes that a packhorse must bear more than one hundred pounds incur a further fine of fifty *solidi,* not only the courier, but also the muleteer. **6.** Moreover, we additionally expect you to have regard for those of the office of the post who are present in the city, to the extent that any digression from these mandates that is detected should be punished by your action according to the above-cited measures. However, if any intemperate person prefers the fine, we want the amount collected by the deputy assistants to be given to the purchasing agents of the changing stations,[5] so that the transport circuit might have a remedy where thus far it has assumed only inconvenience. **7.** Thus in worldly affairs prosperity often emerges from adversity, and when men desire to cause damage they often impart something good. But fulfill everything thus, efficiently and diligently, so that, incited by your good accomplishments, we ought to entrust greater things to your devotion.

5. Presumably for the purchase of new horses.

LETTER 11.6 (C. 533)

Cassiodorus here appoints a *cancellarius,* or bailiff, charged with managing admission (including screening potential entrants) to the audience hall of the praetorian prefect.

Praetorian Prefect Senator to John, Cancellarius

1. Although every public service is discharged according to its own stipulated rank, and those who occupy them by appointment of magistrates observe tenures appropriate to each, your distinction is acknowledged not to be held by established practice, for you have deserved to supersede your own superiors. Indeed, those who are known to precede you in official rank render services to you, and, in a reversed condition of justice, you appear as one who must be respected by those to whom you clearly ought to be subservient. You conduct this fair inequity, a special ordinance and a particular benefit, with the appearance of a judge; nor is what seems to be claimed from a faultless arrangement able to be reasonably censured. **2.** No man prescribes the nature of your tenure. Your duty is a transgression of the public roster, and you alone confidently ignore what you compel others to observe. But such privileges have been conceded to you on account of your outstanding merits; one known to be our choice ought to be trusted to surpass all men in diligence and good faith. For no man proves himself ready to advance except one to whom a commendable virtue attaches itself; it is shameful to elevate a lesser man, unless he should seem to excel other men in merits. **3.** Therefore, the dignity of a *cancellarius* grants to you this commendable miscarriage of justice, a preferential sentence and a domestic service, from the twelfth indiction, so that you may protect the intimate chambers of our office with complete fidelity. Let those who must be admitted approach through you; let the desires of petitioners become known to our ears through you. May you expedite our orders without attention to private gain, and may you accomplish everything else, likewise, so that you would be able to commend our justice. For your service is the reputation of your own judge, and just as the interior of a home is able to be known correspondently from its street front, thus the disposition of a head of office is thought to be depicted through you. Cause no insult, since such a thing would bring all men to decide for themselves what kind of a response they should expect. **4.** Would it not be a disgrace to us if the very garments that are placed on our bodies were soiled with some filth? How much more pleasingly are they truly seen to adorn us when they shine with commendable purity! Thus does the secretary before the private chambers of the judge either decorate or besmirch the reputation of his president. Those who oppress others certainly sin against us, and when the privilege of the one serving is prostituted, the reputation of the magistrate in office is ruined. **5.** Consider if we ought to ignore how it is that we would come to censure. It is senseless beyond everything that we would not seek to punish one who is known for plotting to our own shame. Behold by what title you are named. It is not possible to conceal what you will do behind screens.[6] Indeed, you maintain a transparent store front, an open enclosure, windowed doors; and although you may close them carefully, it is necessary that you present yourself to all. For if you were to stand outside, you would not be free of my scrutiny; if you should step within, you could not avoid the observance of those in the court. **6.** See where antiquity determined to place you: you who bask in such brilliance at every turn will be seen from all directions. Thence, turn your ears and heart to our admonition; fix everything that we have ordered in your mind. Let not these words pour through you as though through an empty pipe which appears full only so long as the water flows in it. Be, rather, a receptacle that preserves what is heard because it does not pour out what was received; for it will profit nothing if whatever words having crossed the thresholds of your ears should please and yet not fasten themselves in the chambers of your heart.

LETTER 11.36 (C. 533–38)

A *delegatoria* was a writ authorizing the payment of public funds. This letter is a *delegatoria* ordering a *cancellarius* to disperse a pension to the chief legal aide of an official following his discharge from service. The pension was to be paid out of the tax revenues of the province of Samnium. The letter includes a digression on natural philosophy and a testimonial to Cassiodorus's own record as a magistrate.

---

6. The title *cancellarius* derived from the *cancellus* (lattice) that formed a barrier to the presence of a judge.

Praetorian Prefect Senator to Anatolicus,
Cancellarius *of the Province of Samnium*

1. The one who invented laborious vigils and duties requiring great exertion quite reasonably also established limits of tenure, so that the reward set for the term of active service should have no uncertainty. Who would otherwise be able to continually serve and attend, when the very light withdraws itself from mortal affairs? For which reason, civil service is certain in an uncertain life, lest one who deserves to reach that appointed term without offense be apprehensive about what he holds.[7] **2.** The very stars, as astronomers claim, although they revolve in ceaseless repetition, preserve the set paces of their courses. What is held confined by its own fixity cannot be inconsistent. Saturn travels the course of the heavens appointed to it in thirty years. The star of Jove illuminates the region assigned it in twelve years. The heavenly body of Mars, seized by fiery celerity, traces its determined course in eighteen months. The sun passes the signs of the zodiacal belt in the span of a year. The star of Venus arches over the space given it in fifteen months. Mercury, girt with speed, rides through the span set for it in thirteen months. The moon, closer to us in our own neighborhood, accomplishes in thirty days what the golden, circumscribing sun completes in the span of a year. **3.** Mortals, therefore, rightly find an end to labor when, as the philosophers say, even those bodies which are unable to perish except with the world have received, quite reasonably, limits to their course; nevertheless, with this distinguishing difference, that they end their own work, so that they may return to the beginning, whereas humankind serves so that it may rest when labors are accomplished. **4.** And therefore, disperse without any hesitation to x, who blamelessly completed the office of adjutant, the seven hundred *solidi* that established custom assigned to him, from the third payment of taxes for the y indiction in the province of Samnium, since it is not possible to question the reward of one whom the formal and genuine discharge of a magistrate commends. For, acknowledged for praiseworthy service, he supervised the judicial chambers of the praetorian bureau, whence his title is derived.[8] By his assistance, we

7. That is, lest he fear being discharged from service without a pension.

8. The chief legal aide to the praetorian prefect was called a *cornicularius;* Cassiodorus associates the title with the *cornua,* or judicial bench.

signed in ink, uncompromised, what used to be done with preference to weighty bribes, we gave preference to those whom the law favored, we rejected those to whom justice offered no surety. **5.** No one grieved for his own victory, since he obtained it with his resources secure, not sold, when the verdict arrived in his favor. You know all that we say, for your personal assistance was not conducted in our private chambers; what we did, the bureau knew. No doubt, we caused grievances as a private citizen, but we represented honor as a magistrate. Our discipline was considered in words and our kindness was felt in deeds. We became wrathful for peace, we threatened harmlessly, and, so that we could not do harm, we were seen wielding terror. As you were accustomed to say, you have a magistrate of the greatest purity; I leave you as the most uncorrupted witness.

LETTER 11.37 (C. 533–38)

This letter is a type similar to *Variae* 11.36 (above), ordering a *cancellarius* to award, from the tax revenues of Campania, the pension of discharge from public service to a department head. It also allowed Cassiodorus to wax effusively on the virtues of state service.

Praetorian Prefect Senator to Lucinus, Clarissimus *and* Cancellarius *of Campania*

1. It has been well provided by ancient regulation that those who serve the public weal should receive in return the value of their services, lest anyone who must be commended for upstanding duty be passed over. For from what office would remuneration be expected, if rewards are withheld from praetorian servants? For almost everything that is accomplished in the republic is completed with their exertion, for this office requires every other to comply, thus that it may not be permitted to transgress; and, what is the most difficult kind of service, it attends the needs of the army: it is subject to armed forces and carries favor there, where another office would find censure. **2.** How would we order tax payments, planned with great precision, to be collected by complex procedure? And who exacts from those whom none dare to offend? Not only must the rations that are stored for distribution at a distance be attributed to their exertions, but without complaint they gather at the royal city those goods native to the provinces, so that when something is sought at the appropriate moment, it is not considered a loss to the one giving. 3. The service of such men is our glory, the reputation of our tenure, the effective strength of our commands, and whatever we receive for the sake of any obligated kindness we justly attribute to their preparations. Those assigned to toil gleam with the practice of that very thing, which always renders men educated; labors: let me call them harsh masters and relentless teachers, through which anyone may be made more careful, when dangers are feared to be incurred. Let someone be educated in oratory and another be taught in some other discipline; nonetheless, that man who is honed in the devotion of continuous service is rendered the more learned. 4. And therefore, what is deserved by such men must be paid with honor, so that one who had always acquired profit for the republic may at some point receive it for himself. Concerning which, we order you to give to that department head already discharged from the labor of service the appropriate amount of *solidi* from the taxes of the third payment from the province of Campania, so that man may fully enjoy just labors and his successors may find an example of willing servitude, when they know him to have been well accoutered on account of his own fidelity.

LETTER 12.1 (C. 533–38)

The first three letters of Book 12 constitute a triad mobilizing the fiscal apparatus for the annual collection of taxes. The first is a forceful letter addressed to the *cancellarii* who acted as praetorian representatives administrating tax collection in each province. It focuses on mutual responsibility for a shared reputation that corruption might impair. The designation of the indiction year as *x* may imply that this was intended as a form letter that would have been dispatched to *cancellarii* on an annual basis.

Praetorian Prefect Senator to the Various Cancellarii of Individual Provinces

1. How could someone who is sent from the inner counsels of his judge not be considered important, since anyone is thought to love justice more in proportion to how often he is known to have audience there? The judge is known by his public servants, and, just as students

spread the teaching of the master, thus does the conduct of our servants expose us. The precipitate man is not thought to have heeded a
careful one; the greedy man is not believed to have obeyed a man of
restraint; the fool is not considered to have attended men of wisdom.
2. I confess that we are judged by our actions, if you follow bad intentions, and, what affects none but you, the scandal of other men spreads
to our disgrace. We endure such a downfall as we could not inflict
upon others, and the law, by which all men prosper, cannot safeguard
us. But, on the other hand, we have consolation through the role
played by others, because your good deeds are accounted as our mandates and whatever glory develops from your service is attached to us
without effort. **3.** For if anyone should observe you acting wisely, it
immediately exalts the reputation of your teacher, since the type of
deeds witnessed are likewise assumed to have been learned. However
you happen to be judged will be the unanimous opinion of the people
concerning your judge. And so, particular care must be taken, lest the
one whose reputation you have previously damaged begin judging
you. Whatever you release to common gossip will be avenged with
punishments, and whatever a goaded populace amplifies will be
exacted from you with torments. How dangerous it is to endure a justifiably wrathful judge and for him, whom you have grievously incited,
to decide your future well-being. Therefore, take great care, so that
you will instead be praised by our voice, since just as the negative sentence of a judge is capable of oppressing you, thus may a favorable
decision elevate you. **4.** Therefore, hasten to that province for this
indiction with God's blessing, decorated with the ostentation of a *cancellarius* and girt with a dignified severity. Though you be far away,
know the honor of our presence. For what baseness would you, who
serve in office, dare to attempt? The *fasces* of magistrates obey you, and
while you are thought to bear the orders of the praetorian seat, you
assume some measure of that very authority by the reverence due to
you. Above all, observe our edicts; demonstrate the best course to
those serving under you. For whose responsibility is it to preserve the
mandates of the magistrate if our servants are seen to ignore things
properly decreed? **5.** Flee avarice, that queen of shameless vices, whom
all crimes service with reprehensible devotion, who, once she has
crossed the threshold of a man's heart, also admits a crowd of wicked
attendants. Once received, she cannot be removed, since she knows

not how to be solitary. She has the most flattering troop of followers; she takes up arms from money and sweetly overcomes those whom she captivates with bitter deception. Accordingly, be on guard for the public weal; discharge your obligations with moral vigor. Someone insistent upon reason accomplishes more than a dreaded man is able to coerce. Let your role be one of refuge for the oppressed, protection for the weak, and defense for one stricken by any calamity. For thus do you properly administer our legal domain, if you open the impious closures to the stricken.[9]

9. Cassiodorus here reminds the *cancellarii* of their role as wardens of the court by contrasting the "legal domain" of the prefect (*nostros cancellos*) with the illegal exclusion (*impia claustra*) of the needy.

Section IV

Taxes and State Finances

*Letters Describing Fiscal Organization and the
Collection and Distribution of State Resources*

The primary function of an elaborate state administration was the redistribution of wealth, collected primarily as taxes, for the maintenance of the military and the allocation of payments and privileges that buoyed the loyalty of officials and magistrates involved in state service. The *Variae* provide testimony for a number of different taxes (such as land and sales taxes), the methods and personnel used for their collection, and their redistribution as salaries and public rations to the military and other public personnel. The *Variae* further disclose how the payment or deferment of taxes could become a moment to renegotiate and reaffirm loyalty to the state when a community experienced financial or even environmental strain. They also reveal the extents to which both state officials used the administration for personal profit and the Amal court attempted to curb such deeply engrained practices.

LETTER 1.14 (C. 507–11)

Addressed to the praetorian prefect, who was ultimately responsible for the collection of taxes, this letter approves a request from a municipality to pay its taxes in one installment, as opposed to the customary schedule of three portions (*tertiae*).

King Theoderic to Faustus, Praetorian Prefect

1. With pleasure do we extend our complete consent, so just is the voice of those petitioning, since it is hardly possible for a favor to be difficult that does not diminish liberality. **2.** And therefore, in regard to the manner of the *tertiae* which is born by the Catalienses,[1] let your lofty splendor cause it to be paid in total as a single annual tax, nor hereafter should those petitioning endure any requisition beyond this share. For what does it matter under what name the landowner bears a responsibility, provided that he pays what is owed without reduction? And thus we remove from them the mistrusted title of the *tertiae,* and by our mildness we banish discomfort from those paying.

LETTER 1.16 (C. 507–8)

This letter grants a deferment of rents owed by tenants on state property for one tax cycle (an indiction). The deferment is couched in the language of reciprocity so common to descriptions in the *Variae* of the relationship of governmental authority to the obligations of the governed.

King Theoderic to Julianus, Count of the Patrimony

1. Let us share more fully, to our own benefit, in what we grant on behalf of human misfortune. For the resources of the ruler would then become more enriched, when it remits something and acquires a distinguished treasure of more noble coin by means of denying parsimony. Hence it is that we extend means to the weak and a hand to the overburdened, so that, stirred by the humanity of our policy, those who sink down under the calamity of their own fortune may rise up by the remedy of our devotion. **2.** Not long ago, the state tenants of Apulia complained bitterly to us in a sorrowful petition that their crops had been burned in enemy raids,[2] requesting that they, for whom the substance of payment has been reduced, not be compelled to make full payment of rents owed. Therefore, we declare, on behalf of what must be considered out of innate kindness, that we are unable to accuse those of idleness whose fortune we deem must be restored.

1. Possibly the Catali, a people of Venetia or Istria.

2. Apulia's proximity to ports of the eastern empire makes it more likely that these were eastern imperial attacks, although Vandal attacks are also plausible. For a similar complaint concerning enemy raids, see *Var.* 2.38 (below).

For now, we wish to assume their regular debt, whence subsequent payments should occur at the appropriate time. 3. And therefore, we order that your eminence diligently inquire into this matter, so that, however much less it will be determined for them to have sold, you should detract this with accustomed moderation from the remaining payment on the first indiction. Nevertheless, let no fraud be associated with our beneficence, lest you be obliged to restore anything overlooked, you who have always pleased us by your inclination to foresight, because just as the losses of supplicants touch us, so ought their profits be payments to us.

LETTER 1.19 (C. 507–11)

One of many letters addressing various forms of fiscal corruption. In this case, Theoderic responds to a petition from the town counsellors of Adriana, where, it seems, some citizens spurned the assessed payment, with the result that the difference fell disproportionately on poorer landowners. The official appointments held by the addressees of this letter are unknown.

King Theoderic to Saturninus and Umbisuus, Spectabiles

1. We wish to protect the legal advantage of the fisc, since our generosity is seen to be maintained by means of our own property, and just as we desire to burden no one, so we ought not to lose debts owed to us. We justly avoid want, which it is a pleasure to exceed, while poverty in one ruling is a ruinous state. And here moderation must be praised. For why should a censurable carelessness descend upon one's own property or an execrable greed extort from another? 2. And therefore, we instruct you in the present order that with respect to the petition received from the curia of the city of Adriana, whoever declines to pay to the fisc of the Goths you should constrain to the equity of redress, lest the poor man be compelled to pay from his own property because the other man held back the appropriate amount without paying. With this evident reason observed, such that if anyone should prefer to impede our command with criminal obstinacy, since he could gain much because he will not need to submit the obligatory amount, in a just age let bald temerity not be left unpunished with such an indecently impudent spirit.

LETTER 1.35 (C. 507–11)

One of the more fascinating examples of natural history in the collection, this letter fulminates against the praetorian prefect for delays in the shipment of taxed grain for which nature herself could offer no excuses.

King Theoderic to Faustus, Praetorian Prefect

1. Although the dryness of the current year, which customarily ravages this region in certain seasons, has hardened the inland areas with excessive heat, it is not so much that it produces a harvest of crops that must be abandoned as that it brings forth only partial fruitfulness. This crop, which is normally expected even in abundant times, now must be demanded with greater eagerness. **2.** And therefore, we are irritated not to have received in the autumn, by any manner, the public grain, which is customarily to be sent in the summer from the Calabrian and Apulian shores by your *cancellarius*. With the course of the sun rushing back to southern skies, the measured arrangement of nature revives the tumultuous storms with an agitation of the atmosphere, which is given from these same months in order to know when preparation for the amount of rains to come should be suitably undertaken. Why, therefore, such a delay? Would not ships sent out into such calmness be swift? Would not the clear position of stars dipping into the sea invite sails to swiftly spread, and would not faith in calm skies fail to deter the promise of hastening? **3.** Or, perhaps, with a favorable southern wind and oarsmen assisting, remoras fetter the course of the ships, delayed even now among the waves. Or do the conchs of the Indian Sea fasten their lips to the bottoms of the ships to similar effect? It is said that the gentle hold of these restrains a vessel more than the disturbed elements are able to drive. A winged ship would stand unmoving with swollen sails and have no course: even though the wind should be favorable, it stands fixed without anchor, it is fettered without ropes, and so a small animal holds it back more than the assistance of fair weather may compel it. Thus, while submissive waters prepare the course, it happens that the hull of the ship stands transfixed beneath the sea and by a marvelous means is restrained, swimming motionlessly, while the water is driven along by innumerable waves. **4.** But let us mention another kind of fish: perhaps the

sailors of the aforementioned ships languish on account of the para-
lyzing touch of the eel, by which skilled hands are weighed down by
such fixedness that it thus corrupts the hand as though stricken
through by a spear (to which it would be vulnerable), to the extent that
a portion of the living body is stunned and immobile without any feeling. We believe that these sailors who are unable to move themselves
have acquired such an affliction. But for them the impediment of the
remora is venality, the bite of the conch is insatiable greed, the eel is
the pretense of fraud. Indeed, these very men have fabricated delays
with a perverse eagerness, so that opportunities for embarking should
seem adverse. Let your greatness, for whom it is especially important
to be concerned about such things, cause this to be corrected by the
most expedient emendation, lest the poverty native to this region
seem to be not so much from the bareness of the season as from negligence.

LETTER 2.4 (C. 507-11)

The recipient of this letter, addressed as "honorable gentleman" (*vir
honestus*), apparently possessed neither rank nor title and should be
regarded as a familiar at the Amal court. The letter awards him the
administration of sales taxes, including the support of a *saio,* a Gothic
retainer of the king, for which reason the addressee is warned not to
abuse the mandate of the present writ.

King Theoderic to Ecdicius, Honorable Gentleman

1. We are delighted by the inventions of antiquity and we gladly
embrace the following of established rules, since however much established practices are safeguarded in accordance with reason, a place
is not allowed for deceitful practices. And therefore, we decide in the
present mandate on a course suggested by your petitions, so that
whatever pertained to Antiochus concerning the administration of
titles to the *monopolium* or *siliquaticum* taxes, by our order should be
transferred in similar measure to you, now fortified with sound fairness by the present mandate against the treachery of any false claim-
ants. Moreover, our authority solemnly assigns you to have the support of a *saio,* for the purpose of assuming the aforementioned titles.
Nevertheless, your legal protection thus should become less entangled

with private business. For what we have granted for support should in no way be perceived as contrary to justice, since the *saio* reasonably regards you as beyond blame, if, through your influence, he should feel another whom you request to be brought before you to be injurious to himself.

LETTER 2.12 (C. 507–11)

The agents who regulate commerce and ports in Italy are forbidden to allow the export of cured meats.

King Theoderic to the Count of the Sales Tax Agents and to the Agent of Port Affairs

1. If foreign commerce serves our needs, if foreign obedience is attained with offered gold, how much more ought Italy to abound in its own goods, since it is assumed that no obstacles to obedience would be tolerated? And therefore, we command that under no circumstance should any kind of cured meat[3] be sent to foreign regions, but that it should serve higher purposes in our use, lest criminal neglect be seen to have diminished what is produced in our realm. **2.** Therefore be warned, lest the smallest opportunity whatever present itself for blame, knowing well the severest consequence if you should strive to support this injunction only half-heartedly. The sin is a matter of kind, not quantity. Indeed, injury requires no measure. If even some small measure of *imperium* is despised, then it is violated in every portion.

LETTER 2.17 (C. 507–11)

Addressed to all citizens directly involved in the collection of taxes at Trento, this letter resolves issues arising from the tax immunity granted to a local priest, Butila, absolving the community from the amount that his property had previously contributed to the calculation of total taxes owed from the municipality.

---

3. *Laridus* translates as either "cured pork" or "lard"; *species laridi* is even less specific. Cured meats were crucial sources of protein in periods of scarcity.

King Theoderic to the Leading Citizens, Landowners,
Public Defenders, and Town Counsellors of Trento

1. We want our beneficence to stand out as a loss to no man, nor should what is conferred upon one man be applied to the expenses of another. And therefore, be aware by the present dictate that nobody ought to make payment from the calculation of fiscal revenues for that portion which, in our liberality, we have applied to the presbyter Butila, but in that payment the amount of *solidi* owed is satisfied. Consider it to be removed from your collection of the taxes. Nor do we want anyone to be responsible for what, in our kindness, we have removed from another person, lest, it is criminal to say, a gift for the well-deserving should happen to become an expense for the innocent.

LETTER 2.23 (C. 507–11)

A contract with three officials for the management of a pottery works, confirming protection against suits that would transfer the contract to other persons or transfer the competence of the officials to other endeavors.

King Theoderic to Ampelius, Despotius,
and Theodulus, Spectabiles

1. It befits the discipline of our reign that those who provide service to the common weal should not be loaded with overabundant burdens. Nor is it right that the jealousy of any person should harm arrangements made by our intention. On that account, apply yourselves energetically to the operation of the pottery works granted to you by royal authority; nor should you fear it possible to be passed on to other offices, from which we trust you have been disentangled already by the present order. Therefore, the shameful presumption of bad persons around you will cease and our authority will destroy anything caused by concealed treachery. For he is hated in vain, to whom the kindness of a *Princeps* has offered itself as protection.

LETTER 2.38 (C. 507–11)

Responding to a petition from merchants at Sipontum, this letter orders the praetorian prefect to suspend compulsory purchases and debts owed until the merchants could restore property damaged during an enemy attack, referring perhaps to Vandal or Byzantine raids along the Italian coast. For a similar complaint concerning foreign attack, see *Variae* 1.16 (above).

King Theoderic to Faustus, Praetorian Prefect

1. We desire our wealth to be increased by a treasury of devotion, cursing advantages to us that have been acquired by the misfortunes of troubled people. That payment which is lamented burdens our clemency, since whatever attaches to the reputation of the one receiving is measured by happiness. 2. And so the merchants of Sipontum[4] claim that they have been devastated by an enemy raid, and since we would rather appraise our wealth in terms of solace to the needy, let your *illustris* magnificence cause those named[5] to be troubled by no compulsory exactions for two years uninterrupted. 3. But since it profits nothing to have relieved the downfallen if another burden of payment should then accrue, let your eminence be advised concerning those of the aforementioned merchants who are known to have borrowed money, lest within this span of two years someone think the amount owed must be demanded. Thus, under the provisions of this judgment they should be able to restore the money given and in some measure the property of the debtors should be sound enough to be restored. For what does it profit the creditor to goad himself when he strains to compel the destitute in vain? We foresee a greater advantage for them if we cause them to collect a loan by extending it.

LETTER 4.38 (C. 507–11)

This letter responds to a petition from two groups of people (it is unknown whether these were citizens of a municipality or farmers of estates) claiming that their tax assessment was not proportionate to the low yield of production. It decrees that they should return to the tax assessments paid in the time of Odoacer's reign (476–89).

---

4. In Apulia, on the eastern shore of Italy.

5. *Nuncupatos* here may refer to a list of exempt merchants that had been attached to the original letter.

King Theoderic to Faustus, Praetorian Prefect

1. While we desire all regions of our republic to be enriched equally, yet the increase of fiscal tribute must be considered with the fairest possible judgment, since an increase of revenue is the diminishment of those serving, and however much one region produces, it detracts as much from its own strength. But the ever-harmful increase of taxes must be prevented by us, who want the utility of a stable fisc to be well established for all time, lest by swelling with its own increase the fisc begin to weaken the more enormous it seems to grow. 2. Thence, let your *illustris* greatness be aware that the citizens of Gravassius and Pontonis have petitioned us, that they have been burdened with unjust assessments by Januarius and also by Probus, the auditors, while the excessive unfruitfulness of their estates permits no surplus to accrue to them. Because any amount of hard work yields to the resistance of nature, it does not profit them to expend the effort of toil that the fertility of the place is known not to support. Where cultivation will produce, there the census may be increased. Thence, even tribute is variable, because the fertility of the fields is not consistent. 3. And so, we have determined that the former practice must be restored for them, so that the tribute they paid in the time of Odoacer may now be a service by them to public weal. And if anything is shown to have increased, we would yield more in favor of their depleted resources. For we do not want any such thing proclaimed that would later be necessary to remove.

LETTER 5.6 (C. 523–26)

This letter orders the restitution of overdue rents from an individual who had contracted to manage several royal estates. A *comitiacus* is ordered to assign a lien on the individual's private property in satisfaction of the debt. Because the matter concerned royal estates, the *comitiacus* was an agent of the count of the patrimony.

King Theoderic to Stabularius, Comitiacus

1. A measure must be taken that does not act contrary to public advantage and that seeks a remedy encompassing the desires of private individuals, so that these concerns may not seem to produce a loss to us.

And so, we have learned in the complaint of the *clarissimus* John that Thomas has taken responsibility for certain estates of our household, that is, x and y, and now has postponed the return of ten thousand *solidi* for our advantage and, through diverse ploys, does not pay the owed amount. This has also been made perfectly clear to us by the report of our court officials.[6] **2.** Therefore, we believe that provisions must be made for such a remedy, that you ought to apply a lien to all the property of the aforementioned Thomas on behalf of a public debt, to the extent that if, by the kalends of September, less than what is reasonably expected will have been paid by Thomas, let the aforementioned property be deeded to the *clarissimus* John, who has promised to pay the debt owed to our treasury. But if the aforementioned Thomas should somehow be able to pay his obligation within the predetermined time, let all property that has been taken from him be returned undiminished, so that thus, our fisc may not be seen to suffer a disadvantage and we may be known to offer the expected justice to our subjects. We would be able to delay even beyond this point if anything were produced in favor of this most irresponsible individual, whom we have ever found to be unwilling for such a very long period of time.

LETTER 11.39 (C. 533–38)

This letter orders a reduction of the tax burden for citizens of Lucania and Bruttium, with the additional treat of Cassiodorus's digression on the history of how this province contributed to the provisioning of Rome.

Praetorian Prefect Senator to Vitalianus, Clarissimus *and* Cancellarius *of Lucania and Bruttium*

1. It becomes apparent how great was the population of the city of Rome, as it was fed from abundant provisions from even distant regions, to such an extent that the immediately surrounding provinces sufficed for the victuals of visiting foreigners, while imported plenty

---

6. Whereas John was a treasury official in charge of balancing accounts (*arcarius*), the other officials who confirmed his report are here described as *proceres*, which is a general term ("court officials") rather than a specific appointment.

served the city itself. For how could those who possessed dominion over the world manage to be small in number! **2.** For the vast span of the walls, the strained circuit of spectacles, the wondrous mass of the baths, and the numerousness of water mills, which are known to be associated especially with provisioning, all bear witness to the crowds of citizens. For if this last apparatus had not been useful, it would have no importance, when it is able neither to furnish ornament nor to complement any other part of the city. In sum, these things are thus tokens of cities, as though the precious garments of bodies, since none rest from creating the excesses that are known to advertise themselves by their great cost. **3.** For hence it was that mountainous Lucania provided pigs, hence that Bruttium offered herds of cattle from its native wealth. No doubt both are wondrous, that these provinces would suffice for such a city and that, by their services, such a full city should have no lack of provisions. Indeed, it was their glory to supply Rome— but it was known that they were able to deliver at great loss what was offered by weight through so many journeys, while nobody was able to reckon what was proven to decrease! **4.** The levy was reduced to a payment, because it was neither diminished by traveling nor stricken by exertion. Let the provinces know their own blessings. For if their ancestors were loyal even in loss, why would these today not be generous in paying from profits?[7] And therefore, your diligence will direct both assessments to the public taxes, now reduced to the established payments, lest those who had obeyed nonresident officials with commendable integrity seem to be neglected during my tenure. **5.** For although I have endeavored to restore other provinces as well, nonetheless, nothing has been accomplished in these provinces that I would wish to claim. These provinces have experience of me as their governor, and those whom I represented as a private citizen, following my grandfather and great-grandfather, I tenaciously strove to assist in my official capacity, so that those whom I noticed rejoicing with well-intended adulation at my promotion should acknowledge I retained affection for my homeland. Therefore, let them obey not from any

---

7. The tax was formerly paid in kind with the delivery of livestock to Rome, and the journey naturally reduced the weight (and value) of the animals; later, with the tax value converted from weight to a set price, the provincials satisfied this burden with profits received from the local sale of their livestock.

compulsion, but from love, when I have reduced for them even the amount that was customarily offered. For while twelve hundred *solidi* had been dispersed in annual payment, I have reduced the payment again, to one thousand *solidi,* through royal generosity, so that they may celebrate, with an increase of joy from the diminishment of their burdens.

LETTER 12.10 (C. 533-38)

This letter warns about a familiar form of peculation: officials accepting bribes to defer the payment of taxes, resulting in spiraling debt for landowners and the state. Here, *cancellarii* charged with collecting taxes in the provinces are threatened with the loss of personal property and degrading removal from office should the practice persist.

Praetorian Prefect Senator to Various Cancellarii *of the Provinces*

1. The neglected portions of public accounts must be compared to an unfortunate sickness. What burdens also enfeebles, unless quickly discharged. Indeed, it is a kind of condemnation to be in debt, nor is it possible for one who is known to be indebted to truly be called free. The wise man compels himself; less careful is the man who is urged by another. For what does harassment endured for an entire year accomplish? The amount owed consumes the payment of future indictions. 2. You do not spare them by holding back payment; you weigh them down by releasing them, and when you seek delays purchased with bribery, you double the burden of taxation. Abandon, then, this cruel mercy, a kindness completely steeped in accursedness. One who connives by being kind strikes more severely, and one who delays collecting taxes within the accustomed time injures with generosity. And so, desist from selling the losses of the landowners at any time, since you render entirely constrained by disadvantages what you disregard with harmful postponements. For after such practices, do not expect that you will be warned again with words, but that you will be compelled by irrevocable distraint. 3. Therefore, if you have neither sent to our treasury on x day the amount that is annually required from the provincials, nor balanced the difference in the accounts from your own resources, you will instantly be dishonorably discharged from the

province where you know you have been dilatory, since it is exceedingly corrupt that the public account should fall to your negligence and that the treasurer should constantly pay out money borrowed from public use.

LETTER 12.28 (C. 535–36)

In this last letter of the collection, Cassiodorus communicates a royal decree to remit half of the taxes normally imposed upon the provinces of Liguria and Aemilia. The letter dwells on the themes of warfare and famine, thus connecting it to both the prevailing environmental conditions and the politics of maintaining loyalty in Italy during the Gothic War.

An Edict

1. Who does not know that divine providence elects to remove certain things from our use, so that it will be able to test the integrity of humanity? For if it should happen that nobody was in deep need, then generosity would have no place. Penury is given to provincials for the praise of our king; fields have been made barren so that the fruitfulness of our ruler might become manifest. It would be a less appreciated gift if some hardship had not preceded it. Rejoice, provincials! Give thanks instead for your misfortunes, when you have proven the spirit of the *Princeps* to be such that he yields before no adversity. Behold such remarkable duty, which everywhere opposes our disadvantages. **2.** For, as you will doubtless remember, when the savagery of the tribes had roused itself in a previous time, your Aemilia and Liguria were troubled by an incursion of the Burgundians, and a war of raids was waged across the border, the fame of the present *imperium* immediately shone forth as though from a rising sun.[8] Having been forced out with arms, the enemy lamented his own presumption, when he recognized that man whose excellence he had tested in the

---

8. It seems likely that by *praesentis imperii,* Cassiodorus means the contemporary administration during the Gothic War, in which the Franks were induced to make incursions into Italy (Procopius, *Wars* 5.1.13); the reference to "Burgundians" may be explained by the fact that the Franks had annexed the Burgundian kingdom by 534.

capacity of a soldier to be the ruler of a celebrated people.[9] How often did the Burgundian wish he had not left his own borders, so that he would not contend with our *Princeps* as an adversary, whose presence it was permitted for him to avoid, once relieved of spoils, so that even the downtrodden should incur some blessing? **3.** For as soon as the Goths gathered themselves together with their native vigor for pressing war, thus was the band of raiders cut down in victorious battle, as though it had happened with unarmed men arrayed on one side and armed men on the other. By the equity of divine judgment, the plunderer fell in the very fields that he had presumed to lay waste. Rejoice, O province, adorned with the corpses of your adversaries; find cheer in the heap of dead that the ruin of your enemy clearly created. Liguria is better cultivated, having been denied its own crops—the enemy now provides a harvest of grain;[10] for even though your tribute had been reduced, you have demonstrated triumphs blessedly conceived in your province. **4.** To these events may be added the raid of the Alamanni, routed some time ago, which was proven to be overwhelmed in its very initial attempt, so that it simultaneously combined arrival and departure, as though purged by the salutary operation of a scalpel, to the extent that both the wicked disregard of those transgressing the law was punished and the plundering of subjects did not spread unchecked. I could easily enumerate for you how many hosts of enemy have fallen in other places, but being eager for your happiness, after the nature of the human heart, you will want us to speak only about that which you feel pertains specifically to you. **5.** Therefore, let us return to the delightful edict of the *Princeps,* since one who has defended you from the blows of war could not permit the dangers of poverty to abide; for one who ejects the enemy from the province likewise commands famine to depart. O struggle proclaimed throughout the world! The humanity of a glorious *Princeps* fights against cruel indigence, whose heaped granaries truly are military camps, which, if he intended to keep closed, an unbearable enemy would then enter; but because he has opened them more, he has already routed a cruel adversary. **6.** I know not for which war the world admires our *Princeps*

9. Witigis, king of Italy, 536–40.

10. This refers to either Burgundians taken as slaves or, more gruesomely, the fertilization of Ligurian fields with Burgundian dead.

more. Nonetheless, let me say what I feel. It is in the nature of brave men to conclude battles favorably, but it is clearly beyond human strength to conquer poverty. But even with these great feats and such favors, nothing has prevailed to satisfy the prayers of the needy, for which he has seen fit to remit half the payment of the taxes, lest he cause grief in some region where he has already bestowed so much happiness. 7. Thus we read that Joseph gave permission for grain to be sold even in the face of a disastrous famine, but the price was such that, being eager to render assistance, he was about to trade himself rather than sell the food.[11] What a time it was, I declare, to live then in such miseries, from which it was a bitter release to sacrifice one's own liberty, when the free man groans no less than the captive would weep! I believe the holy man was constrained by this necessity, that he should both satisfy a greedy *Princeps* and assist an endangered populace. Let me speak by leave of such a father:[12] it is so much more excellent to sell wholesome grain in liberty and to relax taxes on account of impoverishment! 8. Such is a pleasant kind of bribery, when thus it both yields to those buying and imposes a price that would please you. And so, public munificence will sell the amount of twenty-five *modii* for the price of ten, whenever the landowner is unable find it. Humanity has altered the nature of the world: we are ordered to sell cheaply when the man desirous of food would be prepared to purchase more dearly. O strange outcome of a proclamation! By the acceptance of a loss, both a sale is made and it is the wish of the seller to lose even more, so that by selling he ought to find profit. It is perfectly fitting for the king to conduct commerce such as this; such commerce agrees with the exercise of devotion, so that he should consent to receive less when the purchaser is predisposed to offer more. 9. It is fitting to remark what affection you should have for the one ruling, since he first consented to the amount he believed necessary and now he has doubled again what was requested. It was shameful for you to hope for anything after such gifts, when the kindness of the *Princeps* had thus far been held in reserve for favors. He does not despise things requested when he himself has witnessed the sight. It is a fortunate calamity that first finds a pitying man as witness, so that he should not afterward consider a

11. Genesis 41:50–57, 47:13–26.
12. That is, Joseph.

harsh judgment. Therefore rejoice, O Ligurian, already accustomed to favor: a second blessing arrives for your use. For by your remarkable good fortune you have surpassed the Egyptians compared to you; you have avoided a time of hardship and have not lost the gift of freedom. In contrast to that time, you have been rendered free of enemies, when you are also known to be secure from the peril of famine. **10.** However the aforementioned story honors you, it is surpassed by the present measure. For it is read that Joseph returned the price paid to his brothers only in bags of money. Does it surprise that by nature's compulsion he is seen to have been kinder to his own kindred? This ruler, however, has sold generously to all men; he has abandoned claim to an owed obligation and has conferred more to taxpayers in common than the other is known to have offered to his brothers alone. Let broadly cast blessings be proclaimed briefly: hence may the state learn of its own good fortune, when our age is compared not to that of kings but to that of prophets. But lest we delay the object of royal kindness any longer, know that our instructions have been published for those whom it concerns, so that according to the tenor of the command you may obtain the generosity of the *Princeps*.

Administration of the Provinces

*Letters Concerned with Ostrogothic
Affairs in Regions outside Italy*

The *Variae* not only provide a robust profile of administration in Italy
(itself comprising about twelve distinct provincial jurisdictions) but
also reveal attempts to maintain control of provinces outside Italy
proper. Sicily was a major source of revenue, and the provinces of Dalmatia, Pannonia, and Raetia were important as buffers to the military
opportunism of the eastern empire. Additionally, after the death of the
Visigothic king Alaric II in 507, Theoderic annexed the Visigothic territories of Gaul and Spain, thus achieving his ambition to rule regions
of the former Roman provincial system beyond Italy.

LETTER 2.19 (C. 507–11)

This sentence declares the servants of a murdered master to be out-
lawed. Although the place of the murder is undisclosed, the fact that
the letter is addressed to Goths and Romans at ports and border towns
suggests it was known or at least suspected that the assailants intended
to flee beyond Italy.

*King Theoderic to All Goths and Romans or Those Who
Preside in Ports and Border Fortresses*

1. Indeed, we rightly detest all crime, and the merciful man is repulsed
upon hearing everything that is perverse, but our censure especially
rouses itself against what is polluted by the letting of human blood. For
who would bear for danger to have a place in an inviolable household

and to have found the end of sweet life there, where assistance ought to have arisen in defense? **2.** And so, we command in the present dictate that you should detain by the severity of the law those from the household of Stephanus who, in a crime deserving punishment, slaughtered their own lord and, by leaving him exposed, defiled his burial. Look to it that those who would be roused to the most evil deeds would be enclosed by punishments. For the sake of grief! Familial devotion is found among the birds, which are separated from the human condition. **3.** The very vulture, for whom nourishment is the carcass of another creature, having a stature of such great size, is not seen to be hostile to lesser birds but rather strikes down for others the hawk, that bird keen for the lives of feathered animals, tearing at it with beak and striving with its entire bulk to subdue the dangerous creature. But men know not how to spare those whom they recognize to be kindred to themselves. A man should not wish to snuff out the one by whom he had been fed, yet these servants preferred to murder one who was accustomed to nourish those around him. Let them, therefore, become nutriment for the pious vulture, whoever is so cruelly capable of desiring the violent death of a shepherd. Let one who paid his master with an uncovered death instead get a tomb of that kind.

LETTER 3.16 (C. 508)

This letter appoints a vicar, or an assistant, to the praetorian prefect of Gaul, the southern portion of which had recently come under Ostrogothic rule. Although Liberius was later named the praetorian prefect of Gaul, subordination to a senior prefect is not mentioned in this letter or in the subsequent announcement to provincials in Gaul (*Variae* 3.17, below), indicating that the court at Ravenna had not yet made the important senior appointment.

King Theoderic to Gemellus, Spectabilis

1. Our judgment is decided, for which an example is at hand, nor is there room for ambiguity where credible experience approves. We have tested your ability through diverse stages of difficulty, but you, equally proven on various assignments, have earned like praise in each. **2.** Hence it is that, at the present time, our authority sends you to Gaul, now subject to us by God's will, as vicar. Whence may be seen what sort of opinions we hold concerning your measure, when you would be sent for guiding those people, whom we believe especially to have garnered our praise. The glory of a *Princeps* is costly, and it is necessary to be even more protective concerning those victories whence we have found ourselves arriving at an increase of triumphs.[1] Therefore, if you desire our esteem for you to advance, take this commission. Cherish not controversy and avoid avarice, so that an exhausted province may find you to be the kind of judge that it would expect a Roman *Princeps* to send. United by its own defeats, the province desires distinguished men. **3.** Make it so that the province would delight to have been conquered. Let it experience nothing like what it had endured, when it would long for Rome. Let it leave behind all the sadness of ruin; let a darkened countenance finally brighten. Let it happen that Gaul now rejoices, upon arrival at its own desires.

LETTER 3.17 (C. 508)

Presumably sent to the municipal assemblies of southern Gaul, this letter announces the appointment of Gemellus as vicar in Gaul (see *Variae* 3.16, above). It assumes the tone of a return to Roman civilization for Gallic provincials.

King Theoderic to All the Provincials of Gaul

1. You should gladly yield to Roman ways, to which you have been restored after long duration, since the return to where your forebears had their first advancement is welcome. And therefore, having been recalled by God's will to ancient liberty, clothe yourself with togate habits, move beyond barbarity, cast off a cruel disposition, since, under the equity of our reign, it is not fitting for you to live with foreign customs. **2.** Hence, thinking about your needs with the gentleness innate to us, what is said happily, we have decided that the *spectabilis* Gemellus must be directed to you as vicar, for the purpose of arranging matters in the province for us with diligence and good faith. We

---

1. A convoluted way of saying that Theoderic wished to be protective of the means by which his military glory had increased, with *illis* ... *unde* referring to either the "victories" whence the recent triumphs had arrived or the Gallic people over whom Gemellus was being sent.

hope that it would be in no way possible for him to fail in his duty, he who knows that wrong-doers severely displease us. **3.** Therefore, follow his administration by our command, since we believe he has determined what would be in your best interest. Return to lawful habits gradually. A novelty which is righteous could not be harmful. For what could be more fortunate than that men trust only in laws and not fear continued misfortunes? The certitudes of public order are the safety of human life, assistance for the weak, and a curb to the powerful. **4.** Cherish these, and security will come and good conscience will prosper. For foreign manners thrive upon self-gratification, where one who is able to take what he pleases more often finds his own death. Show yourselves now secure in riches. The blessings of your forebears, now recovered from long neglect, are brought forth into the light, since however much one reflects the gleam of upright morals and brilliant dignity, the more celebrated he will be. **5.** For this reason we have directed a vicar to you, so that we may be seen to have settled a means of civil conduct with that very kind of office. May you enjoy the likes of which you had only heard. Come to know men who prefer not so much bodily strength, but rather the force of reason, and know that those who are able to demonstrate righteousness to others wax deservingly in good fortune.

LETTER 3.23 (C. 507–11)

This letter appoints a count to govern the province of Pannonia Sirmiensis (roughly the northern Balkans and Hungary) with careful instructions to temper provincial administration with civil, not martial, law. It is noteworthy that the letter characterizes the provincials as "foreign nations," not Romans, the implication being that the Goths had restored Roman order to the province. Whereas other appointments appear in paired letters to the appointee and to the Senate, this letter is followed by an announcement to the provincials of Pannonia (*Variae* 3.24, below). A similar pattern is seen in *Variae* 3.16 and 3.17 (above).

King Theoderic to Colosseus, Illustris *and Count*

1. It is a comfort to entrust those things requiring proper disposition to proven men, and indeed, the decision to appoint such men is a delight and the property of people that has been entrusted to such approved men is secure. For just as we select him to be the one who would be acceptable, thus do we take care that one who will be acceptable would stand out in merit. **2.** Consequently, commencing with favorable portents and being girt with the dignity of an *illustris* belt, set forth to Pannonia Sirmiensis, the former seat of the Goths,[2] and protect with arms the province entrusted to you; arrange matters according to law, so that a province which knows that it obeyed our forebears happily will be fortunate to receive again its former protectors. **3.** You know with what integrity you may commend yourself to our company. Your only path to pleasing us would be if you should imitate that which we have accomplished. Cherish equity and defend the innocent with virtuous spirit, so that you would be able to represent the justice of the Goths amid the perverse practices of various peoples. They have ever been set in the middle course of honor, as they had adopted the wisdom of Romans and possessed the strength of foreign nations. Roll back the detestable customs that have appeared. Pursue legal cases not by arms, but rather by words. Do not allow the affairs of family members to end in death. Let the fraud surrender what he stole from another, not his life. Nor should the interests of the community exact more than wars would consume. Let shields be raised against the enemy, not kin. **4.** And lest, perchance, poverty be seen to sentence anyone to death, take a completely honorable loss for the sake of such persons. You would gather a bountiful profit of gratitude from us, if you could graft an example there of civility and the true dignity of our judges, and if the judge would accept loss to himself in order that one about to perish should acquire life. Therefore, let our habits be implanted in uncultivated minds; thence may a cruel disposition become accustomed to live in a refined manner.

LETTER 3.24 (C. 507–11)

This letter announces to the provincials the appointment of a count as governor of Pannonia (see *Variae* 3.23, above). The emphasis placed

---

2. Goths settled in Pannonia after the breakup of the Hunnic Empire following its defeat at the Battle of Nedao in 454.

on their loyalty and the maintenance of order may indicate that the province was not thoroughly integrated under Amal authority.

King Theoderic to All Romans and Barbarians Settled throughout Pannonia

1. Our foresight will not fail your needs, since it continually arranges the future welfare of subjects, so that those who recognize us to have taken pains for them would be stirred to greater devotion. 2. Hence it is that we have entrusted your governance and protection to Colosseus, an *illustris* great by name and in strength, so that one who has already given much proof of his virtue may increase yet in deeds to come. And so, now show your obedience, so often proven before, to this same man, to the extent that he will commence upon these affairs which must be accomplished for the advantage of our reign according to reason, and so that they may be accomplished with devotion worthy of approval, since constancy renders good faith and that man proves the integrity of his own intentions who persists in perpetual obedience. 3. Additionally, we feel you must be reminded of this, as you may prefer us to rage not upon you, but upon the enemy. Let not small matters lead you to extreme dangers: acquiesce to that justice which the world enjoys. 4. Why should you who do not have a corrupt judge return to trial by combat? You who have no enemy, lay aside the sword. Worse, you raise your arm against kindred, for whose sake it should happen one would rather die honorably. What use is the human tongue if the armed fist settles litigation? Where is it believed that peace would exist if it were battered along with civil harmony? Let yourselves openly imitate our Goths, who know to wage wars abroad and to exercise restraint at home. We want you to live thus, by that very means by which you perceive our kin to have flourished, with a distinguished master.

LETTER 3.25 (C. 506–7)

This letter appoints a count to govern the province of Dalmatia. While *Variae* 3.23 and 3.24 (above) make clear that the governor of Pannonia would be required to maintain military discipline, this appointment is more concerned with the assessment of taxes and the management of the province's mineral resources. Based on the indiction periods given, this was to be a three-year appointment.

King Theoderic to Simeon, Clarissimus *and Count*

1. We love to involve in public affairs those officials conspicuous for the probity of their habits, so that the increase of utility may grow through the obedience of those faithful to us. Thence, as we know the purity of your mind through outstanding testimony, our mandate entrusts to you the title to the *siliqua,* which we have granted for the lawful assessment of state taxes in the first, second, and third indictions in the province of Dalmatia. Thus, wheresoever by your examination the trail of fraud will have revealed a loss to public taxes, let it be born by our treasury without penalty, since it is not so much that we seek wealth, as that we hasten to comprehend the morals of our subjects. **2.** Additionally, we order you to examine the ironworks of the aforementioned Dalmatia with the shaft of truth,[3] where softened earth brings forth the rigidity of iron and it is baked in fire so that it is altered to a hard substance. Whence, God willing, comes the defense of the homeland; whence utility is derived from the fields and extends convenience to human life in countless uses. Iron lords over gold itself and compels the wealthy to serve the stoutly armed peasant. And so it happens that this substance is carved out with careful searching, by which both our wealth is produced and destruction is purchased for our enemies. Therefore, be eager regarding the previously discussed administration and be moderate with public resources, so that our reasonable gain will be able to procure an advantageous means for your own increase.

LETTER 3.26 (C. 506–7)

This letter announces to the resident count of Dalmatia the arrival of another count, assigned to manage fiscal matters and mining (cf. *Variae* 3.25, above). Presumably, the first count had been appointed primarily to handle military concerns, as was apparently the case in *Variae* 3.23 and 3.24 (above).

3. The phrase *cuniculo veritatis* ("[mine] shaft of truth") is an obvious pun on the subject of mining.

King Theoderic to Osuin, Illustris *and Count*

1. Although it may be necessary for your prudence to offer protection to those assigned to public administration, we nonetheless heap admonitions upon admonitions, so that it may become more firmly rooted where respect ought to accommodate itself to our commands. And so, we have sent to the province of Dalmatia the *clarissimus* Simeon, whose fidelity to us has been recognized for a long time and whose devotion is proven, for the administration of the *siliqua* and also the ironworks according to our direction. You should not deny any comforts sought by him. In this way, your eminence may become more highly valued by us, when it hastens to display itself for the sake of public affairs.

LETTER 3.40 (C. 510)

Another in a series of letters responding to what seems to be a deepening crisis in Gaul, this time expanding the remission of taxes previously granted to citizens in Arles (*Variae* 3.32, not included in this volume) to all provincials in Gaul. Regions unaffected by the war were to continue supporting the military.

King Theoderic to All Provincials Settled in Gaul

1. Although a multitude of tumultuous considerations intrudes upon the perspicacity of our devotion and would command the diverse portions of the kingdom with the usual labor, nonetheless, we have considered the remedy of your utility hastily, since in the view of our good conscience, it is a kind of injury to delay good things, nor are we able to consider anything as pleasant that will have been delayed by unwanted postponement. For an injury is permitted to rage with worsening sickness when the medicine is deferred. **2.** And so, consider the taxes for the fourth indiction suspended on account of the nature of the injuries to you from the savagery of the enemy's devastation, since we are not pleased to exact what an aggrieved contributor is known to offer. But nevertheless, military expenses should be assisted by those areas that remain unharmed, since duty ought not to abandon altogether those whom it knows to labor on its behalf. Because a meagerly . provided defender is powerless, nor does the spirit aid bravery, when prowess has been deprived of bodily strength.

LETTER 3.41 (C. 508–11)

A letter ordering that grain shipped from Italy to support the military in Gaul be transported to armed encampments along the frontier with the Burgundians and Franks through labor requisitioned equally from among Gallic communities. The following letter (*Variae* 3.42, below) announces the same to Gallic provincials. The official charged with executing the order was the vicar of Gaul (see *Variae* 3.16 and 3.17, above).

King Theoderic to Gemellus, Spectabilis

1. Everything that is arranged by fair administration becomes bearable, since a burden shared in common is certain not to oppress subjects. Indeed, a very small portion falls upon any one person when the total amount includes everyone. **2.** And so, the amount of wheat that our foresight sent from Italy to meet the requirements of the military, lest an exhausted province be harmed by furnishing from itself, should be transported from the granaries at Marseilles to the forts positioned above the Durance. **3.** For this reason, we order that the exertion of transporting the above-mentioned amount be undertaken in common, to the extent that what is seen to be assumed by the application of everyone may be accomplished swiftly.

LETTER 3.42 (C. 508–11)

This letter assures provincials in Gaul that the Gothic army has been supplied with pay and provisions from Italy, thereby not increasing the fiscal burden on Gallic landowners. Not only was the measure intended to enhance the image of Amal rule in Gaul, but it also tacitly informed provincials that attempts by the military to exact support would be contrary to present policy.

King Theoderic to All Provincials Settled in Gaul

1. It should not befall the generosity of a *Princeps* that a remedy prosecute subjects, since kindness precedes the entreaty and, in a miraculous way, desires become fulfilled before they arise. Indeed, recently we had been stirred by justice to order that certain unharmed regions of the province offer available provisions to our Goths. But since it is fitting that the *Princeps* always reckon the greater good, because what will remain unchanged in respect to its benefit does not carry the vice of variability, and so that landowners should not be burdened by the least payment, we have sent military provisions from Italy, so that the army sent for your defense out of our kindness should be supported and the provinces should experience only assistance from so great an assemblage. **3.** Moreover, we have sent a sufficient quantity of money to the commanders and to senior officers, so that their salaries,[4] which it had not been possible to convey, ought to be provided there, without loss of any kind, since by our choice we do not want to impose that which, as we perceive it, you would have been able to offer.

LETTER 3.43 (C. 508–11)

This letter illustrates yet another consequence of the war in Gaul: displacement of property, including slaves. In this case, it alleges that slaves have used the confusion as an opportunity to abandon servitude and seek the patronage of others, probably landowners offering better conditions. The letter orders the man serving as the king's sword bearer, likely an honored position among *saiones*, to investigate and return runaway slaves. Uncorrected, the situation could impact agricultural production.

King Theoderic to Unigis, Sword Bearer

1. We are delighted to live under the law of the Romans, whom we desire to protect with arms; nor is attention to moral behavior less of a concern to us than matters of war. For what does it profit to have banished barbaric disorder, except that life is lived according to laws?[5] **2.** Therefore, since the time when our army, by the grace of God, entered Gaul, if any slaves turning away from their duties have carried themselves to others, for whom this seems agreeable, we order them to be restored to the prior masters without any hesitation, since laws ought

4. Each duke (*dux*, a senior field commander) and *praepositus* (a senior officer ranked under a *dux*) received a *praebenda* (regular salary). It is not clear whether the *praebenda* discussed here would also go to regular Gothic soldiers, but soldiers were customarily assigned portions of the *annona*.

5. A reference to the political confusion that attended the war in Gaul.

not to be confused by dictating justice, nor is a defender of liberty able to favor the common slave. **3.** Perhaps the battles of other kings aim at either the spoils or the ruin of captive cities. It is our intention, with God's blessing, to conquer so that subjects should lament that they acquired us so late as a master.

LETTER 3.44 (C. 508–11)

A letter promising both funds to repair the fortifications at Arles and the shipment of provisions from Italy, likely to relieve the impact on agricultural production of the siege of Arles by a Frankish and Burgundian army, which the Ostrogothic army ended in 508. The urban repairs and the relief of food shortages would have been factors key to the loyalty of the large landowners to whom the letter is addressed.

King Theoderic to All Landowners of Arles

1. Although the first priority should be to restore the inhabitants of cities and then to offer an indication of our devotion to the greater extent of humanity, nonetheless, our kindness combines both, so that we both take care of the interest of citizens with the remedy of beneficence and strive to lead ancient cities back to being habitable. For thus it may happen that the happiness of a city, which rises in its citizens, is demonstrated also in the charm of its buildings. **2.** And so, on behalf of the restoration of the aged walls and towers of Arles, we have sent a determined amount of money. **3.** We have also had provisions prepared, which should relieve your costs, so that they should be sent to you when the season for sailing has arrived. Now lighten your concerns and, being relieved by our promise, hope for future abundance and have confidence in divine favor, for what is contained in our words is not less than what is contained in our granaries.

LETTER 3.50 (C. 507)

This letter grants warrant to provincials in Noricum to trade cattle with the Alamanni. These Alamanni may be the same settled under Amal rule after conflict with the Franks (see Section 1, *Variae* 2.41), although it is more probable that official license would be needed to exchange cattle with Alamanni beyond the frontier.

King Theoderic to the Provincials of Noricum

1. An order that assists the one giving and cheers the one receiving in time of need must be gladly undertaken. For who could think it a burden, where more is derived with a shared benefit? **2.** And therefore, we have decided in the present decree that it should be permitted to exchange the cattle of the Alamanni, which are more valuable on account of their ample bodily size but have become weak from lengthy travel, with your own, which, although of lesser stature, are nonetheless better suited to labor. Thus, their task should be assisted by healthier animals and your fields should be furnished with larger cattle. **3.** Thus it will happen that their beasts will acquire robustness of strength, yours more outstanding stature, and, what is accustomed to occur rarely, you both will be seen to attain the desired advantage in the same transaction.

LETTER 4.7 (C. 509–10)

Possibly related to the transport of grain to alleviate famine in Gaul, this letter orders that grain sent from Sicily and lost in shipwreck be credited to the public accounts of the bonded agents involved.

King Theoderic to Senarius, Illustris and Count of Private Properties

1. It is the purpose of our devotion to alleviate the fortunes of those unjustly stricken, since we are unable to find fault with what happens to be imposed by adverse force. For it is unjust that what is not under a man's control should be attributed to his own fault, and that what is rarely possible to avoid should be charged against the stricken. **2.** And therefore, let your loftiness be aware that the agents of the grain, who were sent to Gaul from Sicily, have moved us with a woeful petition, to the effect that their cargo was overcome by hostile weather at the time when they had advanced it to the open sea, where, with the seams of wooden beams sundering, the violence of the waves consumed everything, nor was anything returned to the poor men from the expanse of sea except their tears alone. **3.** Whence, advised by the present dictate, let your *illustris* loftiness bring it about that the allotment of grain, which has been proven to have perished in this misfor-

ADMINISTRATION OF THE PROVINCES   113

tune, be credited to the accounts of the aforementioned agents any without delay. For it is a kind of cruelty to want to exact punishment harsher than shipwreck and to compel payment from those men from whom the monstrous elements are known to have stripped a comfortable life.

LETTER 4.26 (C. 508–11)

This letter cancels a tax payment for the citizens of Marseilles for the remainder of the year, illustrating the strategic importance of a major port city to the control of southern Gaul. The letter is perhaps unusual in that it is not addressed to the count of Marseilles.

King Theoderic to All Inhabitants of Marseilles

1. With a giving spirit do we safeguard those favors formerly granted to you, since we desire to bestow new ones for your advantage. Indeed, kindness knows not how to observe limitations, and it is fitting that benefits restored after so long a time may encourage new ones. **2.** Thence, we grant you, by this dictate, an exemption which applies to your territory, following the special grant of former *Principes,* nor shall we permit any new kind of requirements to be imposed upon you, whom we want to be protected from all burdens. Let the generosity of a *Princeps* release you from the property tax for the remainder of the present year, so that you will be able to receive what you have not demanded. For it is the very perfection of devotion that knows to have regard for troubled things even before they are shaped into prayers.

LETTER 4.49 (C. 507–11)

A curiously short letter announcing the appointment of a man (probably as count) to govern the Pannonian provinces of Siscia and Savia. Maintenance of order in this region seems to have been a recurring problem (see *Variae* 3.23 and 3.24, above). The reference to "long-haired" public defenders may indicate that those in Balkan provinces had assumed tasks other than the traditional urban duties suggested for defenders in Italy elsewhere in the *Variae.* At the time, Frankish kings were also styled as "long-haired," as a marker of status.

*King Theoderic to All Provincials, the Long-Haired
Public Defenders, and the Town Counsellors
Living in Siscia and Savia*

1. Strict observance of a royal decree ought never be undermined, so that dread may restrain the audacious and hope for future blessings may restore the afflicted. For often, announcing a warning accomplishes more than punishment settles. And therefore, with God's guidance, we have decided to set Fridibad over your territories, one who may compass the rustlers of livestock with legal severity, cut away homicide, condemn theft, and offer you, in place of criminal daring, a peace which excessive presumption now rends to bits. Live in a well-ordered manner. Live instructed by good morals. Let no claim to birth or to distinction be a substitute for honorable reputation. It is necessary that one who falls into depraved habits may be subject to the rod of punishment.

LETTER 5.14 (C. 523–26)

Addressed to an *illustris* senator who probably held the position of governor of Savia, this letter directs attention to a wide range of issues plaguing the province. Fiscal corruption is the main focus, but it also mentions abuse of the prerogatives of provincial officials and marriage between Romans and "barbarians." The sweeping problems facing the provincial administration in Savia are quite similar to those illustrated by *Variae* 5.39 (below), concerning Spain.

King Theoderic to Severinus, Illustris

1. The reason of justice urges to restrain those transgressing, so that it may be possible for the sweetness of peace to spread to all men. For by what means is equitability achieved if the resources of ordinary citizens are not permitted to increase? And so, we have often learned in the complaints of our provincials that the wealthy landowners of Savia have not only abandoned to a tenuous fate the duty of taxes on their houses, but also even attached something of a criminal commerce to their own profits, so that public payments have become a private enterprise. 2. We truly desire this to be corrected by as many officials as possible, but thus far it seems to have been delayed to your own glory, inasmuch as fidelity is considered more welcome when you so

thoroughly prove your enthusiasm after the negligence of many. And therefore, we order you to investigate all landowners with the wisdom for which you are noted and with deliberate justice, and herein to measure the equity of the tax with reason, so that the public tax may be imposed according to the standing of the man and his property, and with that corruption which has been practiced by some thoroughly removed from everything. For thus is justice achieved and the resources of our provincials supported. **3.** Those, however, who are found to have imposed a tax assessment without our instruction and who, according to their own pleasure, have cast the burden of certain obligations onto others, let the severity of the law follow hard upon them, so that they may mend every injury to those to whom they have heedlessly caused losses. We further order that this must be investigated, so that the amount of tax payments among the public defenders, the town counsellors, and the landowners may be ascertained and, likewise, whatever a landowner should prove he has paid beyond the contribution of *solidi* for the recently collected eighth indiction, lest it happen that he has not declared in correct measure the payment made to our treasury or for the expenses necessary to managing the province. Let unjust seizure be corrected to the fullest extent. **4.** Moreover, do not suppose that this measure should be ignored, so that if this expense which the accountant reckons is not reasonably disclosed in our privy chamber, let it be returned from the one unjustly withholding it. For is it not so absurd that our generosity, which we want to be of use to all, is now hampered by the profit stolen by a few? **5.** Also, the judges of the province, both town counsellors and public defenders, are said to impose unwarranted expenses on the landowners as much for travel as for other matters. We order you to investigate this and to correct it under the measure of the law. **6.** Let the former barbarians who have chosen to be associated with Roman women in the bond of marriage and whom it pleases to have sought legally documented estates be compelled to pay the fisc for the ownership of land and to obey the imposition of extraordinary imposts.[6] **7.** Furthermore, let a

6. The "former barbarians" (*antique barbari*) are likely federated allies settled in the region, or their direct descendants, who previously maintained certain immunities from public obligations on account of their military service. This clause of the edict seeks to clarify their status and obligations to the state.

Roman judge approach each town once per year, and, on account of expenses to the provincials, which are reported to burden the poor, he may be offered no more than three days' provisions, just as was furnished by the precautions of the laws. For our ancestors intended the circuit of the judges to be not a burden but an advantage to the provincials. **8.** The attendants of the count of the Goths and also of the managers of the royal estates are said to have stolen certain things from the provincials by ingenious threats: with these matters determined under legal inquiry, your justice will discover whatever has been done unjustly by these parties and will arrange matters legally with delays avoided. **9.** Therefore, concerning these matters that pertain to both the provincials and public resources, we want you to conduct everything with investigations that, in every step, ought not to depart from our mildness. Our foresight has reflected upon this matter sensibly, so that the public records may be ordered to be updated with everything found by your careful and diligent examination, to the extent that evidence may reveal your good faith and, after this, nothing that we would want to avoid may crop up from seeds of deceit.

LETTER 5.39 (C. 523–26)

With the Ostrogothic occupation of southern Gaul, Theoderic assumed control of the former Visigothic administration of Spain. This letter illustrates the difficulties at the outset of Ostrogothic involvement in Spain, similar in many respects to the problems of administrating the province of Savia (see *Variae* 5.14, above). The two recipients, a prominent Roman senator and a Gothic count, are instructed to address a wide scope of corruption, including tax fraud, misuse of the public mint and public post, unrestrained violence, and extortion of the locals by Goths sent from Italy.

King Theoderic to Ampelius, Illustris, and to Liuvirit, Spectabilis

1. It is fitting that the provinces, now subject to our rule by God's will, should be arranged according to laws and good character, since truly is the life of men bound by the order of law. For it is the practice of beasts to live by chance; they fall prey to unexpected mishap while engaged in a cycle of violence. And so, the experienced cultivator clears his own field of thorny scrub, since it is to the credit of the careful cultivator if something wild should be made pleasing from its sweet fruits. Likewise, that delightful peace of the people and the tranquil management of a region are deemed to be the reputation of those ruling. **2.** And so, we have learned of the complaints of many in the province of Spain that, what is the worst among moral crime, the lives of men are despoiled by random lawlessness and many fall, ground down by chance of unfounded litigation. And thus they are ruined by a corrupt kind of peace, as though it were sport, falling to such an extent as they could hardly expect under the duress of wars. Furthermore, the fortunes of provincials are allowed to be subject not to public records, as is customary, but to the authority of those in a position to compel. It is a species of obvious plunder to give something on account of the personal inclination of one hastening to compel something more to his own advantage. **3.** On which account, wanting to assist with royal foresight, we have decided that your sublimity must be sent throughout all Spain in official capacity, so that nothing of their accustomed behavior will be permitted under the novelty of your administration. But so that, in the manner of physicians, we may grant a hastened remedy to cruel sickness, let our cure commence where the harm is known to be the greatest. **4.** We order the crime of homicide to be restrained with the authority of the laws; but however much more severe the penalty, the inquiry ought to be considered with that much more care, lest the innocent seem to endure harm to life on account of a zeal for punishment. And so, let the guilty alone fall for the correction of many, since it is even a kind of piety to imprison the crime in its infancy, lest it increase with maturity. **5.** Further, those collecting the public tax are said to burden the property of landowners with inconsistent weights, so that it seems to be not so much a payment as plunder. But so that every opportunity for deceit may be removed, we order all tax payments to be weighed on scales from our privy chamber, which at present have been given to you. For how much more execrable is it that lawlessness should be permitted to sin even against the very nature of scales, so that what has been accorded its own innate justice is known to have been corrupted by fraud? **6.** We have decided that the contract farmers of the royal domain, from whatever family they may be descended, should pay as much in correctly assessed rent as our estates are determined to produce. And lest the burden on each property seem unprofitable to anyone, we want the rents to be set for them by your equity, according to the quality of the property leased. For if the measure of payment occurs according to the inclination of the one being contracted, the farms must not be called ours, but theirs. 7. Furthermore, we order you to attentively collect the import duties, where no small amount of fraud is reported to have befallen the public advantage, and to determine the amount assessed according to the quality of the goods, since a useful corrective to fraud is to know what has been imported. 8. Next, we have learned that the coin minters, who happen to have been established for collecting taxes, have changed practice for the profit of individuals. Concerning the perpetration of this illegality, let them devote themselves to the public assessments according to the capacity to pay. 9. Moreover, take care that the annual tribute of the customs house is not corrupted by any kind of private use, but, so that it may show a regulation useful to business, censure those abusing their freedom in commerce with a measured fairness, lest the ambitious appetite of the collectors extend itself indefinitely. 10. Further, we order that the administration of Laetus,[7] whose best intention is stricken by unpopularity, should be investigated with our usual equity, so that neither fraud may be concealed with clever intrigues, nor the innocent burdened with false accusations. 11. Indeed, let anyone whom you find to have been involved in illicit activities return the concealed money in place of possessions, according to your estimation. But if this property happens to be dispersed among others, let those who knowingly permitted themselves to be involved in such an affair be nonetheless held liable for punishment, for even those who had not committed the act of theft have shown themselves to be accessories to the crime. 12. The prescribed distribution of salaries which our kindness has granted to various persons is reported by the provincials to be an intolerable cause of loss, when it is exacted in kind and then brazenly demanded in money. Such acts are evidence of detestable greed conspiring to exhaust itself and soon to increase the shamelessness of the one making demands. What is seen to be exceedingly corrupt is also exceedingly foolish, that they would both ignore our policies and be found

7. Otherwise unknown, but probably the previous representative sent by Theoderic to administrate the province.

harming the property of taxpayers who must be supported. Let them, therefore, be satisfied with the predetermined measure, whether fixed in kind or all the same converted; let them hold power over the free man to expect only one of the two, while they should not burden the property of others with a double exaction. **13.** It is also said that the liberty of the collectors wrenches much more from the provincials than happens to be paid to our privy chamber. We have decided that you, having dispelled this with careful inquiry, should refer to the exaction of the taxes that happened to be collected in the reigns of Alaric and Euric.[8] **14.** And so, we have learned from the complaint of provincials that those who have been assigned horses demand the conveyance of extra pack animals. You should permit no man to take this entirely for granted, when the landowner is worn down by the most shameful transactions and even the speed of those traveling is impeded. **15.** We also want to be utterly removed the kind of stewards that they lament having found to the ruin of their wards, with respect as much to private property as to public, since it is not protection when it is offered to the unwilling. It is noteworthy that the unwilling have endured. For it is a blessing in a real sense, if something is accepted without complaint. Therefore, we have decided to dispense with the services that they had offered uselessly to the Goths posted in cities. For it is not fitting that those whom we have sent to fight on behalf of liberty should seek servitude from native-born citizens.

LETTER 7.1

Taking great care to describe the temperance needed with martial authority, this *formula* announces an appointment as count of a province. It is not clear from this or other *formulae* whether the authority of a count substituted for or complemented that of a civilian governor.

Formula *for the Count of a Province*

1. Although the duties of every public office are excluded from military service, and those who are instructed to manage public discipline may be seen clothed in civilian garb, only your office is equipped with threats that are girt with the sword of war even in peaceful affairs.

8. Previous Visigothic kings of the region.

Behold by what judgment you enjoy this promotion, when we may seem to entrust the vigor of the *fasces* to others; to you, however, by these very same laws it is permitted to extend iron. They surrender ensanguined business with a pacified heart, so that both the guilty fear greatly and the stricken rejoice at a deserved punishment. On the other hand, the ancients were reproved if all things were not done with restraint. But since you know yourself chosen for measured governance, do not lightly covet the ruin of men. 2. He is called a defendant who would be judged. Know that the remedy of punishing has been given to you for the well-being of many. Such arms belong to law, not to rage. Without a doubt, such a display is deployed against injurious men, so that terror may correct more than punishment would consume. One who deflects mild offenses with words is not compelled to follow upon more hardened deeds with the sword. Such is a civilian dread, not military, which you would thus cause to be glorified, provided it is not deemed excessive. 3. Moreover, you still have a bloodless sword. Let those who stir plots of slight crime be bound with knots of chains. One who decides the issue of a life ought to be a procrastinator: another sentence may be corrected, but crossing over from life is not permitted to be changed. Let cattle rustlers dread your insignias, let thieves quake with fear, let brigands shudder, only let innocent deeds look to happy ends, when that which the discipline of the law conveys anticipates that assistance will come from you. Let no man turn your will with bribes. The sword is despised where gold is taken. You render yourself unarmed if you replace a manly spirit with greed. 4. For which reason, we grant you the dignity of count in this province for the present indiction, so that as a praiseworthy man you may pursue your entitlements by maintaining civic harmony; nor should you presume to do anything except what you would be able to defend by law as a private citizen. For it is this very kind of upstanding governance that is defended without force, so that a man is deemed to have been just when an adversary may oppose whatever he wants. 5. For all that, you need not abandon your aspirations in distaste; for if you should preside well over provincial administration, the laws have rightly consented that you may hope for the fullest distinctions. Whence, what is known to have been promised to you by such authority already seems almost a debt.

LETTER 7.4

This *formula* appoints a duke to govern a province where military readiness and campaigns were more important to stability than was administration provided by civilian magistrates: Raetia was the province north of the Alps that had served as a buffer between the earlier Roman Empire and "barbarian" lands beyond.

Formula *for the Duke of Raetia*

1. Although the distinction of *spectabilis* rank would seem to be of one sort, nor is it customary that anything would be required for that rank except a certain time in service, nonetheless, with the nature of the matter carefully weighed, it seems more should be credited to those who have been allotted the borders of the people, since pronouncing the law in peaceful regions is not the same thing as providing protection from hostile nations, where not only crime is anticipated, but war, and not only the voice of the public crier sounds out, but the blast of the war-horn often assaults. 2. For the Raetians are the rampart of Italy, and the gates to the provinces, for which, not without reason, we deem them to be named,[9] when they are arrayed against fierce and uncivilized nations as though a kind of obstacle to floodwaters. For there, foreign raids are intercepted and the raging presumption is chastised with hurled shafts. Thus, foreign raids are your quarry, and the campaign that you wage successfully you know has been done in vigorous sport. 3. And so, for the present indiction, knowing you to be capable in both skill and strength, we make you duke of Raetia, so that you may both command soldiers in peace and with them patrol our boarders with careful attention, since you know that you are entrusted with no small matter, when the tranquility of our kingdom is protected by your care. Nevertheless, let the soldiers entrusted to you live with the provincials according to civil law, lest armed arrogance become overbearing, since that shield of our army ought to offer peace to the Romans. Therefore, this is fitting for those stationed there, that

9. With the phrase "gates to the provinces," Cassiodorus refers to the *claustra provinciae,* the defensive network of the Alpine region to which Raetia had been integral since the time of Augustus. The name *Raetia* has no relation to the *claustra provinciae.*

within the province a more fortunate prosperity may be harvested with assured liberty. **4.** Therefore, answer our injunction, please us in fidelity and diligence, so that you would neither receive foreigners without careful consideration nor recklessly send our men against foreign nations. Indeed, it rarely comes to the necessity of arms where a carefully planned strategy is enough for defense. By our injunctions will you truly preserve the privileges of your office.

LETTER 8.6 (C. 526)

This announcement of Athalaric's accession is addressed to Liberius, who had been serving as praetorian prefect of the Gallic provinces under Ostrogothic control since 510. His absence from earlier letters of the collection that treat the administration of Gaul is notable, as is the contrast between the present letter and the more lavish ones about the appointments of provincial counts.

King Athalaric to Liberius, Praetorian Prefect of Gaul

1. We know your heart is vexed with harsh grief for the fall of our lord grandfather of glorious memory, since everything seems to gravely lament good things lost; for an esteemed master is missed more when he is removed. The man lost, however, releases the afflicted mind from its expression of devotion and comforts it with a compensatory remedy, since one who is not succeeded by a stranger is hardly felt to be absent. **2.** For he thus arranged it by God's own design, when even after death he would be the provider, that he would leave peace to his domains, lest any novelty disturb tranquility. He has made us master in the seat of his kingdom, to the extent that the grace of his lineage, which flourished in him, should henceforth shine out in his successors with equal illumination. The desires of Goths and Romans have coincided in this ordination, such that under the bond of oaths they have promised to preserve their fidelity to our kingdom with devoted hearts. **3.** We have decided that this must be brought to the knowledge of your *illustris* magnitude, so that a similar example may be rendered by those who are devoted to the kingdom of our piety in Gaul, and, just as they do not want our consideration to make less of them, thus should they be held bound by the same conditions.

LETTER 8.7 (C. 526)

Following upon *Variae* 8.6 (above), to the prefect of the Gallic provinces under Ostrogothic control, a somewhat more elaborate letter was delivered to the Gallic provincials, presumably via the municipal assemblies of towns and cities in the region.

King Athalaric to All Provincials Settled throughout Gaul

1. Although the downfall of our lord grandfather of glorious memory may seem sad to you on account of his outstanding merits, nonetheless, while he succumbed to the human condition, he left us for maintaining the governance that he had managed with such singular ability. Lest you feel the loss of a good *Princeps,* his offspring is acknowledged as ruling over you. For no man loses in our presence what that ruler had promised him, but rather we will pay his debts with the liberality of redoubled munificence, and for future loyalty we borrow kindness from our native devotion. 2. And therefore, he now conjures you to demonstrate the former fidelity with greater devotion, since one who serves well at the beginning of a reign anticipates the state of affairs in the future, since that very man who is felt to support the advent will be trusted to persevere throughout the remainder of the reign. Moreover, we have been indicated by divine favor when we attain the eminence of kingdom. Everything thus has turned out happy and tranquil for us, so that you would believe that what one man pronounced[10] had resounded among all the people, nor could it be thought humanly possible that the will of so many diverse peoples was proven to have no disagreement. 3. Whence it is fitting for you to imitate the aforementioned wish, as Goths offer oaths to the Romans and the Romans confirm by oath to the Goths, make yourselves unanimously devoted to our kingdom, to the extent that your integrity may become commendably known to us, and in return the promised concord may advance your prosperity. Let the tranquility set by laws go among you; do not let the strong cause disquiet for the weak. Harbor a peaceful heart, you who have no foreign wars, since thence you will be able to please us, if you first provide for yourselves by this measure.

10. Theoderic's designation of Athalaric as heir.

LETTER 9.10 (C. 526)

This letter concerns the overhaul of tax assessments in Sicily, intended to encourage loyalty to the new regime of Athalaric. All supernumerary taxes formerly instituted by Theoderic were cancelled and oppressed landowners encouraged to appeal unfair assessments for the regular exaction. This letter initiates a series of communications (through *Variae* 9.14; all but 9.13, not included in this volume, are below) about corrupt fiscal practices in Sicily.

King Athalaric to the Leading Citizens, Landowners, and Public Defenders of Syracuse and to All Provincials

1. It was indeed some time ago that we decided the commencement of our *imperium* must be announced to you; it is now fitting that a benefaction follow for increasing the happiness of all, so that, to those for whom our accession was most welcome, royal devotion may be liberal in another fashion. We desire all things to increase for us, with God as witness, since that tax assessment is reasonable to us which the landowner pays cheerfully. **2.** Thence we draw away the money that would increase glory, and, greedy for praise, we strive to assist cultivators lavishly. Some time ago our lord grandfather of divine memory took great measures for benefactions in his own name; since long peace and the cultivation of fields flourished and the population had increased, he established that a property assessment be required within the province of Sicily, according to the practiced moderation of his wisdom, so that duties would increase with you, whose resources had expanded. But the famous justice of that man prepared a place for our generosity, so that what was rightly offered to him we grant with a kind heart, as though it were an earned salary; and by a kind of foresight of divine mind, he brought about the piety of the man for whom he had prepared *imperium*. **3.** And so, our liberality readily remits for the fourth indiction whatever used to be sought from or paid by you under the title of an increase beyond customary payment.[11] Because even if you are reasonably able to pay, we order you to accept instead the glory of our largesse. **4.** But so that our clemency may be extended further and you should know the sweetness of our rule

---

11. In other words, Theoderic's increase to property taxes was repealed, but the basic assessment remained in place.

from allocated benefactions, whatever has been determined by the tax collectors for the next assessment, of the fifth indiction, we give them notice to remove, so that what will have been rightfully estimated you should produce with an unburdened spirit, since justice served harms none. **5.** But lest you think you have been burdened on account of a large assessment of the tax assessors, if anyone believes that he will be overwhelmed by what they have assessed, let him hasten to the succor of our devotion, so that we who have also kindly conceded unexpected favors may correct those estimating the taxes. For even our lord grandfather of glorious memory had been disturbed concerning the tardiness of those men, so that, having the perception of the highest wisdom, he thought those whom he had already commanded to return with repeated orders had resided for too long in the province, to your burden. **6.** But we, for whom it is fitting to finish anything that man had arranged for equity, now complete those measures begun for you with God's assistance. Return the intention desired from this measure of our generosity, the fidelity of obedience. You have a *Princeps* who has arrived for you with assistance and, what is even sweeter for subjects, who will increase in native generosity while growing in age. Concerning this, we have seen fit that our *saio* Quidila should be sent, through whom directives may be disclosed to you with God's grace.

LETTER 9.11 (C. 526)

This letter communicates to the count of Syracuse the tax reform initiated by *Variae* 9.10 (above), asking for cooperation with the two tax officials sent to Sicily for that purpose. The letter following (*Variae* 9.12) directly addresses the corrupt officials named here (Victor and Witigisclus).

King Athalaric to Gildila, Lofty Count of Syracuse

1. We have directed to the tax assessors of the province of Sicily, the *spectabiles* Victor and Witigisclus, our mandate that they should not exact from the landowners whatever had already been determined by them for the taxes of the fourth indiction, since the payment of this tribute is heavy and the justice of this assessment thus far has not been proven. **2.** We have, in fact, issued instructions canceling their assessments, so that, if these have been arranged equitably for the men assessed, they should remain moderate, but if they happen to have overburdened anyone beyond fair measure, he may be relieved by our decision; nevertheless, if anything is shown as paid for the fourth indiction, let it be restored to the landowners without any reduction, since an imposed burden that it is known must be carried for all time should not cause complaint. **3.** Let what is restored now serve to remind your provincials that we have granted assistance to those whom we find devout in all things and that what is owed to a *Princeps* may be paid with a grateful disposition.

LETTER 9.12 (C. 526)

Variae 9.10 (above) acknowledged to the provincials of Sicily the recalcitrance of two officials who had evaded Theoderic's attempts to recall them from the province. Here, the fiscal measures initiated by *Variae* 9.10 are communicated to the same two officials.

King Athalaric to Victor and Witigisclus, Spectabiles

1. Your tardiness rightly caused you to be suspect to our lord grandfather of glorious memory, you whom he believed must be admonished by a second set of dictates, so that you would finally hasten to his court, thus relieving the inconvenience of the provincials. And now the increase of suspicion has made you not want to be present at the commencement of our reign, which an unfettered conscience would prefer. **2.** And therefore, we have determined in the present dictate that, if you have exacted anything from the provincials beyond the tribute of *solidi* assessed for the fourth indiction,[12] you should restore it to them without any reduction, since we want them to experience no loss beyond the former assessment for the above-mentioned indiction. **3.** Moreover, we believe that this must be added (because we do not want to find faults attached to the affection of clemency, lest being so constrained, we would instead eliminate what we are not able to conceal from sound justice), that, if you have harmed anyone with depraved ambition, you will pay even more in our judgment, since it is proper to correct, and not to cause, what has been left unresolved.[13]

12. The additional exactions cancelled by *Var.* 9.10.

13. That is, should Victor and Witigisclus attach any infamy to Athalaric's policies, they would lose their positions.

4. And lest you believe, perhaps, that these acts may be passed over, owing to the difficulty of the distance, we have promised to the Sicilians the assurance of one who will succeed you. See now if you are able to bear the complaints that our authority invites. We therefore admonish those for whom it is fitting to be dutiful; let one who has not wanted to be corrected of his own free will be found accused by his own crime.

LETTER 9.14 (C. 527)

The last in a series of letters pertaining to the administration of Sicily (beginning with *Variae* 9.10, above with 9.11 and 9.12), here addressed to the count of Syracuse and concerning a wide range of peculation and distortions of comital authority. The tone of the letter suggests that correcting these abuses would allow the count to remain in good standing with the royal court.

King Athalaric to Gildila, Lofty Count of Syracuse

1. It has been reported to us in a complaint of the provincials of Sicily that certain matters have resulted from your exercise of authority, whence it would seem their prosperity has been stricken. But we have taken the report lightly, since they themselves do not want past events to be punished. For a claim yielded by a hostile party is known to be dubious, and one whom the plaintiff prefers to ignore is not legally punishable. But so that we may abrogate suspicion of wickedness in future cases, we have decreed things that must be continually observed according to the present injunction, so that these people need not fear anything in the future, nor may you enact anything for which you would be accused through ignorance. **2.** First, money for the reparation of the walls is said to have been extorted from various provincials, whereupon the promised construction has accomplished nothing. If this has been knowingly permitted, either henceforth let the walls be built for their defense, or let each person receive what is proven to have been unreasonably exacted. For it is exceedingly absurd to pledge fortifications for the citizens and to give them shameful waste instead. **3.** Moreover, they maintain that you have distrained the property of certain deceased men under the warrant of caducous property of the fisc, without any discretion of justice, while this right may be entrusted to you only in the case of foreigners for whom neither a legal nor a testamentary heir may be found. For it is criminal that a right granted to us should be appropriated by you with injury to our name. 4. Furthermore, they groan that they have been burdened by every manner of judicial proceeding, such that those who must bring a case to court seem to lose almost as much in fees as they prove themselves to have sustained from the grievance. Indeed, the vocation of the judge ought to be the hope of justice, not profit. For such a judge is rightly rendered suspect even before the difficulties of litigants are heard in court. Whence we have decided that if our decrees call for the punishment of litigants, let the court collector receive as much in fees as our most glorious lord grandfather determined, in the prescribed amount that *saiones* ought to receive for the defense of persons according to their rank.[14] For the apportionment ought to be in proper proportion:[15] if it exceeds the measure of fairness, it lacks the virtue of its own name. 5. If a legal proceeding is convened by your order, precisely in those cases and concerning those persons where the edicts permit your involvement, then let the officer receive half the payment that he would have been able to claim according to royal precepts, since it does not agree with justice that he should be granted as much from your directive as he would be offered for reverence to our command. 6. However, if anyone has brazenly flaunted such a wholesome constitution, we order the payment to be remitted fourfold, so that what was lost to the delight of greed should be vindicated by the severity of a fine. We certainly want the edicts and general ordinances of our glorious lord grandfather, which he intended to instill good habits for all in Sicily, to be protected with such strict obedience that whoever, urged by his own brutish motives, would attempt to overthrow the defense of these injunctions should be considered answerable for sacrilege. 7. You are also said to call cases between unwilling Romans to your court,[16] in which case, if you know this has been done, presume to do

14. A court official collected fees from defeated litigants; the schedule of fees allowed for legal defense by *saiones* is not elsewhere recorded.

15. *Commodum . . . debet esse cum modo,* a play on *commodum*'s meaning of "legal fee."

16. Because the count was a military official, cases between civilians could have been heard by a magistrate of the civil administration should they have preferred.

so no longer, lest while seeking a judgment where you lack jurisdiction, you instead find yourself a defendant. You ought to be mindful of the edict before anyone else, since you prefer cases that must follow to be settled by you;[17] otherwise, all authority for deciding cases will be removed from you, if these regulations are preserved the least by you. **8.** Unrestricted authority is retained by the circuit judges for their own administration. Let legal contentions be attended to by their own designated judges. Do not allow envy of their official role to consume you. The preservation of civic harmony is the distinction of Goths. Every honor of reputation will converge upon you if the litigant rarely notices you. You defend state constitutions with arms—let the Romans practice litigation with civil law. **9.** They report that you detain the goods conveyed by ships, and, from the ambition of hateful greed, you alone determine steep prices; even if this is not a crime in fact, it should not be thought far removed from suspicion. Therefore, if, as would be proper, you hasten to avoid a rumor of this sort, let the bishop and the people of the city assist as witnesses to your good conscience. Let what necessarily pertains to the fortune of all be pleasing. Prices ought to be determined by shared deliberation, since it is not to the delight of commerce that they are forced upon the unwilling. **10.** Concerning which, we have ascertained that your sublimity must be reminded by the present ordinances, since we do not want those whom we love to transgress, lest we bear anything wicked to be said about such men, through whom we have supposed the conduct of others would be corrected.

17. The singular *edictum* may be a reference to the *Edictum* of Theoderic, which governed the adjudication of legal matters between civilians (Romans) and military personnel (Goths).

Section VI

Goths and the Military

Letters concerning Gothic Settlement and the Organization of the Military

In many ways, military service and Gothic identity were one and the same. Although many of the people who immigrated to Italy with Theoderic in 489 either were Gothic (the language is well attested in sixth-century Italy) or at least had some kind of Germanic origin (such as the Herules), the primary determinant of Gothic "ethnicity" was military service. Inasmuch as a military system may be reconstructed, it is clear from the *Variae* that active-duty garrisons were maintained in key cities and reserve populations were settled throughout northern and central Italy. Goths not on active duty were expected to remain prepared, and the *Variae* describe the movement of military personnel for training, for the muster at which men of military age received their annual salary (the donative), and for deployment to theaters of war, such as Gaul. This level of military preparation justified both the maintenance of the state's fiscal regime and the subordination of "Romans" as a civilian class.

LETTER 1.17 (C. 507–11)

This letter exposes some of the interesting features of Ostrogothic military culture. The inhabitants of Dertona (modern-day Tortona) are ordered to relocate to and fortify a nearby site in preparation for war. Noteworthy is the fact that both Goths and Romans in the area were expected to shoulder this burden as a community. For a similar directive, see *Variae* 3.48 (below).

King Theoderic to All Goths and Romans
Settled in Dertona

1. Stirred by reason of public advantage, for which we are continually and willingly concerned, we instruct you to strengthen the fortress situated near you, since preparation for war is properly arranged however well it is managed in time of peace. Indeed, a particularly strong defense is prepared then, when it will have been strengthened by long-thought planning. Anything erected quickly is carelessly done, and to seek a site for building then, when danger already threatens, is bad. **2.** Furthermore, that same mind-set already agitated by various cares will not be well disposed to bold action. The ancients rightly designated this an *expeditio*,[1] since the mind given over to battles must not be occupied by other considerations. Therefore, a goal that is addressed in advance out of consideration for the commonality must be embraced, nor is it appropriate to bring delay to a command which is known to especially assist devoted citizens. **3.** And therefore, we decree by the present order that you should eagerly construct homes for yourselves in the aforementioned fortress, making recompense for our attention to these matters, so that, just as we determine what must be done for your own benefit, so would we feel you have adorned our reign with the most admirable structures. For then would it happen that you would want to assume expenses suited for your personal homes and it would be a dwelling not unpleasing to you, in which the very architecture is worthy of compliment. **4.** I ask, what will it mean to be in your own households, then, while the enemy is seen to endure the roughest accommodations? Let him lie exposed to the rains while roofs cover you. Let want consume him while abundant stores refresh you. Thus, with you favorably disposed, your enemy will suffer the lot of being despoiled even before the outcome of battle. For it happens in a time of need that the man who does not divide himself among many concerns is proven the most valiant. Who would judge him to be wise, if he began giving attention to the service of construction and to storing provisions then, when it behooved him to conduct war?

---

1. One of several obscure etymological references in the collection, here seemingly referring to the single-minded preparation involved in a military campaign.

LETTER 1.18 (C. 507–11)

This letter addresses two outstanding legal issues, one requiring a general decision applicable to the entire kingdom and the other pertaining to a specific case. In the first instance, Theoderic rules against soldiers' assuming ownership of property subsequent to the initial settlement of Goths in 489. The second matter is a man's assault against his brother. Concerning the letter's addressees, Domitianus's office is unknown, while Wilia is elsewhere referred to as count of the patrimony.

King Theoderic to Domitianus and Wilia

1. It is fitting that you who have undertaken to advocate impartiality on behalf of the people should honor and defend justice, while it is unfitting for one who is entrusted to restrain others under rules of impartiality to commit a crime, lest someone acknowledged as chosen for a praiseworthy purpose become a corrupt example. And therefore, we have taken the care to offer a response to your question, lest you be allowed to err through uncertainty—unless, on the contrary, you wanted to deviate. **2.** If, from the time when we first crossed the River Isonzo and by the grace of God undertook the *imperium* of Italy, a presumptuous barbarian has occupied the estate of a Roman without the writ of any assignor,[2] let him restore the dispossessed property to the previous owner without delay. But if he is found to have occupied the property before that assigned time, since he is then proven to obviate the thirty-year limit,[3] we decree the petition of the plaintiff to be nullified. **3.** For we want those cases which have taken place in our reign led back into full view, since we disapprove that a condition for accusation not be abandoned when the obscurity of a long time has passed. **4.** Concerning the man accused only of assaulting his brother, and not also of killing him, although he is condemned by the common

2. A *pittacio delegatoris,* which would have assigned newly arrived military personnel allotments of land.

3. The *praescriptio trecennii* acknowledged the status quo of property ownership after thirty years. The statement here aligns the occupation start date with Theoderic's entry into Italy in 489, and hence this was not a literal *praescriptio trecenni*—otherwise, the letter would have to originate sometime after 519, and Cassiodorus is believed to have held the quaestorship only until 511–12, after which he did not assume any office again until c. 523.

law of all and only parricide would exceed so tragic a crime, nonetheless, our humanity, which finds evidence for itself in an instance of criminality as much as in an instance of devotion, determines by the present order that monstrosities of this nature should be driven beyond the borders of the province. For whoever detests the company of family does not deserve to have the society of citizens, lest the pleasant serenity of a pure civic body be polluted with dark blemishes.

LETTER 1.24 (C. 508)

This letter calls Goths enrolled in the army to muster on June 24 under the direction of a *saio* for a military campaign in Gaul. The Frankish defeat of the Visigoths under Alaric II at Vouillé and Alaric's marital connection to Theoderic initiated the Amal annexation of southern Gaul. The sentiments of the letter disclose something of the military culture of Ostrogothic Italy.

King Theoderic to All Goths

1. It is more fitting that battles must be known to Goths than that they must be advised by Goths, since it is a delight to be established from warlike stock. Indeed, one who covets the glory of martial excellence flees not from toil. And therefore, with God's blessing (the source from which everything prospers) and for the common weal, we have determined to send the army to Gaul, so that at the same time you will have an opportunity for advancement and we shall offer what we are known to confer on the deserving. For praiseworthy bravery lies hidden under leisure, and the full light of deserving deeds is overshadowed when it lacks the place for proving itself. **2.** And thus, we have given attention to what must be advised through our *saio* Nanduin, so that, in the name of God, you should set out for military duty sufficiently equipped with arms, horses, and all necessary gear according to customary practice on the eighth day before the kalends of this July. With God's favor, display in yourselves the excellence that had been your fathers' and successfully perform our command. **3.** Bring your young men forward to the practices of Mars; let them see under your attention what they should strive to represent to posterity. For what is not learned in youth remains unknown at a mature age. The very raptor whose meal is always had from the spoils of battle casts its own young from the nest, feeble with inexperience, lest they become accustomed to prefer leisure. The raptor buffets the unmindful with its wings, compelling the tender young to flight, so that they must come forward as the kind of offspring maternal devotion should demand. You, however, whom nature stirs and love of reputation goads, strive to leave behind such sons as your fathers prepared to have in you.

LETTER 1.40 (C. 507–11)

This letter orders a military count to procure arms for soldiers stationed in the province of Dalmatia and offers interesting justification for military preparations during peacetime from natural history and military theory.

King Theoderic to Osuin, Illustris *and Count*

1. Our preparation should not be impeded by delay, lest that which depends upon being advantageously arranged encounter an obstacle through the fault of tardiness. And therefore, arms must be distributed before necessity can demand it, so that, when the occasion requires, those more prepared should overcome the unprepared. For the art of waging war is a skill that, if it is not trained in beforehand, whenever it should become necessary, will not be at hand. Consequently, by our order, your elevated *illustris* will procure all necessary arms for the soldiers of Salona, so that the capacity for warlike expeditions will have been made available to them, since the true security of the republic is an armed defender. Let the soldier learn in peace what he will perform in war. They will not rouse their courage for arms in a crisis unless they entrust themselves to what is suitable to that very activity beforehand. Bull calves wage battles, by which they satisfy the requirements of a more vigorous age. Puppies play at unfamiliar hunts. We begin lighting fire in our very hearths with tender kindling, but should you apply full wood to the first sparks, you would extinguish the small fire that you strive to encourage. Thus, the courage of men, unless they are first accustomed gradually to that which you intend, will fail to be suitably prepared. All beginnings are fearful, and timidity will not be overcome by other means, except when unfamiliarity with inevitable things is removed.

LETTER 2.5 (C. 507–11)

This letter orders the praetorian prefect to arrange the distribution of provisions for soldiers stationed along the defensive network of the Alps.[4] The payment must have been delinquent, as soldiers typically received rations and salary on a thrice-annual schedule. Noteworthy is the court's attitude toward foreign incursions, which the state depended upon reliably paid soldiers to repel.

King Theoderic to Faustus, Praetorian Prefect

1. When our kindness is seen to search out a suitable occasion for munificence and may sometimes lavish desired gifts on persons less intimate with the affection of our mildness, how much more it delights to spend on the weal of the republic, where whatever is contributed multiplies the utility of the one giving. Therefore, we order your *illustris* magnificence by the present dictate to immediately present without any delay provisions for the sixty soldiers settled at the fortress of Augustana, just as has been determined for others also, in order that the weal of the republic, which is supported by wages paid from taxation, should be supplied from a willing spirit. **2.** It is indeed appropriate to think of the payment of a soldier who is known to toil on behalf of the common peace on the farthest frontiers and who is deemed to bar, as though a kind of gate, the passage of peoples from the provinces. He who strives to hold back barbarians will ever be girt for battle, since he alone represses that dread which promised fidelity does not restrain.[5]

LETTER 3.38 (C. 508)

A brief message intent on reminding an official of unspecified title to preserve order in Avignon. Because the letter does not address specific problems, it probably served as an appointment to a military post.

4. Augustana in the letter is probably Augusta Praetoria, or the modern Aosta, which was part of the fortified defensive network protecting Liguria and northern Italy; see also *Var.* 1.9 (Section 9) for this location.

5. Referring to treaties the Ostrogothic kingdom maintained with peoples outside Italy, which nevertheless relied upon the maintenance of military strength.

King Theoderic to Vuandil

1. Although it may be consistent with the intent of our devotion that where civility may be practiced, there too would moderation be practiced, nonetheless, we especially want matters conducted well in Gallic regions; both areas where the recent devastation did not convey harm and areas at the very origin of the conflict ought to instill the good report of our name. Therefore, let the safeguarded security of the subjects spread the reputation of the *Princeps* far and wide, and wherever the army is sent, let them reckon it done not for burdening, but instead for defending. **2.** And so, we have decided in the present dictate that you should permit no violence to occur in Avignon, where you take quarters. Let our army live in harmony with the Romans. Let the protection sent to them be to their advantage, nor permit those whom we have striven to free from enemy occupation to suffer anything from us.

LETTER 3.48 (C. 507–11)

An order to Goths and Romans to prepare a local hill fortress under the direction of a *saio,* this letter is fascinating for its perspective on physical attributes of topography, examples from natural history, and the potential for political change. For a similar directive, see *Variae* 1.17 (above).

King Theoderic to All Goths and Romans Settled near the Fortress of Verruca

1. The provident command of one ruling ought to be the delight of everyone, when you see us providing what you ought to need. For what is more pleasing than that human affairs should always have the support of precaution, which is both necessary and does not burden when exceeding necessity? And therefore, we have sent our *saio* Leodefrid with this present order, so that according to his supervision you may build homes for yourselves in the fort of Verruca, which derives its name appropriately from its own position.[6] **2.** For in the midst of a plain, it is a rocky hill rising with a rounded shape; with steep sides and cleared of woods, the whole mountain effects the likeness of a

---

6. An etymological reference to the word *verruca* ("projection" or "hillock").

lone tower, whose base is narrower than the summit, which expands above in the manner of a graceful mushroom, since it attenuates at the narrower portion. A rampart without rival, a secure stronghold, where no opponent may attempt anything surreptitiously, and where one enclosed need not fear anything. Distinguished by reason of its defensibility and its charm, the Adige flows by here, honored among rivers for the purity of its pleasant current. A fort practically separated from the world, maintaining the defenses of the province, for which it is therefore deemed to be more important, since it stands opposed to savage nations. **3.** Who would not desire to inhabit this miraculous haven, this so-called stronghold, which even foreigners are delighted to visit? And although we believe the province to be secure in our reign, with God's blessing, it is nonetheless wise to take precautions even for that which is not thought likely to occur. **4.** Defense always must be commenced in time of leisure, since it would then be badly required when necessity should demand it. The gulls, whose name is derived from the fact that they share habitation with the fish,[7] being aquatic birds and naturally farsighted, seek dry havens from approaching storms and abandon their ponds. The porpoises dwell among the waves of the open main, fearing the shallows of the shoreline. The urchins, which possess a honey-like flesh, a succulence encased within hard ribs, that saffron-hued delicacy of the rich sea, when they become aware of an approaching storm, desiring to change position, embrace pebbles equal to their size, since they have no faith in swimming, on account of the lightness of their bodies, and saved by the ballast of anchorage, they seek out those rocks which they believe will not be harassed by the waves.[8] **5.** The very birds change their native country with the approach of winter, requiring nests suitable to the harshness of the season. Should it not be the concern of men to anticipate what might be required in adversity? It is not a world without change: human affairs are shaken by mutability. And therefore, providence dictates what should be carried out for the future.

---

7. *Mergi* ("gulls") derives from the verb *mergere* ("to plunge"), referring to the fishing habits of waterfowl.

8. See Ambrose, *Hexaemeron* 5.9.24, for the same example, although Cassiodorus's treatment lacks a verbal reminiscence that would allow firm attribution to a reading of Ambrose.

LETTER 4.14 (C. 507–11)

This letter assigns a *saio* to compel Goths settled in Picenum and Tuscany to pay taxes owed on land. Because soldiers received an allotment of land immune to taxation as part of the privilege of military service, it should be assumed that these were properties purchased by wealthier Goths in addition to their allotment. The behavior described here resembles the senatorial disdain for tax payments visible in *Variae* 2.24 (see Section 2).

King Theoderic to Gesila, Saio

1. The greatest kind of sin is for one man to be overburdened with the debts of another, so that one who is able to be compelled should not deserve to receive a hearing. Let debts reflect upon their owners, and let the man who is known to have the advantage of property pay the tribute. And so, we have elected you by the present dictate, so that the Goths settled throughout Picenum and the two Tuscanies should be immediately compelled by you to pay the taxes owed. 2. For this digression from lawful practice must be restrained at its very origin, lest shameful imitation, like an unsightly disease, gradually take hold of the rest of men. Therefore, if anyone relying on his boorish nature casts our commands aside, using the strength of our resources, you will lay claim to his homes with their documented pertinences, so that one who is unwilling to justly pay a small amount can reasonably expect to lose much more. Who, indeed, ought to be more zealously dedicated to the fisc than one who has seized the benefit of the donative,[9] especially when much more is received from our kindness than is demanded in payment by law? For if the taxes are managed for the sake of our generosity, it is rather we, elevating the fortunes of all men, who pay voluntary tribute.

LETTER 5.10 (C. 523–26)

A letter to a *saio,* ordering him to arrange transport for Gepid soldiers for the continued protection of Gaul. The soldiers have been awarded a stipend to prevent them from forcibly seizing needed supplies dur-

9. The bonus paid to soldiers annually at Ravenna.

ing the passage to Gaul. A shorter letter (*Variae* 5.11, below) announces this provision to the Gepids.

King Theoderic to Veranus, Saio

1. While that most fortunate army is led forth, with God's blessing, for the common defense, it must be provided for, lest either the very soldiers be worn out with unexpected lack of resources or, what is heinous to say, our provinces be seen to endure a depredation. For the first step of prosperity is not to be harmful to one's self, so that we should not seem to afflict the wealth of those for whose benefit we toil. **2.** And therefore, we have chosen your devotion in the present dictate, so that you might make the multitude of Gepids, whom we have caused to hasten to Gaul for the sake of its protection, to pass through Venetia and Liguria with every restraint. Lest an opportunity be provided for destroying anything, our generosity has arranged a payment of three *solidi* for each household,[10] so that instead of a desire for pillaging our provincials, there would be the capacity for commerce. **3.** Our indulgence openly grants this to those laboring on behalf of peace for everyone, so that if their wagons are stricken by the long route or if their beasts languish, having been worn down, they may exchange with landowners without any oppression, according to your supervision and guidance, so that they should be given animals better in size or quality, although they may be satisfied with animals of poor health, since life is uncertain for those who are exhausted with excessive fatigue. Let it happen thus, lest transports fail their needs and any man find himself in such a reversal of fortunes.

LETTER 5.11 (C. 525–26)

Following from the directive sent to a *saio* (*Variae* 5.10, above), this letter grants to Gepid soldiers a stipend of provisions to satisfy their needs during travel to Gaul.

---

10. The word *condama* appears elsewhere (Gregory the Great, *Epistulae*) as a measure of land; hence, the phrase *per condamam*, used in reference to an unspecified number of soldiers, likely indicates a unit of Gepid soldiers traveling as a "household." This was a one-time payment for travel expenses, not a soldier's salary.

King Theoderic to the Gepids Sent to Gaul

1. Indeed, it was by our arrangement that we ordered a means for spending the provisions for your activities. But lest payment in kind prove difficult either in itself or from spoiling, we have chosen to arrange a payment for you in gold, of three *solidi* per household,[11] so that you will be able to choose lodgings, and an appropriate amount of fodder should be available to you, and, what is even more fitting for you, you ought to purchase it. For this measure will cause even the landowners to hasten, if it is known that you pay for necessities. Set forth with good fortune; travel with moderation. Let your route be the kind that befits those who labor on behalf of the health of all men.

LETTER 5.13 (C. 523–26)

Addressed to two individuals connected with the distribution of public provisions (*annona*) and probably attached to the office of the praetorian prefect, this letter orders the delivery of supplies to the army. The location of the army is not indicated, but the officials are reminded that soldiers are wont to seize supplies when their daily needs are neglected.

King Theoderic to Eutropius and Agroecius

1. You ought to expend your enthusiasm for the republic with a cheerful disposition, since we have known well from experience how to offer many blessings to the deserving. For we promise an exchange in consideration of devotion, even when we arrange everything on your behalf. And so, we believe that you must be reminded in the present order that you ought to offer the appointed provisions to the army, to the extent that they should not be overlooked by an intention adverse to them, nor ought harmful plunder burden the provincials. For it is most advantageous that the army is restrained under the law of expenses, as it would waste everything if permitted. Rash seizure neglects to observe moderation, nor can it be restrained under any measure, for which license will have been granted. For which reason, let the army obtain the designated amount of sustenance, lest on that account a region be permitted to endure the injury indicated.

11. *Per condamam;* see the previous note, in *Var.* 5.11 (above).

LETTER 5.16 (C. 523–26)

A fascinating letter ordering the praetorian prefect to assemble a fleet to serve Italy's commercial and military needs. Furnishing timber and sailors for one thousand light war vessels may also have been connected to the deterioration of relations with either the eastern empire or the Vandal court at Carthage.

King Theoderic to Abundantius, Praetorian Prefect

1. Although it is by continual habit that we ponder things profitable for the republic, and to that end we command what would be the most pleasing to all, since potential benefits are known to all, it must nevertheless be accomplished in such a way that the intention of the *Princeps* ought to appear onerous to none. For even things that have been very clearly considered, if not acted upon well, are unrewarding; moreover, only that which is praised for both its intention and its execution is said to have been perfectly accomplished. 2. Therefore, since it vexes our mind with frequent anxiety that Italy possesses no ships, where such a great abundance of timber would assist, so that she might export goods sought after even by other provinces, we have determined, with God's guidance, to take upon ourselves the immediate construction of one thousand dromonds, which would be able to convey the public grain and, if necessary, to oppose hostile ships. But we seek the completion of a project so great that we believe it must be administered by the attention of your grandeur. 3. And therefore, let instructed craftsmen seek throughout all Italy for the wood suitable for the work, and wherever you should find cypresses and pines near to the shore, let there be regard for a given price agreeable to the owners. For this is the only timber which may be designated by an assessed value; others do not need to be appraised, by virtue of their own worthlessness. 4. But lest our foresight languish, abandoned in the midst of the endeavor, we order you at the same time to prepare, with divine assistance and with due moderation, a suitable number of sailors. And if someone considered necessary for this project happens to be the slave of another man, either hire him for service in the fleet or, if he should want more for this, grant the right of his own freedom for a reasonable price according to market value. If a selected individual enjoys his own freedom, let him receive an appropriate portion

of provisions and a donative of five *solidi*. **5.** And those who have put off their former masters must be likewise treated in this manner, since it is a kind of freedom to serve a ruler (for often is it thought by those enduring labor, whom the collar of a strict master has oppressed). Thus, for this reason, the above-mentioned sailors ought to receive from your office two or three *solidi,* depending on the quality of the man, in the name of a commission, to the extent that anyone, because he has been paid, ought to be prepared to present himself for duty. For certain, we conclude that fishermen should not be included in this provision, since one who is retained for providing delicacies would be grievously lost, when it is the custom of one to furrow the teeming shoreline, and of the other to hazard the raging winds.

LETTER 5.20 (C. 525–26)

The last in a sequence of letters written to facilitate the construction of a fleet (beginning with *Variae* 5.16, above), here ordering a *saio* to superintend the removal of timber from private and royal lands and also to remove fence works that had been placed across navigable rivers by fishermen.

King Theoderic to Aliulfus, Saio

1. We have ordered timber, suitable for constructing dromonds, to be found along both shores of the Po, and therefore we select you by the present order, so that, following the arrangements of their magnitudes the praetorian prefect, Abundantius, and the count of the patrimony, Wilia, you should unhesitatingly set out for the designated places with artisans and, whether it will have been found on royal domains or private property, you should arrange for it to be prepared without any delay, since we believe that what is prepared by God's will and for the common good extends a burden to no man. **2.** Thus, we truly want you to execute this unfinished endeavor in such a way that nothing may seem to be eagerly sought to the detriment of the landowner, but only that may be claimed which is necessary for the sake of our utility. Let nothing be taken from an owner that afterward may not be deemed acceptable in public. We order the timber of woodlands to be felled, not that anything related to other resources should be impetuously seized. Such an endeavor is an advantage to us that does not cause a burden, concerning which, what the landowner does not seek in person, he should not believe himself to have lost. **3.** We have learned that certain men have cut across the course of rivers with fence work, namely on the Mincius, Ollius, Anser, Tiber, and Arno Rivers, to the extent that it impacts application to sailing. We want you to clear these away in every instance, at the direction of his magnificence Abundantius, the praetorian prefect, lest you permit anyone to presume anything beyond such a deed, but so that the course of the riverbed should be left unimpaired for the passage of ships. For we know that fishing must be done with nets, not with fence work. For thus also is a detestable avarice produced, such that it hastens to enclose only for itself what had provided passage for many.

LETTER 5.23 (C. 525–26)

A brief letter ordering the praetorian prefect to release ships and rations to a *saio,* who will organize the transport of archers to a count for the purpose of training.

King Theoderic to Abundantius, Praetorian Prefect

1. We have determined that our *saio* Tata must be sent to the *illustris* Count Wilia with the archers, so that an increased army may obtain greater strength. Let our young men demonstrate in wars what is said of manliness in the gymnasium. Let the school of Mars send a throng. One who accustoms himself to practice in leisure is prepared to fight only in sport. And therefore, we have decided that your *illustris* magnitude should offer them ships and rations following the established practice, to the extent that, with God's blessing, they ought to be prepared for travel. We have indeed given the effectiveness of our order into your care, since it is acknowledged that what is begun, with God's blessing, by your arrangement may in no way be forsaken.

LETTER 5.26 (C. 523–26)

A general summons for all Goths from Picenum and Samnium to assemble for the annual distribution of the donative. The letter at least suggests that even by this date, some among the military class may have never had an audience with the king. It does not specify the location of the muster, although Ravenna may be assumed.

King Theoderic to All Goths Settled in
Picenum and Samnium

1. Although our generosity may be most pleasing to all people everywhere, nonetheless, we believe what is conferred in our presence is far more gratifying, since people gain something more from viewing the *Princeps* than the benefits that they obtain from generosity. For one who is ignorant of his own master is almost like one dead; nor does he live with any kind of distinction, whom the fame of his own king does not defend. **2.** And therefore, we command in the present order that on the eighth day before the ides of June,[12] God willing, you come before our presence. You will receive the royal donative according to custom, if you hasten to come immediately. It is nonetheless necessary that we advise that none of those coming will be permitted to make detours, lest you ruin the fields or meadowlands of landowners, but rather by hastening with every restraint of disciplined precaution will your gathering be pleasing to us, since thereupon we would willingly take upon ourselves the cost of the army, so that civic harmony may be preserved intact by armed men.

LETTER 5.29 (C. 523-26)

A fascinating letter ordering an investigation into the case of a former Gothic soldier who had been reduced to servitude by two other men. The Goth was blind and therefore unable to defend himself. The recipient of the letter was likely a Gothic military commander.

King Theoderic to Neudes, Illustris

1. An entreaty poured out by Anduit has sincerely moved us. Once decorated, he now returns as a more wretched man, bereft of his own sight. Indeed, it is unavoidable that his calamity should stir us more amply when seen rather than heard. For, lingering in perpetual night, he has hastened to our consolation with the assistance of shared sight,[13] so that he who is unable to see should at least feel the sweetness of kindness. Indeed, he clamors that, irrespective of his birth, the condi-

12. June 6.
13. Likely a servant.

tion of slavery has been imposed upon him by Gudila and Oppas, when not long before he had followed our army freely. **2.** We marvel that such a man has been dragged into servitude, who deserved to be discharged from service by a true master. It is a strange ambition to harass the kind of man whom you would dread and to call a servant one whom you ought to serve out of pious consideration. He adds, moreover, that the false accusation of these men has been refuted by the investigation of the celebrated Count Pitzia. Now, however, restrained by the difficulty of his own infirmity, he cannot avenge himself with the hand once deemed a protector to stand in battle with strong men. **3.** But we, for whom it is fitting to preserve equitable justice between men of equal and unequal standing, have decided in the present order that, if he has formerly proven himself to be freeborn in the opinion of the above-mentioned Pitzia, you will immediately censure those falsely accusing him. Let those for whom it was already fitting to be condemned by their own desire to injure not dare to mistreat him any further with hostile attacks.

LETTER 5.36 (C. 523–26)

This letter grants discharge from military service to a soldier who has grown infirm with age. The *spectabilis* rank of the recipient indicates some status, probably a minor military command. The letter offers interesting insights into the conditions of military service and is an interesting comparison to *Variae* 5.29 (above).

King Theoderic to Starcedius, Spectabilis

1. You affirm that a body worn with continuous labors has brought a feebleness of the limbs to you, so that you, who were formerly suited for military decorations, are now scarcely fit for a leisured life. You therefore request that you not be compelled to those fortunate expeditions, from which you would be led away not by will but from necessity. And because you have requested with your petitions for too long and we have been convinced of the truth in this matter, we grant you an honorable release with the present order, since the wretched misfortune that excuses you is not the fault of cowardice. **2.** But even though we grant your return to civilian life, thus, by the present dictate, we deprive you of the donative, since it is not fair that, while you are recognized as deserving regarding your request, you should receive while at leisure the wage of those toiling. Therefore, as a free man with our protection, enjoy a life secure from the plots of various persons. Nor should anyone accuse you of the disgrace of desertion, as those who happen to be suspended from military service for the sake of illness must be regarded on the basis of former deeds and must be respected by law. For it is not fitting that someone who has deserved to be released from duty by our judgment should be reproved by anyone.

LETTER 7.3

This *formula* appoints a count for a single (unspecified) city. Here, the ideology of separate legal jurisdictions for Goths and Romans is clearly articulated, although this should be understood as preserving the traditional imperial distinction between the military and civilians. Unlike previous examples (*Variae* 6.22 and 6.23, not included in this volume), this *formula* is addressed to both the count and the citizens of the city.

Formula for the Count of the Goths of a Particular City

1. Since we know that, by God's blessing, the Goths live intermingled among you, lest any trouble arise among partners, as is accustomed to happen, we deemed it necessary to send you a count who, being a lofty man and hitherto having proved his good character, ought to decide litigation between Gothic parties according to our edicts, and even if any kind of dispute arises between a Goth and a freeborn Roman, by summoning to himself a wise Roman advisor, he will be able to disarm the dispute with fair reason. Between two Romans, however, let those Romans whom we have sent to the provinces as legal representatives hear the case, so that each may be served by his own laws and a single justice may embrace all people under a diversity of judges. **2.** Thus by the grace of divine authority may both peoples enjoy sweet prosperity and a shared peace. Know, though, that for us there is but one equal affection for all men; but that man who cherishes the laws with a moderate intention will be able to commend himself more amply to our heart. We have no love for anything uncivil; we condemn wicked arrogance as well as its authors. Our piety execrates violent men. In legal cases, laws have force, not arms. For why would those who are known to have courts at hand elect to seek violent measures? For that reason have we granted salaries for judges, for that reason have we maintained so many staffs with diverse donatives—so that we should not allow anything to increase among you that pertains to hatred. **3.** Let one desire for living embrace you, by which there is permitted one *imperium*. Let both peoples pay heed to what we cherish. Just as the Romans are neighbors to your properties, so should they also be conjoined to you in affection. You, however, O Romans, ought to cherish with great enthusiasm the Goths, who in peace make you a populous people and who defend the entire republic in wars. And so, it is agreeable that you obey the judge sent by us, so that you may fulfill by any means necessary whatever he will decide for preserving the laws, to the extent that you would seem to have satisfied both our *imperium* and your own interest.

LETTER 8.5 (C. 526)

Following the death of Theoderic in 526, his successor Athalaric issued a series of commands that inhabitants of the realm swear oaths of allegiance to the young ruler. Although Athalaric came to power at the age of ten and real power lay in the hands of his regent mother, Amalasuntha, rule by minors was not an unusual phenomenon in this period. Taking an oath of loyalty at the accession of a new ruler was a piece of imperial pageantry with its foundation in the reigns of earlier, Roman emperors.

King Athalaric to Various Goths Settled throughout Italy

1. We would indeed want to relate to you the joys of our lord grandfather's lengthy life, but since he has been removed from those who cherish him by hard circumstance, he has made us the heir to his kingdom, by his own decree and according to God, so that, with the succession of his own bloodline, he would make perpetual those benefits conferred upon you by him, while we desire both to protect and to increase those things that we recognize were done by him. As it thus stands in the royal city,[14] by his decree, the wills of all men have been united by the introduction of an oath, so that you would think one

---

14. *Civitas regia*, probably Ravenna.

man promises what the commonality was seen to elect. **2.** Act on this now, following their example with like devotion, lest we seem to have done anything less for those in our service, for whom it is believed that we satisfy everything possible. Indeed, we have ordered Count X[15] to render oaths to you verbally, so that, even as you reveal your most loyal intention to us, you may thereby hear the desires of our inclination. And so, reclaim a name always prosperous for you, the royal stock of the Amals, a source dyed in the purple, a child clad in regal hue, through whom our kinsmen have been appropriately advanced with God's blessing, and who, among such extended ranks of kings, always attained increase. **3.** For we believe in the grace of divine authority, which fittingly assisted our ancestors and now extends the grace of its favor, so that you, who under our forebears have flourished with full praise for your virtues, would also receive the sweetest fruit of happy affairs from our rule.

15. A different count was probably dispatched to each community.

Section VII

Urban Life

*Letters Describing Attention to
the Urban Environment*

One of the features that distinguished Italy from other successor states of the western Mediterranean was a relatively high urban population. Not only was the regional demographic landscape scaffolded by urban centers, but a fair number of cities, such as Syracuse, Naples, and Ravenna, probably boasted populations well over fifty thousand (large by comparison to most urban centers of the former Roman West). Rome may have provided a home for as many as half a million souls at the beginning of the sixth century, a population that could still compete with that of any city of the eastern Mediterranean, including Constantinople. The concentration of urban populations in Italy supported fairly elaborate civic institutions—such as the curiae of town counsellors, who facilitated tax collection at the local level and local interaction with the central state—and depended, at least in part, on continued access to urban amenities familiar from the earlier Roman Empire. The *Variae* describe the provision of many of these amenities: the construction of city walls and baths, the repair of aqueducts, the restoration of bridges near cities, and the expenditure of state funds for public spectacles (mainly chariot races, but also theater performances and wild animal hunts).

LETTER 1.6 (C. 507–9)

The first of many letters dealing with public building projects and the maintenance of antique heritage, here directing the urban prefect to send marble workers from Rome to Ravenna for the construction of a new annex to Theoderic's palace. The urban prefect was to assume responsibility for the cost of their travel and materials, presumably from the municipal accounts. The building is otherwise unattested.

King Theoderic to Agapitus, Illustris and Urban Prefect

1. It is fitting that the *Princeps* should consider which efforts would enrich the republic, and it is worthy indeed for a king to adorn a palace with edifices. For it is not fitting that we should yield to the ancients with respect to adornment, when we are not unequal to the prosperity of those ages. 2. Therefore, I have commenced the massive undertaking of the Basilica of Hercules in the city of Ravenna, to which antiquity contributed a suitable name. We eagerly delegate to your greatness whatever should be secured in the palace for praiseworthy admiration, so that, according to the brief affixed below, you will send to us from Rome the most skilled marble workers, who may bind select pieces with fine seams, such that they would counterfeit in a praiseworthy manner a natural likeness conjoined with intertwining veins. From this skill comes that which may surpass nature. The variegated surface of marble is woven with a most pleasing variety of figures. Because it will be graceful and refined, such a thing is prized always. 3. For this endeavor you will furnish the materials and transport, lest our *imperium*, which we wish to be known for its advantage to each and all, burden anyone.

LETTER 1.20 (C. 507–11)

The first of several letters addressing the unrest that attended the popular chariot races in Rome, this one assigns two leading senators to act as patrons for the Green Faction and to select a pantomime for it. These men may have been brothers, as the letter mentions their responsibility as patrons as having been passed down from their father.

King Theoderic to Albinus and Avienus, Illustres and Patricians

1. It is fitting that the least portion from among the honorable cares of the republic and the salubrious tide of concerns for governing should be that the *Princeps* speak concerning spectacles, yet nevertheless it is not distasteful to enter upon this topic for the sake of love for the

Roman republic, since from this we are able to demonstrate what we believe worthy to our way of feeling, especially when the blessing of the times would be the happiness of the people. For by the grace of God, it contributes to our labors that the common populace know themselves to be at leisure. **2.** And so, we have learned in a petition introduced by the Green Faction (and it has been remarked that the people clamor on behalf of this faction) that disruptive outbursts are agitated by the most nefarious types of individuals and that the state of public happiness has been thrown into frenzied turmoil. As it stands, it is not possible for the comeliness of celebration to have a distinguishing quality if it does not deserve to hold peace for all. And therefore, it is also worthwhile that our clemency examine these factions, so that it will be possible to illuminate the probity of good habits everywhere. For we do not dwell upon the idle products of popular banter, but we cut out the seed of harmful discontent. **3.** For this reason, by the recommendation of this present command, let your illustrious greatnesses kindly assume the patronage of the Green Faction, which your father of glorious memory managed. For it ought not to be reckoned injurious to rule the people and to govern Romans. For if it would be considered the cause of all honors, those who deserve to receive the most glorious honors will be chosen on behalf of the utility of others. **4.** Therefore, assemble the spectators, and between Helladius and Thorodon,[1] whichever will be thought most suitable to public delight, with the turbulence of the people subdued, let him be confirmed by you as the pantomime of the Greens, to the extent that we may be seen to bear for those chosen an expense which we shall pay on behalf of entertainment for the city. **5.** The ancients named this the silent accompaniment to the musical discipline, which indeed one speaks with a closed mouth by means of the hands, and which by certain gesticulations makes understood what is hardly able to be expressed by spoken word or written text.

LETTER 1.21 (C. 507–11)

This letter requires two senators to audit the accounts used to fund the workshops (*fabricae*) in Rome that produced materials for the

---

1. Helladius is mentioned again at *Var.* 1.32 (below); these actors are otherwise unattested.

maintenance of public buildings. The order concludes with a short excursus on natural history.

King Theoderic to Maximianus, Illustris, and Andreas, Spectabilis

1. We are called forth for the improvement of the city by an active zeal for its citizens, since nobody can esteem what he knows the inhabitants do not love. For each person, his own native city is more precious, since, beyond anything else, he seeks safety there, where he had lingered from the time of the very cradle. Therefore, we are induced by similar sentiments to make a gift, on account of which, however much we should willingly contribute, we will receive redoubled gratitude. And therefore, it would not be harsh to anyone to give an account of moneys allotted for Rome's architecture, since a pure conscience would desire to prove itself when it obtains the fruit of its own labor, provided that it knows prosperity has reached us through its efforts. 2. On which account, we have decided in the present dictate that you ought to inquire of the workshops of Rome whether the labor of the project agrees with the expenses; or, if it should happen that the money remains idle among some persons, in which case it has not been paid out to the workshops, let them return what must be paid out for the allotted purpose. With this matter clearly expressed, send to us the most faithful account, so that you who have been chosen to track down the truth of the matter may be seen to comply with our directive. For we believe that nobody wants to be cheated of our generosity, when we have deemed him to be capable of managing this kind of business for his own support. 3. The very birds roaming the sky love their own nests, the wandering beasts hasten to the thorny den, delightful fish crossing watery fields follow along practiced trails to their own fastnesses, and all animals know to take themselves back to where their kind have been wont to settle for generations. What ought we to say now concerning Rome, which it is even more appropriate for her own children to love?

LETTER 1.25 (C. 507–11)

This letter combines fiscal auditing with urban ideology by commanding that the riverfront of Rome be returned to its intended purpose of housing the brick-making industry that contributed to, among other things, the restoration of the mural fortifications. The letter loses no opportunity to vaunt the role of the Amal government in preserving Rome's ancient urban heritage.

King Theoderic to Sabinianus, Spectabilis

1. It advances nothing to firm up the beginning of a project if lawlessness will prevail to destroy what has been arranged. For those things are robust and long-lasting which wisdom commences and care preserves. And so, there is more security in conserving something than in arranging its furnishings at the outset, since fame is owed to an invention from its beginning, but praiseworthy completion is acquired through preservation. **2.** Not long ago, it was established by our order that the port of Licinius should be repaired with allotted revenues, so that it should produce twenty-five thousand roof tiles as an annual contribution to the walls of the city of Rome, where it will ever be an unending ambition to expend our efforts. Moreover, at the same time, the nearby docks which of old had pertained to that site now have been overwhelmed by usage of various sorts. **3.** Therefore, the entire shore front is to be returned without delay to its intended obligation. Although it is fitting that our commands should be scorned in no way, on account of the reverence they are due, nonetheless, we especially want to preserve those mandates by which the appearance of the city is seen to be adorned. For who would doubt that by this provision the miracle of architecture is preserved or that, by the covering of roof tiles, rounded vaults of overarching stone are protected? And so the ancient *Principes* rightly owe the praise given them to us, who have bestowed a lasting youth on their buildings, so that they may shine with their former newness, which until now had been blackened by an idle old age.

LETTER 1.28 (C. 507–11)

This is a general decree requiring the transportation of derelict stone to local cities for use in fortifications. Presumably, the order equipped local magistrates with the authority to enforce such labor as a compulsory service, or *munera.*

King Theoderic to All Goths and Romans

1. Construction is worthwhile in that city which promotes royal attention, since the restoration of old cities is the celebration of an age in which both the adornment of peace is acquired and the necessary precautions of warfare are prepared. **2.** And so, by this present command we decree that, in the future, if anyone has stones lying about in his field of any kind that would benefit the walls, in a charitable spirit he should hand them over without any delay. He will then take possession of what is more genuine than many things, since by this he would then contribute to the utility of his own city. **3.** Indeed, what is more agreeable than to witness the increase of public beauty, wherein the common advantage of all is embraced? And even if stones of little worth are brought forth, it is fitting that what returns to their owner should be great in advantage: indeed, more is given back to him because of what is received on behalf of the greater good. For man often embraces his own gain when by necessity he donates according to the needs of the time.

LETTER 1.30 (C. 507-11)

This letter addresses the ongoing problem of maintaining civil order during chariot races in Rome. Senators are reminded that members of their households have been implicated in outbreaks of violence, seemingly in retaliation for various indignities to which senators were subjected during the games. The Senate is also reminded that its members may not shelter individuals from the discipline of the urban prefect and that city dwellers will be made aware of their right to appeal to the prefect for protection from senatorial households (cf. *Variae* 1.31, below).

King Theoderic to the Senate of Rome

1. Our mind, conscript fathers, aroused by cares of the republic and scrutinizing the assemblies of diverse nations, is struck often by the complaints of the people of Rome, which, originating in events of celebration, nonetheless vomits forth severe excesses. For it is lamentable that extremes of danger should transpire on account of the pleasure of the games, so that, with consideration for law driven hopelessly underfoot, a slave's armed fury could harass the innocent. And what our kindness has bestowed upon them for the sake of delight, punishable audacity has turned into sadness. We restrain this with the accustomed foresight of our generosity, lest by gradually relaxing we be compelled to punish a more severe offense. Indeed, is it not for a benevolent *Princeps* to prefer to punish faults, rather than to destroy, lest he be either thought excessively harsh for destroying or considered lacking forethought for acting mildly? **2.** And therefore, we have decided in the present decree that, if the servant of any senator by chance becomes involved in the assault of a freeborn person, that senator should deliver the assailant to the law, so that, with the particulars of the case having been discussed, a fitting sentence may be justly pronounced. If, indeed, the master should in bad faith fail to present to judges a man accused of such a deed, let him know himself to be liable to a fine of ten pounds of gold and, what is far more grievous, liable to enter into the danger of our displeasure. **3.** But, so that the honor of each man should be settled by justice and the esteem for civil harmony should come together with restored conduct, we also direct to the people our instructions, which we have enclosed to be openly shared with you, so that broken concord among citizens may be mended through one of several considered opinions. Accordingly, we have withdrawn the joy of the games from nobody, but we have torn out the seed of dissension, root and all. **4.** Let it therefore be decided between your splendid reputation and more base habits: avoid such servants as would be the bearers of injury, who would strive to ascribe to their love for you what they commit in crime, and who, while they desire to exercise their own willfulness, work to entangle your respectability. You, for whom solemnity has always been seemly, do not answer the empty words of the people with hostility. If the insult is such that it deserves punishment, bring it to the notice of the urban prefect, so that the fault may be restrained by laws, not through vigilantism. For what distinguishes the man who strives to avenge himself to the point of excess from the one transgressing? For the citizen, it is revenge that comes by means of the law that will not be regretted, and he who is seen to have triumphed loftily over insult is the one proclaimed the victor by the judge. **5.** As you know, the first battles were not between armed adversaries, but a contest, however incensed, resolved itself with fists, whence also comes the word *pugna*. Afterward, Belus first produced the iron sword, for which it was pleasing even to be called *bellum*: a savage assembly, a cruel assistance, a bestial disputation.[2] For even if easily overcoming the unarmed was first given a name by him, what posterity was thence wont to abolish must nevertheless be considered a crime. Therefore, you should not permit members of your households to do against citizens what even now ought to be deplored against enemies.

LETTER 1.31 (C. 507–11)

This is a companion piece to *Variae* 1.30 (above), concerning the civil disturbances connected to the chariot races in Rome. Citizens are reminded to respect the dignity of senators who attend the games.

King Theoderic to the People of Rome

1. We want the pleasure of the games to be a joy to the people, nor ought what was established for the diversion of the spirit provoke a motive for anger. For we have undertaken such a burden of expenses for that very reason, that your assembly should not be brazen in sedition, but rather adorned by peace. Reject such foreign behavior; let the voice of the people be Roman, which delights when it is heard. Do not let rejoicing give rise to violent insult, nor let it be engendered out of celebration. It was certainly this that you faulted in foreigners. Do not in any way aspire to adopt the disruptive life which you have observed others to follow.[3] **2.** And therefore, we have determined by public proclamation that, if an unjust voice should presume to commit outrageous injury to any of the senators, he will find himself hearing the law from the urban prefect, so that in response to the particulars of the case having been discussed, he may justly receive a public sentence. **3.** But so that every planted seed of discord should be extracted, we have ordered the pantomimes to practice their arts at assigned locations; but the arrangements given to the urban prefect will be able to instruct you. And thus it is that you should enjoy the delights of the city with

---

2. Cassiodorus here offers ironic exaggerations of the concepts of *pugna* ("quarrel") and *bellum* ("war"), to illustrate how some behaviors have no justification, however described.

3. Perhaps a reference to circus riots in eastern cities.

composed minds. For there is nothing that we want to preserve for you more eagerly than the discipline of your forebears, so that what you always held to be praiseworthy in antiquity should increase more under us. **4.** For you have become accustomed to fill the very air with a sweet clamor and to speak with one voice, which it delighted even the beasts to hear.[4] Produce voices sweeter than a musical instrument and thus resound among yourselves that certain harmony of the cither in a vaulted theater, so that anyone will be able to apprehend musical notes rather than discordant shouts. For what could be seemly amid such brawling and enflamed strife? Let rejoicing cast down raving; let revelry exclude wrath. For even a foreign disposition can be tempered when your applause is sweetly heard.

LETTER 1.32 (C. 507-9)

This letter treats the civil disturbances of *Variae* 1.30 and 1.31 (above) by addressing the urban prefect as the official ultimately responsible for maintaining order in Rome. Here it becomes clear that contention over the popularity of pantomime performers has played a role in the disturbances.

King Theoderic to Agapitus, Illustris and Urban Prefect

1. It is fitting for the president of the most exalted city to be the custodian of peace. For from whom should moderation be expected more, than the one to whom Rome was entrusted? Indeed, that mother of all dignities rejoices that men of virtues preside over her. And therefore, you ought to be equal in disposition to your exalted position, so that what you have acquired from our favors would be credited to your merits. It is fitting that you constantly be on the watch, lest any cause for disturbance arise during the games, since a tranquil people is your public reputation. Let moderate behavior be cause for triumph, so that an honorable license should not squander liberty, nor should discipline lack good conduct. **2.** On which account, just as we have instructed the highest rank and decreed the people to be advised by our proclamations, so by this we recommend your

---

4. Presumably a reference to interactions between audience and animals in the amphitheater.

greatness to observe that, if there is an insult to a senator from any kind of indiscretion, brazen temerity should be punished immediately by the severity of the law. But indeed, should a senator, unmindful of civil harmony, cause any freeborn citizen to be harassed by execrable assault, being immediately apprehended by a summons sent from our court, let him anticipate much trouble. **3.** For everyone should be mindful to thus separate factional politics from zeal for the games, as there ought to be concord in the homeland, nor should disorder be displayed for its own pleasure, from which hostile wrath would begin to seethe. But lest hereafter anything could again provoke outrageous strife, introduce Helladius to the public eye.[5] Let him offer pleasure to the people and hold equal place among the pantomimes of the other factions. **4.** Moreover, we declare by the present dictate that, because it incites frequent riots among the people, Helladius's followers should assign a free opportunity for others to watch him, whom we have selected to dance in public without favor to any faction. Even if the fickle inclination of the crowd should gravitate in favor of one faction, let the people thus enjoy their enthusiasm in the circus as in the theater, with the faction that they love, so that if they presume to pursue prohibited disturbances, the faction itself may be judged.

LETTER 1.33 (C. 507–9)

Following upon the concern in *Variae* 1.32 (above) about the role of pantomimes in maintaining public order during the games in Rome, this letter directs the same urban prefect addressed by the previous one to support the pantomime of the Green Faction with public funds. The letter to Albinus and Avienus referenced here is *Variae* 1.20 (above).

King Theoderic to Agapitus, Illustris and Urban Prefect

1. A judgment of our serenity, once published, knows nothing of uncertainty; nor may that which has been settled by prudent arrangements be altered by the deception of any opportunity. Pursuant to this, not long ago we gave instructions to the patricians Albinus and

---

5. Helladius is likewise discussed in *Var.* 1.20 (above).

Avienus, to the effect that they should select a pantomime for the Green Faction who would befit the games most excellently, which, having been accomplished, they disclosed to us in their own report. **2.** And therefore, we have now decided in this present writ that it be confirmed: to whomever the above-mentioned distinguished men have chosen, you should pay without reduction that monthly salary owed to the Green Faction, so that what our foresight has determined for the sake of eradicating disorder should become an opportunity not for riots, but for peace.

LETTER 2.34 (C. 509-10)

This letter orders the urban prefect to correct the abuse of the accounts intended for the maintenance of Rome's walls, which had been diverted to other uses. This appears to have been an ongoing problem (see also *Variae* 1.21, above).

King Theoderic to Artemidorus, Urban Prefect

1. Our judgment rejoices to have flourished in you. We are pleased to have elevated a worthy patron for the fortifications of Rome, you who with generous intentions would not bear to secretly conceal a friend's fraud, lest either the crimes implicate you or a sense of safety rather encourage greater offenses. And therefore, let that public account which was set aside for Roman builders and according to the report of your magnificence remains perjured, since it neither explains expenses nor has returned to its original condition, be restored without any delay, and let it be applied again to the walls of Rome by your arrangement. For it is scandalous, and not without reason, that Rome should long for those funds stolen from it, which have passed to other uses. **2.** And so, we ought to strike down with unreserved punishments those embezzlers of delegated funds who defraud our generosity in such a manner. But that governess clemency is always at hand and conjoined to our intentions, lest we strike out severely, with unseemly punishment against one urging justice. Let it suffice that the greed which motivated him should not be satisfied. Nor shall the rod of punishment be permitted to extend further, when what he had shamefully decided to take possession of, having been restrained, must seem just as the loss of his own property.

LETTER 2.37 (C. 507–11)

After a lengthy preamble on the relation of liberality to good governance, the praetorian prefect is ordered to release another *millena* (the
fiscal income associated with a particular measure of land) to support
the maintenance of public baths at Spoleto.

King Theoderic to Faustus, Praetorian Prefect

1. The advancement of our reign ought to emulate benevolence, so
that however much human kindness enlarges rewards, thus would the
republic receive increase. For we would not otherwise be able to safeguard a praiseworthy manner of life, except that we should inspire a
design for the contemplation of our administration. For among so
many daily blessings from God, the advance of parsimony would be a
vice eager for meager liberality. And therefore, let your *illustris* magnificence know by the present dictate that another *millena* beyond the
customary amount must be allocated to the maintenance of baths
for the citizens of Spoleto. For we desire to freely spend upon what we
know pertains to the health of the citizens, since the proclaimed happiness of the people is praise for our reign.

LETTER 3.9 (C. 507–11)

Taking up a theme previously rehearsed in *Variae* 1.28 (above), this
letter requests that citizens of Aestuna transport derelict masonry to
Ravenna to facilitate construction there. The location of Aestuna is
unclear, although it must have been within a reasonable distance of
Ravenna.

King Theoderic to the Landowners, Public Defenders,
and Town Counsellors Settled in Aestuna

1. It is indeed our intention to build new things, but also to protect
ancient things even more, since we are likely to acquire no less praise
for the preservation of things than for their foundation. Consequently,
we desire to erect modern buildings without diminishment to those of
previous rulers, for it is not deemed acceptable to our justice that anything should occur through disadvantage to others. **2.** And so, we have
learned that columns and marble stone, cast down by the envy of great

age, now lie without use in your town. And since it profits nothing to protect things cast aside carelessly, those stones ought to rise up, renovated for embellishment, rather than point out sorrows from the memory of the preceding age. 3. And therefore, we have decided in the present dictate that if the testimony of those reporting is true, that none of the material is deemed now suitable for public adornment, let the above-mentioned columns and marble slabs be gathered for transporting[6] by any means to the city of Ravenna, so that, by lovely craftsmanship, the forgotten form may be restored from sunken quarries, and so that what had been blackened with decay could reclaim that quality of shining antiquity.

LETTER 3.30 (C. 510–11)

This letter announces to the urban prefect the appointment of an official to superintend the sewers of Rome.

King Theoderic to Argolicus, Illustris *and Urban Prefect*

1. Concern for the city of Rome always keeps watch over our attentions. For what is more worthy than to demand the restoration of that place which we ought to maintain and which, thus adorned, serves to unite our republic? Consequently, your *illustris* dignity should know that we have sent the *spectabilis* John[7] to the city of Rome on account of the remarkable sewers, which bestow such amazement upon observers that they are able to surpass the wonders of any other city. 2. There you may see floods enclosed, as though within hollow hills, rushing through prodigious plastered channels. You may see, among the waters, torrents being navigated by vessels assembled with the greatest precaution, lest it be possible to sustain a maritime shipwreck in the headlong torrents. Here, Rome, it is possible to understand how much singular greatness is contained in you. For what cities would dare to contend with your towers, when they are unable to find an equal to your deepest foundations? And therefore, we order you to offer the assistance of your office to the above-mentioned John,

6. The gerund *devehendas* suggests water transport, perhaps along the Po River.

7. This may be the same man mentioned elsewhere in the collection (*Var.* 3.27, not included in this volume) as governor of Campania.

since we want officials to implement our public administration, thereby removing the private hands that are so brazenly immersed in illegalities.

LETTER 4.24 (C. 507–11)

This letter donates unused public space adjacent to a local bath to a member of the clergy in Milan. It is not explicit what purpose the deacon intended the space for, but it involved the restoration of architecture, probably for religious purposes.

King Theoderic to Helpidius, Deacon

1. Those things that are fittingly conferred upon the deserving yield a profit, and more is acquired by the very act of giving away when just deserts are bestowed on the best recipients. Thence, we have learned from the tenor of your petition of an area in Spoleto which the decay of great age has already concealed for a long time with grime, and which awaits the splendor of restoration, so that, in a kind of confusion, the face of novelty would be returned to something mature with antiquity, and from your beneficence something renewed would rise forth, which had fallen to ruins with the decline of many years. With regard for your accomplishments and for the long duration of your thankless service, we grant what must be assented to with a free spirit, so that a just outcome may be conferred upon the wishes of those beseeching and so that the adornment of restoration may augment the city. 2. And so we grant strength to your petition with the present kindness, so that you may gain possession of the portico behind the Baths of Torasius, generously given with its precinct, if it still serves no public function, since, with permission to restore buildings, we receive, rather than give, a gift. Therefore, supported by this decree, take faith in building upon the aforementioned places, nor should you fear any complaint in the future, since, on account of you, both the utility of the city is maintained and the desire of the *Princeps* has been respected.

LETTER 4.30 (C. 507–11)

Similar in theme to *Variae* 4.24 (above), this letter grants a patrician permission to restore a portion of the Republican Forum in Rome.

King Theoderic to Albinus, Illustris *and Patrician*

1. It is indeed fitting that each person consider the augmentation of their own country, but especially those whom the republic has obligated to itself with the highest honors, since it is the nature of things that one who is seen to undertake greater things necessarily ought to accomplish more. **2.** And so, you have asked in a submitted petition that permission be granted for building workshops at the Portico of Curva, which fittingly encloses the Forum in the manner of a courtyard, being situated near the Domus Palmata, so that a building for private habitation may be extended and the appearance of newness may arise from the ancient city. Thus it happens that what had been able to decline from neglect may be sustained by the diligence of inhabitants, since the ruin of buildings is easily accomplished by removing the careful attention of residents, and what the presence of men does not look after quickly sunders with the ripening of age. **3.** Thence, we, who desire the city to be arranged with the brilliance of rising buildings, grant the requested opportunity, provided that the project impede neither the public weal nor its comeliness. For this reason, expect to commence untroubled by legalities, so that you may appear a worthy patron to Roman workshops and the completed work may commend its author. For there is no undertaking for which one is better acknowledged for both the inspiration of wisdom and the practice of munificence.

LETTER 5.42 (C. 523)

A fascinating letter presumably sent on the occasion of the recipient's consulship in 523, when he would have offered public spectacles in Rome. It does not, however, congratulate the new consul, but rather dwells upon the gross moral error of paying performers to court death in the arena with wild animals (during staged hunts, or *venationes*).

King Theoderic to Maximus, Illustris *and Consul*

1. If those who wrestle with supple and anointed bodies may invite consular generosity, if the award of prizes is made for performances with a musical instrument, if a merry song comes to a reward, with what payment must the huntsman be satisfied who labors toward his own death so that he might please the spectators? He offers pleasure with his own blood, and, constrained by an unfortunate lot, he hastens to please the people, who do not wish him to escape. A detestable act, an unlucky battle, to want to contend with beasts, which he does not doubt he will find stronger than himself. His only boldness is therefore in deceiving, his one comfort in trickery. **2.** If he should not prevail in fleeing the beast, sometimes he will be unable to find proper burial; while the man stands, his body perishes, and before it is rendered a cadaver, he is savagely consumed. Caught, he becomes a morsel for his enemy, and that man—oh, the horror!—satisfies the appetite of the one whom he had hoped to dispatch. A spectacle so elevated by its edifice, but debased by its performance, was founded in honor of Scythian Diana, who used to rejoice in the flow of blood. **3.** Oh, to have desired to venerate that error of wretched deception, she who was placated with the death of men! First with the prayers of country folk in the groves and woods and with dedications to hunting, they fashioned this tripartite deity with a false image, depicting her to be the very moon in the heavens, the matron in the forest, and Perse-phone in the netherworld. But perhaps only as a power of Erebus did they reckon her correctly, when, deceived by such falsity, they passed, living, into deep darkness with their errors. **4.** This cruel sport, a bloodstained pleasure, godless observance, and human bestiality, as it should thus be called, the Athenians first introduced to the rites of their city, providing it divine sanction, so that what the celebration of false observances had discovered would transfer to the mockery of the spectacle. **5.** The royal power of Titus conceived the commencement of this edifice, with a flowing river of wealth, whereupon the capital of cities could partake in it.[8] And when a theater, which is a hemisphere, as it is called in Greek, appears joined as though two into one, a place for watching is rightly called an amphitheater. It encloses the arena in the shape of an egg, so that it is given an appropriate space for races, and so that the spectators may view everything with ease, since that accommodating roundness has gathered everyone together. **6.** They therefore go to such affairs that human nature ought to avoid. The first man, trusting in a slender beam, rushes upon the mouths of beasts,

8. Here describing the purpose of the Colosseum, begun under Vespasian in 72 and completed by his son Titus in 80.

and he is seen to head for that which he hopes to evade with great impetus. Both predator and prey hasten upon each other in equal speed; nor is it possible for the one to be safe, except that he should meet in that spot the beast that he desires to escape: then, with an elevated leap of the body, his upward-prone limbs are cast into the air, as though the lightest of cloth, and the onslaught of the animals passes under him, while he, poised in a kind of corporeal vault above the beasts, makes a delay of descending.[9] 7. Thus it happens that the animal reckoned to have been mocked can seem much less fierce. Another man flees not by veering away; holding four-part screens distributed in a circle with angles arranged on a rotating mechanism, he does not escape by holding himself at a distance, but pursues the one following him, bringing himself nearly to his knees, so that he might avoid the mouths of bears.[10] Another man, suspended from a narrow beam on his belly, taunts the deadly animal, and except that he is endangered, it is not possible that he obtain there a means to survive.[11] 8. Another man encloses himself against the most savage of animals with a portable wall of reeds, hidden away after the example of the hedgehog, who, withdrawing under his own back and gathered up within himself, thus hides, his body not visible, while he never runs away. For just as the one, having rolled into a sphere against an approaching enemy, is protected by natural spines, thus the other, girt with sewn-together wickerwork, is rendered more defended with the fragility of reeds. 9. Three others, just as I shall describe, each positioned at an assigned portal, dare to call upon themselves the waiting fury, hiding themselves behind lattices in the open arena, now showing their faces, now their backs, so that it is a marvel that you should behold them thus dodging and dashing among the claws and teeth of lions. 10. One man is offered to the beasts on a lowered wheel, while another is raised aloft on the same, so that he is born away from the danger. Thus does this machine, formed in the likeness of a treacherous world, restore some with hope, torture others with fear, but nonetheless smile upon all in

9. Here describing pole vaulting over animals.

10. The performer here seems to wear a harness supporting rotating screens which he must continually shift on a frame to thwart contact with the animal.

11. This seems to describe a tightrope performance, probably on a flexible reed, above an animal.

turn, so that it might deceive them. **11.** It would be tedious to digress in words on every species of danger. But what the Mantuan said concerning the netherworld is aptly appended here: "Who could comprehend all the kinds of crimes, who could peruse every name for punishment?"[12] But you, for whom it is necessary to exhibit such sights to the people, shower rewards generously and with an open hand, so that you may make these offerings to the wretched. Otherwise, it is a kind of savage compulsion to withdraw customary gifts and to order spiteful deaths. **12.** And therefore, grant to the supplicant, without any delay, whatever customarily occurred for a long time with respect to ancient liberality, since it is a case of homicide to be frugal toward those whom your exhibition has invited to death. Alas for so harmful an error of the world! If there would be any consideration for equity, as much wealth ought to be given for the life of men as seems to be poured into their deaths.

LETTER 6.18

A fascinating *formula* that combines history and myth to promote the honor of maintaining the distribution of public provisions in Rome. This operation was the key factor in maintaining the largest urban population in antiquity, possibly even as late as the early sixth century.

Formula *for the Prefect of Public Provisions*

1. If public offices must be assessed by this measure, that one may hold as much distinction as he is known to have benefited citizens, then certainly the one worthy to be selected for the alimentary resources of the Roman people ought to be the most gloried. It is indeed by your attention that the provisions for this most sacred city are furnished, where the abundance of bread may overflow and so great a people may be sated as though at a single table. You hasten nourishment to and from the guilds of the millers, you enforce the correct weight and purity of bread, and nor do you deem it demeaning, whence it is that Rome is able to praise you, and rightly so, when the affection of this city is a singular glory. **2.** And lest anything that you do be thought somehow peripheral, you ascend the carriage of the urban prefect

12. Virgil, *Aeneid* 6.625–27.

with shared gratitude. You are found seated next to him at public games, so that the urban mass whom your diligence feeds may know that you are honored as a tribute to itself. For if complaints over the bread are provoked, as is customary, you, as the guarantor of plenty, settle civic dissension with immediate satisfaction and through you it is planned, lest anything be wanting for a complaining populace. **3.** Not without reason it is reported that Pompey attained the summit of public life with foresight for the extent of alimentary resources, since it is rightly the singular desire of a people that it will be free from want. Hence that man earned popular applause and gratitude; hence was he always singularly loved, and, in the gratitude of every citizen, he surpassed the deeds of the greatest men. Out of appreciation for this role, he was even called "Great," lest he might be spoken of with any dishonor.[13] **4.** May this example encourage you to success, when that man whom blessed Rome admired is known to have acted in the role of your office. However, lest anyone suppose you to rule over abject men, the laws over bakers, which were most widely used across diverse regions of the world, are also subject to you, lest what supplies Roman abundance with praiseworthy servitude be cheapened by causing scarcity.[14] The pork butchers also, devised for the sake of Rome's plenty, are known to be delegated to your administration. **5.** You have acquired privileges in which to glory. Your tribunal is not among lesser offices, when you enjoy the gratitude of Rome and send commands to the provinces. But so that we may scrutinize in whole the efficacy of these deeds, the praetorian prefect procures the supply of wheat; but to manage the approved distribution is not less an honor than collecting the grain, when, regardless of the abundance, complaints do not fail if the refinement of bread is not served. **6.** Similarly, Ceres is said to have invented grain, whereas Pan is attributed with first baking the moistened grain, whence bread is called after his name. And thus, Ceres discovered that by which she is honored, and Pan, who fittingly

13. Cassiodorus was apparently unaware of Plutarch's claim that Sulla gave Pompey the cognomen "Magnus."

14. Those engaged at the lower levels of alimentary provisioning, such as bakers, were regarded as having sordid professions; this passage seems to suggest that the *Praefectus Annonae* could mitigate the legal disabilities of bakers to encourage continued employment.

applied it to consumption by human means, is praised. 7. And therefore, knowing your diligence, which is always a friend to wisdom, we choose to confer upon you the office of prefect of public provisions for the present indiction. Give these matters your attention now, since it is not appropriate that anything be stolen from the people. For what is done to the detriment of the city may not be concealed in silence. The populace knows not how to be silent, when sometimes it even decries what has been perpetrated by no one. Be an equitable judge; correct fraudulent abuses; maintain the weight of bread. That by which the Quirites[15] live is weighed more carefully than gold, because the happiness of the Roman people is more agreeable to us than an abundance of the most precious metals. Consider well what we say. Consider what would be sweeter for you to prefer than to seek from that people the gratitude that even we desire.

LETTER 7.6

This *formula* appoints a count of aqueducts for the supervision of hydrology in Rome. A rare treat among *formulae,* it offers a full digression on the wonders of aqueducts, but says little concerning the actual administration of water in Rome.

Formula *for the Count of Aqueducts*

1. Although the collected buildings of Rome are hardly able to be considered distinct from one another, since the entirety that is seen there is known to be designed for causing wonder, nevertheless, we are convinced there is a difference between what may satisfy necessary utility and what is dedicated only to beauty. To see the Forum of Trajan even frequently is a marvel; to stand on the lofty Capitoline is to see human genius surpassed. But what is nourished by these monuments? And is bodily health refreshed in any way through delight in them? 2. In the aqueducts of Rome, however, both utility and beauty are pronounced, so that the structures are wondrous and the wholesomeness of the waters is unparalleled. For so many rivers are led there, as though across fabricated mountains, you would believe through natural channels with the firmness of stone, when such a flood of water was capa-

15. An archaic and hence poetic name for Romans.

ble of being firmly supported for so many ages. Hollowed mountains are frequently undermined, the courses of rapids are dispersed, and this work of the ancients is not destroyed, if it is served by diligent support. **3.** We may consider how much the abundance of water offers to the improvement of Rome. For what would be of the beauty of the baths, if the city lacked that certain wet charm? The Aqua Virgo, which is believed to be named thus because it has been stained by no filth, courses with the purest delight. For while other courses are polluted by an excess of rain commingled with earth, this gliding flow with the purest water is mistaken for perpetually clear sky. Who is able to describe such a thing in appropriate speech? **4.** The Aqua Claudia is marshaled to the peak of the Aventine on such a mass of arches that when it falls there, tumbling from on high, it seems to water that lofty peak like a deep valley. The Egyptian Nile, swelling in certain seasons, rises boisterously under clear skies, with the flood channeled over level fields; but how much fairer is Rome's Claudia, sending the purest waters over the highest peaks of such dry mountains and through a bounty of pipes to houses and baths. It flows thus continuously, so that the desired amount is never able to be diminished! For when the Nile recedes, there is mud; when it arrives unforeseen, a flood. Who, therefore, would not consider the rivers of our city to be superior to the famous Nile, when its waters either terrorize in coming or utterly forsake in receding? **5.** We have related these matters not in gratuitous digression, but so that you should note what kind of diligence is expected from you, to whom such a great wonder has been entrusted. Concerning which, after much consideration, we have appointed you count of aqueducts for the present indiction, so that you may strive with the greatest effort to accomplish what you expect to be advantageous for such noble and great works. **6.** Harmful trees, which bring ruin to buildings, are akin to inexorable battering rams against walls. We suggest at the very outset that they be torn out at the root, since no injury may be avoided unless it has been destroyed at the source. If anything, however, has fallen to the consummation of old age, let it be repaired with dutiful celerity, lest a cause of expense to us spread from increasing neglect. The management of the aqueducts is the source of your prosperity; should you strengthen them, you will remain unvexed. However much you are proven in devotion to these, you will advance in our presence. Therefore, act with skill and good faith, so that the structure may endure undiminished and the distribution of the waters may be diverted by no venality of the attendants.

LETTER 7.7

This *formula* appoints a prefect for the command of Rome's city watch. Rather than a military garrison, this was primarily an urban police force that patrolled the city. The prefect is clearly described in terms of reduced authority, including the absence of judicial authority.

Formula *for the Prefect of the City Watch in Rome*

1. Although your title ought to rouse you to the security of the city, so that you would be able to fulfill that for which you are called, nonetheless, it does not detract from the customary precaution of our wisdom that we may also sweetly encourage those whom we designate for holding a public position to obey. For what would be more attractive to you than to zealously expend the pains of your diligence in that city, where such distinguished witnesses are seen to reside? Indeed, your guardianship, as soon as it becomes apparent, will course back and forth in the mouths of consuls and patricians; just as it happens that you do anything with care, you will hear the nobles praise you with admiration. You direct a modest post, and you abide in the highest reputation. You will direct the guards of Rome, since you defend the city from an internal enemy. **2.** Therefore, be vigilant for thieves. Even the laws, which advise you not to punish in any way, nonetheless did not revoke the license for finding them. I believe this is because, while thieves are detestable, nevertheless, as they are called Roman, the laws subject them to a magistrate of greater dignity. Enjoy, therefore, office as prefect of the city watch for the present indiction. The horror of inflicting punishment is removed from you, not the authority; for the law wishes the wicked to be seized by one whom it deems they fear more. Therefore will you be the security of sleepers, the fortification of homes, the protector of locks, an unseen investigator, a silent judge, for whom it is right to deceive plotters and a glory to cheat them. **3.** Your activity is the nocturnal hunt, which by wondrous means is first unperceived, then felt. You bring greater theft to the thieves when you strive to circumvent those whom you know are able to ridicule everyone else. What you do is a kind of deception, that you are able to ensnare the wiles of brigands.

For we reckon it easier to understand the riddles of the Sphinx than to discover the current refuge of a thief. How may a man be caught who, watching everything, restless for anything approaching, anxious for any kind of snare, and having no fixed seat, is distinguished by the nature of the wind? **4.** Keep watch with the birds of the night; observation unfolds the night to you, and even as the birds discover their meals in the shadows, thus will you be able to find fame. Now, be attentive to our injunctions. Corruption need not deprive you of that which diligence provides. For while it seems fitting that these things are accomplished in deep darkness, nonetheless, no deed is able to be concealed. And so, protect with good reason the privileges deputed to your office by our authority, since it is necessary that in such a great city, what one man may not accomplish must be done through diverse magistrates.

LETTER 7.10

This *formula* appoints a manager for public games. It grudgingly accepts the necessity of following tradition, although it clearly considers involvement in public spectacle to be degrading as a profession.

Formula *for the Tribune of Spectacles*

1. Although arts of the slippery sort may be removed from honorable habits, and the wandering lives of actors may seem prone to produce dissolute behavior, nonetheless, antiquity has provided a governess, so that they may not completely run rampant, when even these affairs countenance a judge. For the display of public games must be governed with a certain discipline. If not true order, then let at least the semblance of a judge restrain the stage. Let this business be tempered by a kind of law, as though noble conduct could govern the ignoble, and those who ignore the road of correct living might live by some measure of rule. For they strive not so much for their own enjoyment as for the delight of others, and, by perverse compact, when they surrender mastery of their own bodies, they instead have captivated the minds of the audience.[16] **2.** It will therefore be worthy for those who

16. This is a traditional view of acting, in which actors endure degraded status for submitting their bodies to the audience, and the audience, in turn, becomes enslaved to the performance.

know not how to conduct themselves with proper behavior to accept a supervisor. Your position, then, is arranged as a kind of guardian for this flock of men. For just as additional precautions protect those of tender years, thus must hot-blooded pleasures be curbed by you with careful maturity. Manage with proper instruction what the ancients invented with exceeding wisdom. Even if capricious desire and modesty do not agree, predictable discipline will maintain due measure. Let the appointed spectacles be conducted according to their own set of customs, since they will find no gratification unless they imitate something like discipline. **3.** Therefore, our preference appoints you tribune of spectacles for the present indiction, so that you may conduct everything in such a way that you would associate the wishes of the city with yourself, lest what had been established for delight be found transformed to blameworthy conduct in your tenure. Preserve your own good reputation with the infamy of the lowly. One to whom prostitutes are subject must esteem chastity, just as it was said with great praise, "He is a man who pursued the virtues when involved in public spectacles."[17] For we wish that through the governance of something frivolous, you should attain a more serious office.

LETTER 7.11

This *formula* appoints a public defender. During the late empire, this municipal official acted on behalf of underprivileged citizens. Based on the *formula,* it would seem that public defenders regulated prices and transactions at the local marketplace. They were likely selected from among the town counsellors by leading citizens.

Formula *for a Public Defender of Any City*

1. If a man who should be praised for good counsel and seriousness is selected for conducting business of any kind, how much more distinguished ought you be, who undertakes the business of the whole city? For if it is a danger to cheat one man, how would it be to appear unjust in the judgment of so many citizens? For deeds done well for the sake of many ennoble the reputation, when one who is trusted to act

17. Attribution for this quote is not known; given Cassiodorus's tendency to cite authors, this was probably an aphorism without a known author by his time.

entirely according to proper intentions is felt to be favorable to common needs. **2.** And so, moved by the petitions of your fellow citizens, our authority grants you the title of public defender of this city for the present indiction, so that you, who are solemnly announced by so important a title, would want to do nothing venal, nothing disreputable. Arrange commerce for the citizens according to the value of the day and with fair measure. Abide by the limits that you set, since it is not a burden to restrain the highest price for selling, if the prices chastely preserve public statutes. For in a real sense, you fill the role of a good public defender if you suffer your fellow citizens to be neither oppressed by the laws nor consumed by want.

Rural Life

Letters concerning People in the Countryside and Their Obligations to the State

Like much late-antique and early-medieval literature, the *Variae* give sparse attention to rural life. Much of what is known about life in the countryside derives from textual sources concerned primarily with property rights and taxes. In these sources, however, it is clear that the countryside was not populated by a vast, undifferentiated "peasantry." The Gothic military and Roman aristocracy were large landowners in much the same sense as the Roman elite had been in the earlier empire. Small farmers who either owned or leased plots of land are also visible, as are freeborn citizens who were legally bound to state-owned property (*coloni*) and rural slaves. Despite the immense interest that modern social historians may have in this landscape of microregional cultures and legal distinctions, the governmental perspective typically focuses on the administration and productive potential of the countryside, for the simple reason that the late-antique economy was anchored there: agricultural production was the key to wealth. For a traditionalist, landowning aristocrat such as Cassiodorus, the countryside also provided an opportunity to wax nostalgic, and even philosophical, on the idea of familial legacy (the *patria*).

LETTER 1.29 (C. 507–11)

This is a writ sent to a local magistrate, charging him to restore lands that had been used to maintain horses of the public post but were subsequently claimed by local landowners. (The letter's heading addresses the citizens of the community, but its content makes clear that it was directed to a leading citizen of the region.) Although concerning a rural matter, the letter pertains more broadly to communications in northern Italy.

King Theoderic to All Lucristani Settled on the River Isonzo

1. There is no doubt that the protection of the public post pertains to the advantage of the republic, a service through which the swift enactment of our proclamations is made public. And therefore, as greater provision must be made for the horses, so that the post should continue without interruption, let them not wither with unsightly neglect, lest, thin and overcome with weakness, they succumb to their labors and a means designed for speed become affected by delays. **2.** Therefore, mindful of the present command, let your devotion restore to the use of their way stations the tracts of land that formerly had been permitted to the horses, duly claimed from the landowner, so that land lost in small quantity should not harm him and land recovered should be sufficient for the horses.

LETTER 2.21 (C. 507–11)

Theoderic granted a contract to two men of senatorial rank to drain a swamp near Spoleto in Umbria. The present letter responds to complaints from one of the partners that his colleague had withheld resources for the completion of the project and illustrates state concerns for land management.

King Theoderic to John, Assessor

1. It is especially serious that a most diligent man should be cheated of the fruit of his own labor and that which ought to be conferred as a reward for earnest application should be endured as an unjust expenditure. This matter particularly concerns our own liberality, where no kind of neglect ought to be permitted, lest we seem to have sanctioned less for things that would be useful. **2.** In respect to this, some time ago our generosity bequeathed to the *spectabiles* Spes and Domitius lands unprofitably occupied by muddy flows of water, in the area of Spoleto, where deserted depths of waters had swallowed pleasant land in no way beneficial for use. The ground lies shipwrecked in a squalor of messy marshland and, having been subjected to loss of two kinds, had not gained the liquid purity of water and had lost the distinction of earthly firmness. **3.** Now, it is our intention to change all things for the better, and we granted this land to the above-mentioned men on the condition that, if the unsightly flood should be drained by their labor and application, they should gain the liberated countryside from that very work. But a number of the agents of Spes report in a petition the fault of the *spectabilis* Domitius. While unmindful of the order, he firmly withholds the outlay of expense. The work of the laborers is called back at its commencement, while already the soft face of the ground had gradually dried and hardened and an unaccustomed sun kindled an appetite hidden in the earth for so long. **4.** In no way should we suffer this to be ignored, since anything begun well is destroyed by unfavorable inactivity. Thereupon, let your devotion call on the aforementioned Domitius with moderate means, so that he should come forth as the assiduous agent of a project already begun, or, if he has found it too expensive for himself, let him yield his portion of the project to the petitioners. For it is fitting that, if he himself is unable to execute the requirements, he should permit a sharing of the favor to fulfill the glory of our reign.

LETTER 4.8 (C. 507–11)

Frustratingly spare of detail, this letter orders the leading citizens of Forlì to organize the collection and transport of timber to another settlement for unknown purposes.

King Theoderic to the Leading Citizens, Landowners, and Town Counsellors of Forlì

1. What has been decided by our command should not seem grievous, since we know how to reckon what is fitting for you to accomplish. Indeed, to be protected reasonably by that power of ours which has assisted you is not burdensome. Thence, we have decided in the present dictate that, without any delay, your devotions should transport timber to Alsuanum from your area, being recompensed with an acceptable price, inasmuch as it is possible to accomplish this according to our instructions and with wages paid for labor, lest you appear to have sustained a loss.

LETTER 5.9 (C. 523–26)

This is an uncharacteristically brief letter addressing an important topic, in this case the construction of a new city in the region of the Italian Alps. The landowners are ordered to share in building portions of the new city wall.

King Theoderic to the Landowners of Feltria

1. The public concern of many ought to be addressed with devotion, since it is not proper that few should undertake what stands to assist many, lest royal commands weaken from disinterest while a useful undertaking is delegated to those unfit for its completion. Therefore, our authority has ordered a city[1] to be built in the region of Trento. **2.** But since the scarcity of the region is unable to sustain the magnitude of the operation, our disquiet concerning this has ascertained that you, who are near the area, should each undertake an assigned portion of the wall, having agreed upon a fee to be received, to the extent that what was known to have been perhaps impossible for a few may be completed more surely with relative ease. Let it be clearly defined with this stipulation that no man may be excused from this duty, whence not even the divine household is excepted.[2]

LETTER 5.12 (C. 523–26)

In response to a complaint against Theodahad, this letter orders Theoderic's nephew to restore a property seized by his men or to send a representative to court for a formal hearing. The petitioners were family of the deceased former urban prefect Argolicus.

King Theoderic to Theodahad, Illustris

1. If we command all men to respect and cherish justice, how much more fitting is it that those who are glorified by relation to us should conduct everything in praiseworthy fashion, so that they would be capable of demonstrating the brilliance of the royal family? For it is an

1. The term *civitas* at least suggests an urban center with full municipal duties and amenities.
2. *Divina domus* probably refers to the imperial household (i.e., the household of the king), although it may also mean the local church.

unquestioned nobility which is proven to be adorned by good character; it is the sweet advantage of fame to avoid the foul profit of money. **2.** And so, the heirs of the *illustris* Argolicus and the *clarissimus* Amandianus have complained in a petition submitted to us that the estate Pallentiana, which our generosity had transferred to them as compensation, since by this benefit they were paid for the loss of the Arbitana house, has been unbecomingly assailed by your men for no apparent reason, and thence to have caused the crime of illegal seizure where an example of glorious restraint ought to be provided. **3.** For which reason, if these claims are not repudiated as lies, let your grandness restore what has been taken. Furthermore, if you believe anything can be put forward on your behalf, send to our *comitatus* a representative instructed in the law to the fullest measure, so that a formal hearing may obtain an end with civility according to the laws. For certain, no matter what is decided in court there, it will be attributed to your deception, and you will suffer great harm to your reputation, since such things are unavoidable in legal contentions. Here, however, cases are compared according to their own strengths, and any common citizen is given a decision without partiality, when justice is prevailed upon in person.

LETTER 5.38 (C. 523–26)

This letter orders all landowners in the vicinity of Ravenna to provide labor for the maintenance of the city's aqueduct. It is worth noting that the state maintained slave gangs for regularly removing vegetation that would destroy the carefully balanced architecture of aqueducts at Rome, while other urban centers depended upon the seasonal conscription of agrarian labor forces organized by large landowners.

King Theoderic to All Landowners

1. A particular concern for the aqueducts admonishes us, so that we must quickly clear away what has been allowed to grow harmfully, to the extent that, God willing, the strength of the aqueducts should be preserved intact and, because this pertains to young trees, it would be an easy undertaking for you. For what are now only shoots would become, if ignored, even stronger. For such saplings, which are dislodged with the ease of uprooting, later will hardly succumb to blows from axes. And therefore, you ought to attend to this with shared haste, so that you may avoid with present diligence the troubles of future toil. For without opposition, this is the ruin of civil order, a sundering of buildings as though by a battering ram. **2.** For this reason, we order all trees that grow dangerously close to the walls along the aqueduct of Ravenna to be ripped out at the root, so that the restored structure of the plastered channel may decant water for us of such a purity as can be had from springs. Then will the production of water be the embellishment of the baths; then will the fish paddle in glassy pools; then will it be that water washes, not pollutes, after which it will not always be necessary to bathe. Moreover, if waters sweet for drinking should flow, everything would be rendered acceptable to our palate, since no morsel of human fare is made pleasing when the clarity of sweet water is not available. For if we desire to bathe in the cleanest water, how much more should we hasten to be sated by such? If these things are now accomplished for the future, the labor that is undertaken for the delight of all men will cause distaste for none.

LETTER 8.27 (C. 527)

This letter orders a *saio* and a *comitiacus* to investigate claims that the landowners of Faventia have been subject to unspecified abuses.

King Athalaric to Dumerit, Saio, *and to*
Florentianus, Loyal Comitiacus

1. Just as the severity of public discipline ignores the innocent, it is thus necessary that it impose the standard of its own punishment on criminals, since the diverse deserts of various persons do not always merit one judgment. Even the sick are treated with different concoctions of herbs; for some, the physician calls for nourishment as the best remedy, for others the scalpel, and in each case the prescription is determined by the nature of the suffering. **2.** And therefore, let your devotions hasten without delay to the territory of Faventia, and if it is found that any Goths or Romans have involved themselves in plundering the landowners, inflict both fines and punishment according to an examination of the deed, since those who may not be trusted to be obedient to the *Princeps,* either initially or after just admonition, must be punished severely. The better course is to want to serve new masters,[3] so that, having been commended by good behavior at the outset, they would enjoy the gift of security for the remainder of their lives.

LETTER 8.31 (C. 527)

This letter addresses what seems to have been an endemic problem in late antiquity: the retention of leading municipal citizens for civic duties. Here, the governor of Bruttium is obliged to encourage local landowners and town counsellors to return to urban residences, which they had apparently forsaken for rural estates. The topic allows Cassiodorus the opportunity to pontificate indulgently about urban culture and the natural history of his native region. The ideological tensions between town and country were as old as the Roman Empire.

King Athalaric to Severus, Spectabilis

1. Since we believe that you learned everything that pertains to managing the affairs of the republic while commendably engaged with the counsels of the prefect,[4] you especially understand, polished as you are by literary arts, that a city proven to have a host of peoples has a splendid manner. For thus the adornment of freedom shines in them, and the necessary support serves our ordinances. It is given for wild creatures to seek woods and fields, but for humanity to cherish above all their paternal hearths. 2. Those birds that are gentle with harmless intention fly in flocks. The melodious thrushes love the congregation of their own kind; the incessantly noisy starlings similarly attend in armies; murmuring pigeons delight in their own cohorts. Whatever enjoys an honest life does not refuse the pleasantness of association. 3. By contrast, fierce raptors, hunting eagles, and keen-sighted birds above all covet flying alone, since, being violent predators, they have no need of peaceful assemblies. For those who do not desire to come upon their spoils accompanied by another roam in order to act alone. Thus, the disposition of humankind that is known to avoid human sight is generally detestable, nor is it possible to expect anything genuinely good from one whose life lacks a witness. 4. Let the landowners

3. Presumably *novi domini* refers to Athalaric's court.
4. The praetorian prefect is probably implied.

and town counsellors of Bruttium return to their cities: those who endlessly cultivate the fields are peasants. Those to whom we have granted offices and to whom we have entrusted public affairs by pleasing appraisal should endure separating themselves from rusticity, and certainly in that region where luxuries arrive abundantly without labor. **5.** There Ceres luxuriates in great fecundity, and Pallas too rejoices with no less liberality.[5] The plains smile with fertile pasturage, elevated slopes with viticulture. The region abounds in various herds of animals, but it especially glories in droves of horses, and understandably, when the woodlands are so springlike in the season of heat that animals are not vexed by the stings of flies and are fully fed on the ever-green grasses. You would see among the mountain summits the purest running streams, which, as though flowing out of the very heights, rush down from the highest places of the Alps.[6] It may be added that, on both sides, the region possesses rich and frequent maritime commerce, so that it overflows with wealth of its own and is furnished by foreign provisions along its neighboring shores. There the rustics live on the banquets of townsfolk; middling folk, moreover, enjoy the abundance of the powerful, so that the least fortune there is shown not to be lacking in plenty. **6.** Therefore, do citizens confess that they prefer this province only on their own estates, not wanting to dwell in the cities? What does it profit for men so greatly fattened on the literary arts to lie hidden? Boys seek the association of liberal education, and as soon as they would be fit for the court, they immediately undertake the ignorance of a rustic lifestyle. They advance in order to unlearn; they become learned in order to forget; and while they delight in the countryside, they know not how to respect themselves. Let the learned man seek where he may live with glorious reputation; let the sage not cast off concourse with men where he knows he will be praised. Likewise, a good reputation is failed by the virtues if their merits should be unknown among men. **7.** For what kind of desire is it to abandon interaction with citizens, when one may observe that even some birds want to mingle with human society? For the swallows faithfully suspend nests in the dwellings of humankind, and the intrepid bird feeds its chicks amid the commotion of residents. It is,

5. The personifications of grain and olive production, respectively.
6. The Italian Apennines were considered a branch of the Alps.

therefore, exceedingly disgraceful to educate the sons of noblemen in the wilderness, when one may see the birds entrust their offspring to human society. Let the cities, therefore, return to their former dignity; let none prefer the allurements of the countryside to urban walls of the ancients. **8.** How is it possible to flee in time of peace from that place for which it is proper to wage war, lest it be destroyed? For whom would the assembly of nobility seem the least pleasing? Who would not be eager for exchanging conversation with peers, visiting the forum, observing noble arts, representing one's own causes with the laws, being occasionally occupied with calculations of Palamedes,[7] going to the baths with companions, arranging dinners with shared preparation? One who wishes to spend his entire life with slaves will certainly lack all these pleasures. **9.** But, lest a mind tainted to the contrary relapse further into the same habits, let landowners as well as town counsellors offer promises with collateral, with a penalty determined by the assessment of other men, to remain for the greater part of the year in the cities that they have chosen for residence. Let it be thus, that neither would they lack the distinction of citizenship, nor should they be denied the pleasures of the countryside.

LETTER 8.32 (C. 527)

This letter requires the same governor of Bruttium addressed in *Variae* 8.31 (above) to examine the claim that bandits had plundered the stock of a man en route to Athalaric's court. The victim's name, Nymphadius, seems ironically attuned to the main subject of the letter, which is a celebration of the miraculous spring where he was robbed. The letter's perspective on the cognitive agency of nature deserves attention.

King Athalaric to Severus, Spectabilis

1. When the *spectabilis* Nymphadius was hastening to pursue his interests at our sacred *comitatus,* having completed some distance of the journey, he decided to rest at the fountain of Arethusa, situated in the region of Squillace,[8] because here the area abounds in fertile pasturage

7. A dice game (gambling).
8. Then Scyllaceum, Cassiodorus's hometown.

and is lovely for its inundation of waters. For it is said that there is a fertile field at the base of a hill overlooking the sandy seashore, where a wide pool issues from a bed girt with reeds that wreathe the edge of its shore in the likeness of a crown. It is entirely pleasant and remarkable for its reedy shade and for the character of these waters. **2.** For when a man approaches there, remaining silent and taking care to create no sound, he finds the waters of the refreshing font so untroubled that they seem not to flow so much as to lie still, like standing water. But should he produce the grating of a cough or perhaps sound out in a loud voice, at the very same moment, by what agency I know not, the waters immediately churn with excitement. You would see the surface of the pool boil up, grievously disturbed, so that you would suppose placid waters had assumed the heat of burning oil. Remaining still with a silent man, they answer the noise and clamor of one speaking, so that you would be astounded at water so suddenly disturbed which no touch had excited. **3.** A remarkable force, an unheard-of property, that waters are stirred by the voice of men and, as though called, would respond thus to the words projected in human voice, murmuring I know not what. You would believe some animal rests there prostrate in slumber, which, having become roused, responds to you with a deep growl. It is even read that some springs bubble over with various wonders, so that some turn drinking animals to different colors, others make flocks white, and still others change submerged wood to the hardness of stone. But no reason comprehends these causes, since it is known that what thus pertains to natural phenomena lies beyond the human intellect. **4.** But let us quickly return to the complaint of the petitioner: when the above-mentioned Nymphadius had taken respite here, he asserts that his packhorses were driven off by the cunning of the rustics. It is not becoming to the discipline of our reign that the charm of this place should be rendered disreputable on account of such a loss. We want your diligence to search with careful examination for what would seem to agree with both the authority of our court and the justice of the laws, so that you may be seen to avenge what a criminal has done. **5.** Let thieves be approached with complete silence, let furtive men be bound in their own snares, so that, as soon as the executioner has bellowed, their hearts will become distraught, they will project their voices in alarm, and they will throw themselves into disorder with murmuring.[9] Thus will signs determine them to surrender their own waters to punishment.[10] Therefore, let what is exacted from them be fitting, so that these places may be passable. Invite the interest of travelers with strict discipline, lest such a miracle as is known to always gladden the pilgrim be avoided on account of the excesses of brigands.

LETTER 8.33 (C. 527)

This letter responds to disturbances at a local religious festival in which merchants have been victimized by the agrarian workforce of the area. To establish order, the provincial governor addressed in the previous two letters is directed to collect sureties from the property owners who manage peasants on their estates. The affair allows Cassiodorus to digress in lavish terms on the abundance of the festival and on the local sacred springs.

King Athalaric to Severus, Spectabilis

1. Just as the wise want to learn unknown things, thus it is foolish to conceal what has been discovered, especially at a time when harmful circumstances can find the swiftest correction. Indeed, we have learned from repeated attestation that at the assembly in Lucania which received from ancient superstition the name of Leucothea,[11] because there the waters are exceedingly brilliant and clear, the property of merchants has often been vandalized by the hostile plundering and lawless impropriety of rustics, so that those who come to celebrate the most sacred festival of Saint Cyprian and to adorn the countenance of civil harmony with their own merchandise should depart poor and shamefully destitute. **2.** We believe that this must be corrected with a simple and easy remedy, so that, at a previously designated time, your distinction ought to obtain from the landowners and from the managers of various estates advance sureties for the peace of those attending

9. Cassiodorus here recycles much of the vocabulary he used above to describe how the waters respond to sudden disturbance.

10. *Aquas suas,* or "blood"; there is also the sense here that Severus is being told that pursuing the available signs will reveal the thieves, so there would be no excuse for them to remain unpunished.

11. Leucothea was originally a Greek deity associated with initiations, transplanted to southern Italy probably much earlier, in the period of Greek colonization.

the assembly, lest punishment utterly consume those whom it finds accused of savage deeds. But if any of the rustics, or a man from any place whatever, attempts a violent altercation, having been arrested at the very outset, let him be subjected to punishment by cudgeling immediately. Let one who first attempted to excite concealed crime correct his wicked designs with a public spectacle. **3.** Indeed, that very gathering is both celebrated by an exceedingly large throng and greatly profitable to the surrounding provinces. For abundant Campania, wealthy Bruttium, cattle-rich Calabria, prosperous Apulia, and even its own province of Lucania send there whatever they have that is excellent, so that you would rightly expect the plenty native to many regions to be gathered there. For there you may see the widest fields bedazzle with booths of the loveliest kind, and temporary lodgings immediately woven with charming wickerwork, and the happy commotion of boisterous peoples. **4.** Although you may not view works of urban architecture, nonetheless, you may witness the accoutrement of the most celebrated city. Boys and girls are offered for inspection by sex and various ages, those whom liberty, not captivity, brings to be sold. Parents rightly sell them, since they prosper from the very same servitude. Indeed, there is no doubt that slaves who have been transferred from agrarian labor to household service may be improved. What should I say of clothing arrayed in countless variety? What of fattened animals that gleam in their diverse kinds? There everything is displayed at such a price that even the most circumspect buyer would be enticed. Thus, if everything is arranged with proper discipline, nobody departs from that market unsatisfied. **5.** For indeed, the very site extends with the charm of open meadows, a kind of suburb of that most ancient city of Consilinum, which has adopted the name of Marcellianum, from the founder of sacred springs. A swell of sweet and clear waters bursts forth here, where the clear liquidity emanates in an apsidal hollow fashioned in the manner of a natural cave, so that you could mistake for an empty pool what you know overflows. Here clarity persists all the way to the bottom, so that at a glance you would think it appears like air, not water. The most tranquil water emulates clear daylight, for whatever is born in the depths is visible to the eyes with unperturbed clarity. **6.** There plays a school of the happiest fish, which fearlessly approach the hands of those offering food, as though aware they will not be seized. For whoever presumes to dare such a thing is known to immediately attract divine punishment. It would be tedious to describe the wonders of such a spring. Let us come to the most unique portent and sacred miracle. 7. For when the bishop commences to pour forth the prayer of baptism on holy night[12] and springs of words flow from that holy mouth, a wave immediately leaps on high; the pool directs the waters, not through their accustomed channels, but by massing them to a height. The unthinking element surges by its own will, and in a kind of solemn devotion prepares itself for the miraculous, so that the sanctity of divine power may be revealed. For while the spring extends over five steps and submerges only these while placid, it is known to rise above another two, which it is never known to cover except at that time. It is a great and awe-inspiring miracle that lapping shores thus stand or rise at human speech, so that you would not doubt them to be an attentive audience. 8. Let this heavenly spring become venerated in the speech of all; let even Lucania have its own Jordan. Those waters provided a model for baptism; these preserve sacred mysteries in annual devotion. Therefore, reverence for the place and the advantage of the fair ought to recommend holy peace to the people, since the most scandalous, who dare to despise the celebration of such days, must be held in the judgment of all.[13] Let what we have pronounced be read and made known to the people, so that they will not seek the liberty of complete abandon when they believe it to be unpunished.

12. Probably Christmas Eve.

13. Another affirmation that the leading citizens will be held accountable for indiscretions.

Section IX

Religion

Letters to Bishops and Letters Touching upon the Court's Spiritual Sentiments and Involvement in Religious Matters

Two centuries after Constantine elevated Christianity to a position not only of public respectability but also of political power, the religious landscape of Ostrogothic Italy was still complex and diverse. Although in the sixth century "Manichaeism" was probably only a convenient label for the religious "other," as opposed to a gnostic belief, non-Christian faiths and other varieties of Christianity existed side by side with the Christianity represented by the pope and the church of Rome. According to sources such as Procopius and anecdotal evidence in the *Variae*, "paganism" was not extinct in the early sixth century. And major Jewish communities prospered in Rome, Naples, Genoa, and Milan, despite the opposition of Christians that flared up periodically. The Amals, and presumably many of the Gothic military class, followed the Arian interpretation of Christianity, a relic of the long-term affiliation of Germanic peoples with military service in the Roman Empire. Unlike the neighboring eastern empire, the Ostrogothic state was tolerant of all religious faiths, excepting only "paganism" (usually construed as "sorcery"). Indeed, despite adhering to the Arian creed, the Gothic Amal rulers established close, productive ties to Catholic bishops and clergy. The local church, in turn, became a conduit through which the state asserted its ideological imperatives, maintained urban infrastructure, and supported underprivileged citizens. References to the great doctrinal debates of the day and to differences between Catholic and Arian Christianity are absent from the *Variae*.

LETTER 1.9 (C. 507–11)

This letter offers judgment in a treason case against the bishop of Augustana. As his superior in the ecclesiastical hierarchy, the bishop of Milan was directed to restore the accused to his congregation and ensure his safety.

King Theoderic to Eustorgius, Venerable Bishop of Milan

1. The well-being of subjects is preserved where it thrives under the fairness of those ruling; nor is it fitting for one by whom I have established policies that must not change to be dragged down by uncertain rumor. Indeed, we gather faith in matters from reason, which is never concealed from those searching after it, if it is carefully followed according to its own evidence. **2.** And therefore, what we hold to be most agreeable to your blessedness, in the present statement we declare the bishop of the city of Augustana[1] to be accused of treason against the homeland on false accusations; restored by you to his former dignity as bishop, let him hold every right that he held. For nothing in such a dignity must be presumed from rash thinking, wherefore, if something is believed by report, the silent man is excused from harm. Similarly, openly criminal deeds should hardly take faith in such matters; moreover, whatever is said out of jealousy is not deemed true. **3.** Indeed, we want to strike down his assailants with righteous punishment, but since these very men perform in the name of clergy, we commit all that must be arranged to the judgment of your sanctity, whose role it is to establish probity of behavior in such persons and to preserve ecclesiastical discipline.

LETTER 1.26 (C. 507–11)

Vague in detail, this letter nonetheless illustrates a classic case in the devolution of fiscal integrity. An immunity to taxation given to a particular church had been extended to either persons or other church properties, for which reason the praetorian prefect was commanded to restore the former obligations to the fisc.

1. Probably Augusta Praetoria, or the modern Aosta; see also Section 6, *Var.* 2.5 for this location.

King Theoderic to Faustus, Praetorian Prefect

1. It is shameful that trust in a former gift has been diminished for those who it often happens are shown our generosity in other matters. But even though on one occasion we agreed that this gift deserved not to be rescinded in perpetuity, nevertheless, those who obtained our generosity with moderate requests ought not to have transgressed the limits we set for this gift with their immoderate presumption. **2.** Whence, because we were reminded of the deference owed to religious studies, some time ago we offered to the venerable gentleman of the church Bishop Unscila what we deemed should endure in perpetuity. But now we find that your *illustris* magnificence must be reminded how long the aforementioned church has not felt the burden of annual property taxes, on account of this favor, which had been discharged with consistency and pure trust for us from the time the property was released from obligation by the magnificent patrician Cassiodorus.[2] **3.** Let that property, which indeed has been transferred by some persons to our church since the time of the grant, now know the burden of payment common to all landowners, and let it be subject to the fulfillment of that which it is the right of the master to obtain. In no respect will this gift from us be increased for someone who profits from loss to the fisc. Let the payment of rent satisfy the landowner; taxes are for the ruler, not the private citizen. Wealth obtained by deceit is dangerous; how much better to conduct everything moderately, which no man would dare to reproach!

LETTER 2.8 (C. 508)

Damage to private property frequently attended the movement of armed forces; this letter entrusts fifteen hundred *solidi* to a local bishop to compensate property owners for the passage of the Gothic army (probably to Gaul).

King Theoderic to Severus, Venerable Bishop

1. What man is better delegated to the rights of equity than one clothed by the priesthood, who, because of affection for justice, knows not

---

2. Cassiodorus's father.

how to judge for personal advantage and, delighting in everyone alike, does not abandon a case to deception? Therefore, considering the task well suited to your merits, we declare that we have sent fifteen hundred *solidi* to your sanctity in the care of Montanarius, a sum which you should distribute to the provincials according to what you learn concerning any loss suffered during the passing of our army this year, with careful estimation of the damage, so that nobody should receive from our generosity anything beyond what has been aggravated by his own losses. For we do not want to bestow liberally, in a confused manner, what is more fittingly distributed with reason, lest what we determined should be sent to the afflicted out of need be paid unnecessarily to the uninjured.

LETTER 2.27 (C. 507-11)

This letter touches upon the delicate issue of the government's relation to Jewish communities living in Italy. Imperial law since Constantine forbade Jews from expanding the urban fabric of synagogues; this letter concedes a request from the Jews in Genoa to restore damage to a synagogue, while illustrating the minimal level of tolerance for a non-Christian group (cf. *Variae* 4.33 and 5.37, both in Section 9).

King Theoderic to All Jews Settled in Genoa

1. Just as we desire to demonstrate the righteousness of concord when called upon by entreaties, so too we dislike that offenses to the law should occur through our favors, especially in that portion of the laws that we believe concerns divine reverence. Therefore, let those puffed up with pride and destitute of divine grace not be seen to behave insolently. Wherefore, we decree in the present dictate, providing as much license to your petitions as divine constitutions have permitted, that you should erect a roof over only the ancient perimeter of your synagogue. Nor would it be proper to add any adornment or to stray beyond bounds by enlarging the building. 2. And you will know the severity of the ancient sanctions to waver the least if you should not refrain from illegalities in this matter. Indeed, we grant license only for covering or strengthening the walls of the building, if the thirty-year limitation is not able to prevent you. Why do you request that from which you ought to flee? We verily grant permission, but to our own

praise we disapprove of the desires of those so erring. We are unable to command religion, since nobody may coerce the unwilling to believe.

LETTER 2.29 (C. 507–11)

This letter advises a military count assigned to Sicily to be mindful of the protection (*tuitio*) accorded to the estates and clergy of the church of Milan in that region. Like the church of Rome, the church of Milan owned extensive properties in Sicily, which provided revenues and required intensive land management.

King Theoderic to Adila, Spectabilis *and Count*

1. Although we do not want anyone whom our devotion is known to protect to endure any great burden, since the leisured peace of the subjects is the glory of the ruler, nonetheless, we especially desire foreign churches to be delivered from any injury.[3] When fair treatment is offered to the church, the mercy of divine authority is acquired. **2.** And therefore, having been stirred by a petition from the blessed Bishop Eustorgius of the church of Milan, we remind you by this present address that you may be eager to offer protection for the property and persons of this church situated in Sicily in a spirit of sound civic harmony, lest, against sacred law, you allow to be oppressed, by anyone of any origin whatever, those for whom it is fitting to be elevated by considerations of divine authority. It is nevertheless true that they should not postpone answering public and private suits which may have been reasonably brought against them, since, just as we in no way want them to be oppressed by anyone, so too we would not permit them to be found exempted from the path of justice.

LETTER 2.30 (C. 507–11)

This letter grants permission for the church of Milan to appoint a purchasing agent, who would be exempt from taxes imposed on other merchants so that he might obtain the resources needed for the church's care of the poor.

3. The phrase *ecclesias alienas* should be understood as a reference to the church of Milan, which had no jurisdiction in Sicily but nevertheless owned property there.

King Theoderic to Faustus, Praetorian Prefect

1. A personal exemption should not prejudice civic responsibility, since it is fitting that a *Princeps* be generous, lest royal munificence be confined within rules of procedure. Let fickle wrath be coerced by heavy regulations; let impatient ambition be curbed by law. Kindness has no need of law, nor should liberality follow narrow strictures, because it is fitting to be lauded without limit. **2.** And therefore, the public defenders of the patrimony of the holy church in Milan desire that one from among the merchants of their city be made available to them who would have authority in the office of a purchasing agent, being exempt from the impositions placed on merchants so that he may fulfill what he undertakes on behalf of the resources for the poor, which are squandered under an increase of profit.[4] For they remind us in a reasonable petition that we granted to the church of Ravenna that example of our piety which they now entreat also be applied to their own advantage. **3.** And therefore, your lofty and *illustris* magnificence, with public advantage secure in regard to other merchants, by which the civic body is accustomed to be supported, authorize one, whom they will have elected from among themselves, so that he might exercise the trade of a merchant, to the extent that he should not pay any fee for the monopoly, the sales tax, or the exchange of gold,[5] nor should he bear any burden whatsoever from having been permitted access to the market. For why should we delay assenting to this, where it is not possible that we would experience any loss?

LETTER 3.14 (C. 507–11)

A remarkably short letter responding to a complaint that a bishop's dependents (possibly tenants on church property) have assaulted the wife and property of another man. The status of the victims, whether tenants on church property or free landowners, is undisclosed, but their vulnerability is evident, as is the state's position in relegating the case to the care of the bishop.

---

4. The phrase *sub lucre exaggeratione funduntur* describes the inflation that impacted the purchase of resources for the care of the poor.

5. The *monopolium, siliquaticum,* and *auraria* were taxes levied on merchants, as discussed in *Var.* 2.26 (see Section 3).

King Theoderic to Aurigenes, Venerable Bishop

1. Although we may believe that any wickedness would displease your judgment, we especially trust that what would assail the condition of legal matrimony must be condemned by you. For with what hostility is it received by the faithfully married, which is execrated even in the curses of the laity? And so, Julianus has complained to us in a tearful petition that his wife and property have been ravaged in an unjust attack by your men. Whence, if you know the claim of the petitioner to be true, once struck, the crime is not reasonably dismissed. Restrain the author of the deed without any delay. For when a wicked deed remains unpunished, it increases, and a hastened corrective for the transgressor is a healing boon.

LETTER 3.45 (C. 507–11)

Another letter adjudicating confused church property rights. In this case, the public defenders of the church of Rome contest a claim that a house bequeathed by a former member of the church and then in use by clergy had been a Jewish synagogue. It is not clear why this case was addressed to the count in Rome (Arigernus) and not to the bishop of Rome. In *Variae* 3.37 (not included in this volume), a similar matter is handed to the bishop.

King Theoderic to Arigernus, Illustris *and Count*

1. It agrees with our justice that we should not allow chicanery to occur in regard to generous benefactions, and whatever is concealed through misleading interpretation we would uncover from a fleeing cloud of lies. And so, the public defenders of the sacred Roman church have been complaining that Simplicius,[6] of blessed memory, had formerly purchased from the acolyte Eufraxius, with documents drawn up according to custom, a house situated in the holy city, which, by right of no contest, the Roman clergy undertook to inhabit in the course of many years and transferred to other uses with security of ownership. **2.** Now, however, someone hardened by the shameless effrontery of the Samaritan superstition has appeared, who would pre-

---

6. Probably Pope Simplicius, who died in 483.

varicate with perverse intentions that the same place had been a synagogue, while to the contrary one may point to domiciles far and wide designed for human habitation, which this building calls to mind. For this reason, let your greatness dispense this case with diligent examination and according to the proven justice of your own good conscience, and, if you should learn the truth that comes out of this complaint, let it be decided with well-considered equity. For if trickery must be banished from human affairs, how much more we feel that matters judged to be practically an outrage to divine authority must be corrected!

LETTER 4.18 (C. 507–11)

This letter orders a count to investigate claims that a local priest had plundered wealth interred with the dead. Clergy were responsible for maintaining the precincts of the dead; it is not known where this may have occurred.

King Theoderic to Anna, Count and Spectabilis

1. It is the practice of our kindness to entrust issues requiring action to fidelity that has been proven to us, so that, when we choose judges endowed with mature discernment, craven thievery may not find a foothold. Indeed, not long ago it reached us through the report of many that the presbyter Laurentius has been searching among the corpses of men for funerary riches by exhuming the remains, and he has inflicted harm upon those dead that ought to be shown respect from the living. It is claimed that such corrupt contact has not been withheld from hands dedicated to the sacred rites. It is reported that he sought gold in an execrable manner, one for whom it would be more fitting to bestow his own wealth, or at least wealth properly collected, upon the needy. 2. We order you investigate this matter with careful inquiry, so that, if you find that the claims hold truth, you conclude your surveillance of the man only with that end, lest he be able to conceal those things that were illicit for him to find. For we believe that this crime, which we leave unpunished on account of the dignity of the priesthood, must be punished by something weightier.

LETTER 4.31 (C. 507–11)

This letter exhorts the bishop of Vercellae (modern-day Vercelli) to complete the repair of a local aqueduct, a form of public munificence more traditionally undertaken by a secular magistrate. The reference to the project's official sanction ("our authority") may indicate that the court subsidized the project in some manner.

King Theoderic to Aemilianus, Venerable Bishop

1. That which the intention of wise men is seen to have begun ought to be completed, since, just as the completion of something gives rise to praise, so too something unsound which is abandoned in the midst of completion produces censure. For having failed in endeavors, one has proved to have either wavered in plans or fallen short of strength. Therefore, let your sanctity, foregoing any particular objections, quickly bring to completion that charge undertaken by our authority for the satisfactory restoration of the aqueduct. **2.** For what is more fitting than that a blessed bishop should provide water for a thirsting people, and that human foresight should sate those who, moreover, ought to be fed with miracles? Indeed, you would imitate that most ancient Moses, who brought forth abundant streams from a sterile stone for those Israelites, long parched with thirst, and who, by fulfilling a miracle, caused clear waters to rush where there had been dry hardness. You, however, if you lead forth waters channeled by the construction of stone, would bestow upon the people with your own labor what Moses did by his miracles.

LETTER 4.33 (C. 507–11)

One of several letters addressed to Jewish communities in Italy, this brief rescript affirms to the Jews of Genoa the state's commitment to maintain the rights accorded to Jews under former imperial law. The reason that such an assurance was warranted is not clear from the letter.

King Theoderic to All Jews Living in Genoa

1. The maintenance of the laws is the hallmark of civic harmony, and reverence for prior *Principes* also testifies to our sense of duty. For what is better than for a people to want to live under the precepts of justice, so that the assembly of many may be a union of free wills? For this draws people from the life of a savage to a model of human concourse. This separates reason from beastliness, lest those who want to be ruled by divine counsel wander to the arbitration of chance. **2.** And so, you have demanded in a submitted petition that those privileges ought to be preserved for you which the foresight of antiquity decreed for Jews in the institutes of law. We willingly consent to this, we who desire that the laws of the ancients be observed for our own reputation. And so, we have decided in the present dictate that whatever the statutes of law proposed concerning you should be preserved undiminished, to the extent that what is known to have been devised for the conduct of public harmony may be maintained with continuous devotion.

LETTER 4.43 (C. 509–11)

Another letter illustrating the strained relations between Christians and Jews in Rome (cf. *Variae* 3.45, above), the present address to the Senate responds to an outbreak of violence, apparently involving Christian slaves and Jewish masters, to which the urban populace responded by burning a synagogue. The Senate was charged with investigating and bringing to trial the principal parties.

King Theoderic to the Senate of Rome

1. The celebrated reputation of Rome must be preserved by its own practices at the very least, lest it adopt strange vices that it has ever before dispersed with the probity of conduct. Indeed, it is not Roman to want the disorder of sedition and to invite arson in that very city. And therefore, discipline of deeds must be preserved among the authors of laws, lest the detestable appearance of arson compel the hearts of the common people to imitate what must be execrated. **2.** And so, we have learned from the report of the *illustris* Count Arigernus that the complaint of the Jews was roused because the unruliness of slaves had erupted in the slaughter of masters. Although the deed could have been punished for the sake of public discipline, with the controversy immediately enflamed by the populace, they caused the synagogue to be utterly consumed in a reckless fire, punishing the faults of men with the ruin of buildings. If any Jew had been proven to transgress, he himself would have been subject to injury. However, it was not right to rush to the horrible act of rioting, or to hasten to the burning of buildings. **3.** But we, whose desire it is to correct wrongly committed acts, by the grace of God, have decided in the present dictate that you should become acquainted with the above-mentioned case by lawful inquiry, and that you should restrain with the accustomed punishment the few agents of this conflagration whom you are able to discover. In this way, everyone can participate in pleasing conduct. For we do not want anything detestable to occur, whence Roman prestige may deservingly be reproached. **4.** Evaluating the case with equal measure, so that, if anyone reasonably believes that something supports him against the Jews, let him come to be heard at our court, so that whomever the offense will have implicated may be condemned with censure. Know for certain, this has displeased us exceedingly, that such fruitless intentions of the people have accomplished so much as the destruction of buildings, in a place where we want everything to be arranged with beauty.

LETTER 5.37 (C. 523-26)

This letter, addressed to the Jewish community of Milan, ensures the preservation of its legal rights in the face of hostility from the local Christian church. The exact nature of the dispute is not disclosed, but it seems to have required the reiteration of legal distinctions between the two communities.

King Theoderic to the Jews of Milan

1. We have gladly assented to that which is requested without injury to the laws, especially since, for the sake of preserving civic harmony, the benefits of justice must not be denied to those who thus far have been known to err in faith. And in this way may they learn the sweetest taste of good conduct, so that those who strive to attain human justice may begin more eagerly to consider divine justice. **2.** Consequently, since several of you have often claimed to be wounded by infringements, and you claim that rights have been rescinded which pertain to your synagogue, let the requested protection of our kindness bring assistance to you, to the extent that no man of the church, which rightly contends with your synagogue, may incite violent disruption, nor may he involve himself in your affairs with troublesome hostility. Instead, just as there is separation in the observance of religion, let the performance of celebrations[7] be separate. Nonetheless, we grant the benefit of royal assistance in this matter with moderation, so that you should not attempt to disruptively appropriate what the court has determined to pertain to the aforementioned church or to its religious offices by right of law. **3.** On that account, the thirty-year prescription, which is preserved for the protection of all mankind, should rightly be preserved for you, nor do we unreasonably order you to endure the loss of usury practices, so that your petition may enjoy freedom from illegal prejudices by means of the walled defense of our piety. We therefore grant what you have requested, in the usual habit of our kindness; but why, O Jews, thus supplicating, do you seek earthly peace if you are unable to find eternal rest?

LETTER 9.15 (C. 533)

In 532, Pope Boniface II died and was succeeded by John II, the addressee of this letter, according to which the recent papal election at Rome was attended by corruption. The main issue seems to have been the sale of church property by clergy and men associated with the church in order to influence the election for one party or another. The new pope was not directly implicated (his rival's party may have been responsible for the abuses), but the king's decree has a flat declarative tone and refers to a recent public statement (*consultum*) of the Senate intended to curb current practices.

King Athalaric to Pope John

1. If it was the inclination of ancient *Principes* to scrutinize laws, so that subject peoples might enjoy the delights of peace, it is much more outstanding to decide such matters as may agree with sacred law. Let condemnable profits be lacking from our reign. We can call profit only that which divine judgment is known not to punish. **2.** Only recently, a public defender of the church in Rome approached us with the tear-

7. The phrase *conversatione actuum* is vague but suggests the celebration of holy days.

ful allegation that, when a bishop was sought for the apostolic seat, certain men exploited the difficulty of the time with an impious scheme and thus moved against the property of the poor[8] with extorted promises, so that—even to say it is abominable—sacred vessels were seen exposed for public auction. The deed was committed with as much crassness as the glory gained from the piety to eliminate it. **3.** And therefore, let your sanctity be aware that we have established by this ordinance, which we also want to extend to all patriarchs and metropolitan churches, that, from the time of the most holy Pope Boniface, when the fathers of the Senate, mindful of their own nobility, produced a resolution concerning the prohibition of such sales, if anyone is discovered to have promised anything for obtaining the episcopal office, either through his own action or that of any other person, that execrable contract will be deprived of all validity. **4.** Moreover, if anyone is caught being involved in this crime, we grant him no appeal; but even if someone wants to be repaid for the purchase of church property or does not want to return what they have received, let them immediately be held guilty of sacrilege and restore the received property by compulsion of the assigned judge. For even as just laws make legal action available to good people, thus do they close opportunities to people of bad character. **5.** Furthermore, we support whatever the Senate decided in its resolution; let it be preserved in every measure against those who have involved themselves or any intermediary persons in forbidden agreements in any way. **6.** And since it is fitting that everything be moderated by reason, lest something excessive might be considered just, we have decided that when it happens that an accusation concerning the consecration of the apostolic pontiff is made, and the dispute of the people has been brought to our court, those approaching us with a collection of petitions will receive no more than three thousand *solidi*.[9] Nevertheless, we exclude from eligibility for this measure those who are sufficiently wealthy, since it is instead for the poor that a gift of the church must be considered. **7.** But for other patriarchs, we order no more than two

8. The property owned by the church that was intended to support a wide range of individuals: beggars, widows and orphans, monks and nuns, regular clergy.

9. This is a limit to the expenses that any party could impose upon church coffers in order to further their claim with the court at Ravenna.

thousand *solidi,* to be spent on persons for the above-mentioned purpose, when the matter of an appointment in their church comes to our
comitatus. Moreover, let them know that they may distribute no more
than five hundred *solidi* to the poorest of the people in their own cities.[10] Let the penalty of this edict and of the policy recently determined
by the Senate restrain other recipients, but let the severity of church
canons harry those giving church property. **8.** Moreover, since our
decree has freed you from illicit promises, it follows that, imitating
good examples, you, who preside over other churches in the office of
patriarch, may present worthy bishops without any loss to the majesty
of churches. For it is corrupt that the purchase of office, which we have
barred to secular office holders out of consideration for divine law,
may hold a place among you. **9.** Therefore, if any chief official of the
apostolic church or of the churches of patriarchs believes a bishop
must be appointed by the purchase of any votes, either through his
own action or that of his relatives, or of any person serving them, we
decree that he will return what he has received and will suffer every
measure of what is prescribed by canon law. But if anyone fears to
acknowledge what he has given or promised while the same bishop
holds office, let the church reclaim it from either the heirs or the representatives of the one whose sale purchased the ordination of a
bishop. Let those surviving heirs be known by no less disgrace of
infamy. We order that other ecclesiastical offices too will be subject to
the same ordinance. **10.** But if, perhaps by the contrivance of a crafty
scheme, a person has become obligated by hindering oaths, so that,
for the state of his soul's salvation, he neither may be able to prove nor
dares to disclose the offense committed, we grant freedom to any honorable person[11] to report this crime, and whatever he can gather as
evidence, to the judge assigned to the particular city. So that we may
hasten prosecutors to court, let that man who has agreed to prove such
a deed receive a third portion of the implicated property; let the
remainder of the property profit the same churches from which it is
known to have been wrenched, benefiting the buildings or at least

10. In order to limit suborning the poor to a particular party.

11. *Honestis personis* probably means someone of senatorial, decurial, or other rank
determined by public office, such as the public defender mentioned near the beginning
of the letter.

their services. For it is fitting to convert to good use what perverse iniquity wanted to steal. **11.** Therefore, let the depraved greed of wicked men cease. What may those who have been excluded from the font intend? Let the just condemnation of Simon be recalled and dreaded, he who believed the source of all largesse could be bought.[12] Therefore, pray on our behalf, maintaining our edicts that you know agree with divine mysteries. But so that the will of the *Princeps* may become known more easily to those of every disposition, we have ordered this to be announced to the Senate and the people by the urban prefect,[13] so the public may recognize that we pursue those who, instead, are hostile to the majesty of the church. You, who rule by the grace of God, will also publish this to all the bishops, lest anyone be free from blame who was able to acknowledge our ordinances.

LETTER 11.2 (C. 533)

In this letter, Cassiodorus requests spiritual guidance from the pope in Rome for the performance of his new duties as praetorian prefect (see Section 10, *Variae* 11.1). Just as important, the letter serves to remind the pope of his responsibility to the needs of the urban populace, for which open communication with the praetorian prefect was essential.

Praetorian Prefect Senator to Pope John

1. I must implore you, most blessed father, that the gladness which we receive through you, by God's generosity, we may know to be preserved for us through your prayers. For who would doubt that our prosperity must be attributed to your merits, when we, who have not deserved to be loved by the Lord, attain honor and, in exchange for such things as we have not done, receive the blessings of office? Indeed, by the fasting of clergy, famine is severed from the people; by tears of grace foul grief disperses, and through holy men its departure is accelerated, lest what burdens drag on longer. **2.** And therefore, greeting you with proper formality, which is right, I entreat that you pray strenuously on behalf of the welfare of those ruling, to the extent that the

12. Simon Magus, in Acts 8:9–24.

13. The order to publish this edict survives as *Var.* 9.16 (not included in this volume).

heavenly *Princeps* may cause their lives to be lengthy, diminish the enemies of the Roman republic, and grant peaceful times. Then, adorning peace, may he bestow needed plenty upon us from the abundance of his granaries. And for me, your son, may he open a spirit of understanding, so that I may follow what is truly useful and avoid what must be shunned. 3. Let that rational strength of the soul offer us counsel; let the face of truth dawn radiantly, lest bodily blindness cloud our mind; let us follow what is within, lest we become lost to ourselves; let wisdom which is wise in its own truth instruct us; let that which shines with heavenly clarity illuminate us. And thus, may public life receive the kind of judge as the universal church would send out as a son. May holy virtue enclose even us among its services, since we are then exposed to the deadly plots of the ancient adversary when we receive his gifts. 4. Do not leave to me alone the care of that city, which is more secure through your fame. For you preside over the shepherds of the Christian people: in the role of a father, you love all. Therefore, the safety of the urban populace relies upon your reputation, to whom the divinity has entrusted their protection. Therefore, it is appropriate that we have regard for some matters, but you for everything. Indeed, you pasture the flock entrusted to you spiritually; nevertheless, you cannot neglect such things as concern the substance of the body. For just as humanity is known by two natures, it is thus for a good father to restore both: First, by holy prayers avert the seasonal scarcity that transgressions produce. But if it should befall—would that it doesn't— exigency is properly removed when it has been prepared for under conditions of abundance.[14] 5. Advise me as to what must be done with urgency. I wish to act well, even by reproof, since the sheep that longs to hear the calls of the shepherd strays with more difficulty, nor does one whom the careful teacher instructs become wicked easily. I am indeed the palatine judge, but I do not desist from being your student; for then do we manage affairs properly if we depart the least from your principles. But since I desire to be advised by your counsel and assisted by your prayers, it must be attributed to you if anything is found in me other than what is desired. 6. May that throne, a marvel throughout

14. Beyond its obvious spiritual focus, this passage may allude to the papacy's role in managing food stores in Rome.

the world, shield its own cultivators[15] with that affection which, although it may be proffered to the whole world, is known to be more specifically apportioned to us. We hold something particular of the holy apostles—may it not be delivered to another by the sundering force of sins—because Rome has more fortunately deserved to possess in her fold those attestations that the world seeks.[16] 7. Therefore, with such patrons we fear nothing, provided that the prayers of the bishop are not lacking. It is certainly arduous to satisfy the desires of so many, but divine authority knows how to offer great rewards. May that very authority check the envious; may it make citizens grateful to us by heavenly inspiration and by your prayers bestow times which may be celebrated as having divine favor.

LETTER 11.3 (C. 533)

Much like *Variae* 11.2 (above), this letter asks the bishops of the realm to pray on behalf of Cassiodorus's fulfillment of the obligations of his new office, but intriguingly, it also tacitly makes them responsible for reporting to him the actions of subordinate officials whom he sends to act on his behalf. Rather than his own subordination to spiritual matters, *Variae* 11.2 and 11.3 demonstrate Cassiodorus's activation of ecclesiastical networks for the maintenance of public affairs.

Praetorian Prefect Senator to Various Bishops

1. It is a natural habit for a father in the flesh to rejoice in the advancement of his sons, when whatever praise is granted to a distinguished offspring reflects upon the instruction received from the father. You, however, who are spiritual fathers, who behold the author of all things with an illuminated mind, do pray diligently to the sacred Trinity on my behalf, so that it may cause the candle waiting in my mind to shine joyously, to the extent that nothing seen within me should be inadequate and that its appearance may incline others toward me. 2. For

15. The Latin *cultores* can mean both "worshippers" and "husbandmen," so here it may refer to the populace of Rome or perhaps more specifically to the clergy of the church.

16. *Sancti apostoli* ("holy apostles") and *confessiones* ("attestations") refer to the burial cults of Peter and Paul.

what does it benefit for a judge to be transparent to others if he is still rendered obscure to himself? Let one who is worthy to honor a seat of judgment display the dignity of good conscience. Let the judge be untroubled, lest he condemn those wandering astray. Let the Trinity be fortuitously at hand for us, so that unfavorable defects should be rendered absent. Let it bestow its love, so that, having compassion, it would forbid an opportunity for sinning. 3. Therefore, true fathers of the soul, I beseech you in affectionate and honest petition, so that you would pray with silent fasting to the Lord, that he may extend the lives of our *Principes* in flourishing reigns, that as a defender he may diminish the enemies of the republic, that he may give peaceful times, and that, for the praise of his own name, he may bring prosperity with tranquility in all affairs, so that he may deign to render me beloved to you. 4. But so that your prayer may also be heard more easily, be attentive to those whom we send concerning various affairs. What we do not know should not be incumbent upon us. Let your testimony accompany their actions, so that a man commended by you should find gratitude in our presence, or blamed, find censure. Nor should they be able to impute it to us if they are not judged to act wrongly when they transgress, so that they may thereby be encouraged to learn inappropriate behavior. 5. Offer to orphans and widows, against harsh circumstances, those comforts pleasing to God, but not so that—what happens through excessive piety when you seek to assist the wretched—you may remove the role set aside for the laws. For if any punishment should perhaps offend, give such admonishments to all alike, so that you would be able to render the laws unnecessary. Exile, holy fathers, the implacable furies of vice to the realm of unclean spirits; temper violence; impoverish avarice; remove theft and isolate luxury, the disease of humanity, from your people. Thus do you thoroughly overcome the author of iniquity, if you remove his enticements from human hearts. 6. Let a bishop teach, lest the judge punish what he finds. The administration of innocence has been given to you. For if your preaching does not fail, it follows that a punitive course of action may remain idle. And therefore, we who depend less upon secular authority commend our office to you in full, to the extent that our administration should be conjoined to the prayers of holy men. 7. May what is just please me most intimately. I am not a cunning oath taker: what I promise, I do not willingly abandon. Moreover, I fulfill the obligation of honorable greetings to your sanctities and conclude the text of this letter with an affectionate closing, so that sweeter words might abide in your mind, since the soul commends the last words to itself favorably.

LETTER 12.13 (C. 533–38)

This letter responds to a situation in which *canonicarii* were collecting taxes from churches by falsely claiming to execute the authority of fiscal accountants. The churches in question had received certain unspecified fiscal immunities by earlier imperial decree, and Cassiodorus seeks to distance these actions from the policies of his prefecture through repudiation.

An Edict

1. The largesse distributed by our rulers ought to be preserved by the effort of all, when what they are shown to accomplish by the inducement of divine authority is necessary to benefit all people. Indeed, the devotion of the *Principes* safeguards the entire *imperium,* and, provided that fitting compensation is returned to them, the limbs of the republic are preserved intact. Some time ago, indeed, imperial decrees assisted the holy churches of Bruttium and Lucania by a particular offering of gifts. But as it is habitual for sacrilegious intentions to sin even against divine reverence itself, the *canonicarii* have been removing a considerable portion in the name of the tax accountants, making the property of clergy a profit for the laity. **2.** But the tax accountants of our office, repudiating this detestable abomination, report that nothing which impious hands have embezzled by such crime has been paid to them. To what length will you assay with inhuman audacity, if you extend thefts even there where you know you are least able to be concealed? That you may perhaps toy with human witnesses, however shamefully, nevertheless seems to be a particular presumption. But one who assumes that he may perpetrate what divine authority may not condone has been condemned to such great blindness! **3.** But lest similar presumption perchance violate further or repeated transgressions challenge divine patience, we have determined in the formula of an edict that anyone who is involved further in this fraud shall be deprived of official rank and shall lose the enjoyment of his own property. Indeed, one who has extended his own audacity to no less than injury of the divine must be seriously stricken with punishment. Let the poor hold the gifts of those ruling; let those who have no property possess something. 4. Why should the resources of another, established by royal generosity, be plundered? The possession of it is the gift of the *Princeps*. In what way may a subject presume to seize what he beholds the humility of the ruler offering to God? Moreover, not giving to such men is stealing from them, and rightly, when one capable of assisting the hungry condemns them if he does not feed them. Let it be a shame to rob those whom we are commanded to support. Desiring to become wealthy from the poverty of the needy is beyond all perfidy. Let honest profit be loved; let damnable gains be feared. Thus, let no man dare to pilfer what is able to scatter gathered blessings. One who acquires by withholding perishes by increasing, and he instead draws poverty upon himself if he does not reject the money of the needy.

Family and Gender

*Letters concerning Households and Relations
between Family Members and Letters
to Women*

The full range of sixth-century changes to family structure and gen-
dered norms is not easy to discern through the *Variae*. Many of these
modulations in the culture of the late-Roman household responded to
the rise of Christianity, which has a comparatively muted presence in
the collection. In terms of impact on domestic life, changes in the
economy and in social stratification are the most readily apparent. In
most cases, the social and cultural standing of women and children
appears in the *Variae* in connection with landownership, and the letters describe women in very traditional terms, in relation to marriage-
ability, sexual propriety, and the rearing of children. Indeed, much of
Theoderic's diplomatic strategy depended on the marriage of Amal
women to kings of other successor states. Among the women who
appear in the *Variae,* the two who are known to have achieved status
by force of personality are Amalasuntha (Theoderic's daughter) and
Theodora (Justinian's wife).

LETTER 1.7 (C. 507–11)

This letter summons a senator to Theoderic's court to answer for his
role in the mishandling of an inheritance. The property had been
awarded to a parent by Theoderic and had subsequently passed to the
children. It seems that the addressee claimed this property on behalf
of his wife, the sister of the underaged child, Plutianus, who was enti-
tled to it. The following letter (*Variae* 1.8) offers further detail.

King Theoderic to Felix, Clarissimus

1. We know that you have been entangled in litigation with respect to Venantius's guardianship of the inheritance of Plutianus, in a manner unbecoming, to the extent that he whom you ought to have assisted at your own expense you have instead harmed with the loss of property. Indeed, costly consolations ought to have been testimony to your relationship to him. Therefore, what kind of deed would it seem to be between those conjoined by blood, which would be judged criminal between strangers? **2.** And therefore, we resolve by the present injunction that whatever property you know that wanton Neoterius has not so much shared as stolen with willful prodigality, you must restore fully intact to our agent without any delay, lest you compel us, who up to this point have tempered everything with mildness, to avenge a deed of this sort by turning to the law. For we do not permit what we have bestowed upon parents with our praise to be taken from the ward. It is indeed most grievous to steal through chicanery what was conferred by the beneficence of the *Princeps*. **3.** Now, in regard to the remainder of the property, which you assert on behalf of your wife has been divided into shares, contrary to the path of justice—if somehow that division which stands widely known under the original judgment must be addressed—hasten yourself to approach our *comitatus,* so that in your presence we may arrange that which accords with justice. For it is unjust that from one property by which succession occurs in equal portion, some should prosper abundantly while others should groan with the misfortunes of poverty.

LETTER 1.8 (C. 507–11)

This letter delegates the inheritance dispute initiated in *Variae* 1.7 (above) to an agent of Theoderic's court.

King Theoderic to Amabilis, Court Agent

1. It is in our heart to protect everyone in common, but especially those whom we know have been unable to protect themselves. For thus the scales of equality are served, if we liberally bestow assistance upon those without means and, on behalf of children, instill fear of us in the insolent. A lesser fortune requires a *Princeps,* since those who would subvert a gift made publicly encounter our censure. **2.** And so, we have learned through the tearful petition of Venantius, the legal guardian of Plutianus, that his own brother, Neoterius, having forgotten the condition of brotherhood, has attacked the property of this child with hostile madness. This matter has moved us to act severely on behalf of his affairs, since our beneficence, which we would have stand as a statement of our public duty, seems to have been replaced by an illegal audacity. And since it is not doubted that a waste of time would especially result in a repetition of offense, therefore let your devotion, by our firm command, cause the required property to be restored to the aforementioned guardian without delay, if there is nothing that can reasonably interpose punishment. **3.** But if there is anyone who may oppose this with the intention of retaining their own portion by preceding with a legal surety, they should hasten to approach our *comitatus,* so that we may judge with proved representatives according to the custom of our equity.

LETTER 2.10 (C. 507–11)

This is the first in a dossier of letters (also including *Variae* 2.11, below, and 4.40, not included in this volume) resolving a case in which a woman of senatorial rank was seduced (or abducted) and thereby induced to alienate property pertaining to her marriage.

King Theoderic to Speciosus, Loyal Comitiacus

1. It is the royal purpose to relieve those burdened by injustice, just as the punishment of a wicked man should cause justice to be loved more. Nor can that by which the wicked man lives be concealed from a healthy community, such that the cherished association of the marriage bed should endure professional seducers and that sacrament belonging to the engendering of humankind should be polluted by a profane crime. **2.** Therefore, having been moved by the petition of the *spectabilis* matron Agapita, who revealed her own secret sin to diverse witnesses—that these men even threatened the violent death of her husband, by whom instead they rightly deserved to be snuffed—we have decided in the present decree that whatever will be determined to have been claimed by detainers from the time when that deeply shamed woman abandoned the conjugal bond, with respect to any contract which is unable to be valid by virtue of unstable mental state, by which the principle of the laws having been compromised, you should cause to be restored without any delay, lest criminals prevail in defending the advantage of their frauds to the derision of justice. For it is exceedingly absurd that those who deserve to be consumed by punishment should even attempt to defend profits thereby gained.

LETTER 2.11 (C. 507–11)

This letter elaborates on the case of Agapita (see *Variae* 2.10, above) by directing strong language at the patrician Probinus (also former consul of 489). According to the complaint, men associated with Probinus were responsible for Agapita's loss of property. Although the letters hint that Agapita may have been a willing party, the case clearly fits the legal description of *raptio;* nonetheless, the court offers the senior senator involved an opportunity to restore the status quo.

King Theoderic to Probinus, Illustris *and Patrician*

1. Among other burdens of the human condition, conjugal affection provokes its own anxiety, and not without merit, since the source of posterity's renewal deserves to be held in high regard. Every indecency follows its particular author, while the mistake of a mother transfers to her sons, and in a particularly strange case of misfortune one's own disgrace becomes the sin of another. Therefore do husbands take such great precautions that the marriage bond be safeguarded by either divine or public sanction, so that it would be a great flaw of character not to respect the affection shared between others. 2. And so, the *spectabilis* Basilius has complained in petitions that his own wife, Agapita, was led away from their home by the seduction of certain persons, since the female sex lies exposed to the faults of inconstancy. Moreover, the confession of the above-mentioned wife in her own petition has confirmed this to us, adding that when she sought refuge within the precinct of a holy church, unknown to her husband and with all reason set aside, she transferred the estate Arcinatina to your magnificence. And now, having tasted of such burdensome wantonness, she deplores what she has done to herself, condemning her own acts, so that she would make restitution even as a poor wretch to the wealthy man, a deceitful woman to a chaste man, and a fool to a wise noble-

man. **3.** Now, cast away the prize, which clearly does not commend an honorable demeanor, since it is more fitting that you instead acquire that which may increase your reputation. Hence, the order we had issued the first time, we now repeat with a second dictate, so that you will surrender the above-mentioned property without any delay. For the alienation of property requires a firm judgment, and certainly with respect to Agapita's change of heart in these matters, she is shown to have squandered good counsel. For what respectable man will she be able to find, who has abandoned a husband with no obvious faults?

LETTER 4.9 (C. 507–11)

A letter ordering a count to provide guardianship to two orphaned children who had become targets of unspecified legal suits.

King Theoderic to Osuin, Illustris *and Count*

1. It is the role of the innocent to seek our court, where no place is given to violence, and where the injuries of greed are not tolerated. And so, Maurentius and Paula, stripped of the assistance of a father, claim that they have been exposed to the attacks of many. Their youth is deemed an opportunity for misfortunes, especially as it would be easy to steal from young orphans. And therefore, they deserve our protection, because the conniving of the wicked would not restrain itself from them. Thence, your loftiness, recognizing the intention of the present order, if any litigant in a legal contest prefers to vex the above-mentioned youths, they must be sent to our *comitatus,* where, it will be known, the innocent may find refuge and plotters may find the severity of the law.

LETTER 4.35 (C. 507–11)

A young senator was led to make ill-considered contracts, and so his legal representatives appealed to the court; this letter offers to nullify any contracts that the client entered into while a minor.

King Theoderic to the Agents of Albinus, Illustris

1. The foresight of antiquity has deliberately decreed that minors would not have the freedom of entering into a contract, as they are ensnared by the deceptions of schemers, and an insecure age assists their mistakes. Indeed, innocence would be overwhelmed if bold vigil should be eased, and every man would be eager to deceive if the fraud of plotters should succeed at bringing profit. 2. And therefore, you allege in a petition submitted in a respectable manner that your patron, being a minor, has accrued losses to his own resources, since ignorant childishness guides to the contrary whatever he will have considered advantageous, and that now we, adducing his age to have acted thus, should be able to amend a fault of ignorance, so that our kindness may also bestow what the laws have assigned. 3. And furthermore, if your petition does not deviate from the truth and he lives within that span of years for which the sacred laws offer this benefit, and nothing is claimed contrary to this right, then our authority also permits your patron to be duly restituted in full with respect to the considered case. Nonetheless, let everything be carried out according to justice and the laws, since we want to consider entreaties thus, so that we do not burden your adversaries unjustly.

LETTER 5.32 (C. 523–26)

This letter, one of a pair treating a domestic dispute between the households of two Gothic soldiers, censures a man for the conduct of his wife, who had assaulted the wife of another man. In the following letter (*Variae* 5.33), the source of the conflict is revealed as adultery.

King Theoderic to Brandila

1. Patza has sent the same complaint to us time and again, claiming that, while he was occupied on a very successful expedition, his own wife was mutilated with three blows from your wife, Procula, with the result that she escaped only by the grace of sheer chance, since at that time she was believed not to have been exhausted from blows, but to be dead. This audacity, at which we especially marvel in a woman, if indeed it is true, we shall not permit to occur unpunished. 2. And so, we advise you in the present decree, if you openly acknowledge the deed, reflecting upon your own sense of honor, censure the disclosed charge with a husband's severity, to the extent that a just complaint should not return to us concerning the same case. Furthermore, you know it is possible to restrain with laws what would be fitting for you

to correct with domestic severity. **3.** But if you perhaps want to say more, charging a case of unfounded slander, removing any excuses for delay, hasten immediately to our court with the aforementioned wife, there in due course to be either punished for wrongful presumption or vindicated of a wife's bad behavior.

LETTER 5.33 (C. 523–26)

This letter requires a military commander to resolve a dispute, first mentioned in *Variae* 5.32 (above), between the households of two Gothic soldiers. Here it becomes apparent that the source of the conflict was adultery and a bigamous marriage contracted while one of the soldiers was on campaign in Gaul.

King Theoderic to Wilitancus, Duke

1. The intimate complaint of Patza weighs on our sense of forbearance. While Patza was absent and engaged in the Gallic campaign, Brandila is reported to have launched an attack against him, so that Brandila led his wife, Regina, to share his company as his own wife and, in an adultery injurious to our reign, legally contracted the semblance of marriage with her. In no way shall we permit these charges, if they are true, to pass unpunished. For when would anyone hold anything dear if he should be subject to crime then, when he was fighting for the well-being of all people? **2.** Consider, O shameless woman, the most chaste species of the cooing turtledoves, which, if they become separated from their mates by accidental death, confine themselves to a perpetual rule of abstinence. They do not seek out again the delights of marriage, which they lost. Patza served good faith, while Regina ignored the praise of chastity, and, what is honored by no association with widowhood, she was detected speculating on his death. **3.** Wife, take heed of your peril! For those who fail to hold vows, reason urges, the punishment of law imposes, and the terror of a husband demands chastity. Good habits wither away completely if they are not proven by those circumstances that are tempered by reason and want. And therefore, let your loftiness cause those sought out to hasten to your scales of justice and, with the truth of the matter examined in full, just as our laws demand, censure the adulterers in favor of married men, since those who were conjoined in criminal presumption did not want a defender of the republic to return. **4.** Those who attempted to use the laws for scandalous acts had desired all these deeds to be concealed without suspicion. But it is better that the intentions of the wicked be corrected with the condemnation of a few, since every marriage would be abandoned to uncertainty when the husband was away if such a respected institution should be sinned against without any fear.

LETTER 7.39

This *formula* provides an individual with a warrant for legal guardian-ship (*tuitio*). Typically, *tuitio* was assigned for a member of the nobility who was vulnerable for some reason, for example young age. In some cases, it involved the physical protection of a ward assigned by the king, usually to a *saio*. In other cases, the king appointed a prominent senator to manage the property of a ward.

Formula *for Legal Guardianship*

1. Indeed, it seems superfluous to seek protection individually from the *Princeps,* who is intended to protect all alike. But since the execra-ble temerity of certain violent men has threatened your safety, it is not inappropriate to be led by the quarrels of aggrieved men to this role of duty, so that we may most readily confer upon a supplicant what we desire to bestow upon all. And so, with kindness do we remove you from the attacks of various harmful men, for whatever reason you are attacked, to the camp of our protection, to the extent that you may be seen to contend with your adversaries, not in the open field, but from behind a fortified defense. Let it be thus that, pressed by cruel men, you are restored to the battlefield, made equal by royal assistance. **2.** Therefore, our authority confers upon you the guardianship of our name, as the strongest tower against both lawless attack and contrac-tual damage; nonetheless, thus protected from this lawlessness, do not despise offering a lawful response, and do not appear so contemptu-ous as to trample upon public laws, you whom a reprehensible audac-ity oppressed first. And since our precept ought to have able executors, lest it not seem possible to act upon what it is fitting for a *Princeps* to pronounce, by order of the present kindness, let loyalty and diligence readily protect you, the one against Goths and the other against

Romans, since no one labors to defend what is feared to offend, when it is dreaded that the more powerful patron should become displeased. Therefore, enjoy our kindness; rejoice in the privilege received. For if you are threatened with further civil disharmony by anyone, you, being in a stronger position, will satisfy your desires concerning your enemies.

LETTER 7.40

Not all unions had legitimacy in the eyes of the law (or religion), particularly those involving a man and a woman of different classes. This *formula* legitimates a marriage to a woman of lower social status than her new husband and confirms that their children can inherit from him.

Formula *for the Confirmation of Matrimony and Granting Legitimacy to Children*

1. An everlasting gift is one that has been conferred by the blessing of posterity; nor could it be more becoming to a king than that he should provide for human offspring. It is certain that one entering the light of day does not deserve to receive adverse misfortune, lest he first incur the disability of limitations rather than discover the joys of heavenly light. **2.** And so, in the submitted petition you have presented as your wife one whose loving embrace you have gratefully bound to yourself, who ought to be married in honorable matrimony by our award, so that the children born to her may obtain the name of legal heirs. For when a bond unites everything with voluntary eagerness, and what pleases seems to be proper to everyone, it is hard not to have unconditional liberty there, where children have been engendered. **3.** And so, this woman who, even though she was legally taken as a wife, was not deemed to be equal in reputation, we decree to have become your legitimate wife, and we want the sons from the same woman, whether they are already born or will come in the future, to share the rights of inheritance, so that you may cherish without any hesitation those whom you know perfectly well to be your future successors. For it is nature that bestows sons upon you, but we who have caused them to become more precious with this security.

LETTER 9.4 (C. 526)

A letter fascinating for its disclosure of the problems faced by families of decurial status whose male members served as town counsellors. The praetorian prefect is here ordered to remove from the roster of town counsellors a family that pled financial burden—and that would now join the ranks of taxpayers, rather than benefit from including a tax collector.

King Athalaric to Abundantius, Praetorian Prefect

1. It is a happy request when laws are surmounted by piety, and blessed is the condition of the subjects if they recognize one among themselves to be more wretched than the others and choose him to be favored. For the most sacred laws have not debarred town counsellors from anything, except that only *Principes* may free them—that is, they should find a gift of forbearance where the lord dissents from his own resolution in amiable strife, when it is a kind of justice of its own that the one who is called dutiful may be held the least by the strictness of the law. For such a ruler is indeed reasonable to separate from the service of their rank those who are proven unequal to their labors. For the town counsellor is fit only for deception if maintained by no strength of substance; and what will it avail to continue, if he is known to be lacking in resources? It is quite similar to being an absentee, by whom delegated affairs cannot be accomplished. Thence, since the curia enjoys a great multitude, it should not seem stricken from losses with a few separated from so many. **2.** Therefore, let your *illustris* magnificence cause Agenantia, the wife of the learned Campanianus, living in the province of Lucania, and their sons to be immediately erased from the roll of their curia,[1] so that posterity to come may not learn that which it is forbidden to expose, since treachery is not perpetrated where a public record is not maintained.[2] Henceforth, let them instead be counted among the populace of landowners, enduring no less the

---

1. Agenantia may have been a widow with underaged sons, which would account for her request for the family to be removed from the decurial roster, possibly because women could not hold a seat in the curial assembly. Moreover, her sons' youth may have necessitated the appointment of a guardian to oversee her properties.

2. That is, the record of decurial obligation should be so thoroughly effaced that the family would not be held accountable for it at a later date.

exactions that they themselves had inflicted upon others. **3.** Now they will become troubled at the accustomed taxation; now they will dread the appearance of the collector. They will not know rights that come from holding authority. Wearied with their desired ignorance, let it happen that they dread the exactions for which they had formerly been feared. Still, they must be reckoned to have lived out that portion of their lives with good conduct when they would bear to live without office among those whose hatred they are not cognizant of having earned. Likewise, they would not be vulnerable in abiding under those whom they had incited with acts of wickedness.[3] Therefore, let them enjoy a favor from the *Princeps;* let those who were ranked by the quality of their own deeds live forgotten in peaceful tranquility.

LETTER 10.10 (C. 534)

Although merely a letter of salutation that introduced the envoys bearing the matters of true substance, this is nonetheless intriguing as an example of how diplomacy could move through multiple channels at the eastern imperial court, in this case through the wife of the emperor. This is the last letter in the collection from Amalasuntha, whom Theodahad had murdered sometime early in 535, and the first of several addressed to Theodora.

Queen Amalasuntha to Empress Theodora

1. While it may be our purpose to seek what is shown to pertain to the glory of a pious *Princeps,*[4] it is proper that you, who are known to continually increase with every kind of blessing, should be offered the respect of an address. Concord is had not only in immediate presence, for, on the contrary, those who conjoin themselves with the deepest affection behold each other more truly. And so, rendering the affection of respectful greeting to an empress, I hope that, with the return of those legates whom we have sent to the most clement and glorious *Princeps,* you will cause us to rejoice concerning your approval, since

---

3. They had reason to fear reprisal neither from the landowners whom they were now joining as taxpayers nor from the other town counsellors, to whom they would now make tax payments.

4. Here Justinian is meant.

your prosperity is as pleasing to us as our own, and it is essential to obtain that hoped-for approval which we are known to constantly desire.

LETTER 11.1 (C. 533)

In the longest letter in the collection, Cassiodorus addresses the Senate in gratitude for his appointment as praetorian prefect. Although he received the office during the reign of Athalaric, the greater portion of the letter is an epistolary panegyric for Amalasuntha, who acted as regent during her son's minority. The letter is also noteworthy for its commentary on relations with other states at the time of Cassiodorus's appointment.

Praetorian Prefect Senator to the Senate of Rome

1. You commend me in my promotion, conscript fathers, if I know that you had desired this for your order, for I believe that an outcome which so many blessed men had clearly preferred would arrive most propitiously. Indeed, your approval is a premonition of all good things, when no one can receive the commendation of such great men unless divine authority has arranged for him to be advanced. Receive, therefore, my gratitude, even as you exact obedient service. It is in the nature of things to love a colleague. But truly, you exalt your own reputation if you applaud an honor that has been given to a senator.[5] **2.** May concern for the senators drive me unswervingly toward the public weal, so that I may be credited with your acclamation more, when I have earned the pleasure of such solace. After the *Principes,* my next concern is to commend myself to you, since we trust that you love what we feel the masters of the state intend: first, that we judge honesty to be serviceable, so that justice, as though a handmaid, would always attend our public acts, and we would not shamefully barter away an office that we received by integrity, without purchase, from a *Princeps.* **3.** You have heard it spoken already, leading men, what a weight of affairs I have assumed.[6] A celebrated entrance to the summit

---

5. An obvious pun on Cassiodorus's own cognomen.

6. A reference to the announcement, given in Athalaric's name in *Var.* 9.25 (not included in this volume), of Cassiodorus's appointment to the Senate in Rome.

of office requires more than strength. We dare not speak this falsely, but confess the role to be overwhelming: for such judgment does not discover merit, but rather makes it. For we, who know that our masters have wanted to elevate humility, do not boast about this; nor should they seem to bestow such a remarkable distinction on the unworthy. The blessings of a celebrated reign seize us and invite us, as though parched from long thirst, to a draught of the sweetest savor. **4.** O blessed fortune of the age! With the *Princeps* at leisure, it is the favor of the mother, through whom everything is accomplished in such a way that the goodwill of the public may be felt covering us, that rules. To her, the one whom all resources serve[7] offers glorious obedience, and, by a miraculous admixture of concord between them, he now begins to command his own character before he is able to govern the people. It is easily the most difficult kind of imperial reign, for a young man to rule his own passions. It is an entirely rare blessing for a master to triumph over his own conduct and in the flush of youth to arrive at what aged modesty is hardly capable of attaining. **5.** Let us rejoice, conscript fathers, and let us give thanks to heavenly majesty in humble devotion, when, at the arrival of the right time, clemency will not be difficult for our *Princeps,* who learned to serve in devotion to his subjects in his adolescent years. But let us attribute this wonder to the morals of them both: for the maternal genius is so great in her, whom even a foreign *Princeps* by right ought to serve.[8] **6.** For every kingdom most properly venerates her; to see her is awesome, to hear her speaking, a marvel. For in what tongue is she shown not to be the most practiced? She is learned in the brilliance of Greek eloquence; she shines in the presentation of Roman discourse; she glories in the wealth of her native speech; she surpasses all in their own languages, while she is equally inspiring in each. For if it is wise to be accomplished in one's native tongue, what could we claim concerning an intellect so great that it preserves so many kinds of eloquence with flawless execution? **7.** Hence, a great and needed assistance comes to diverse nations, because none lack for interpretation in the presence

---

7. Athalaric.

8. An interesting insight into the view of Amalasuntha's position vis-à-vis Justinian's prior to Athalaric's death. If Theoderic's reign was understood in truly imperial terms, his appointment by Zeno made his heirs senior to Justinian, after a fashion.

of our wisest matron's hearing. For neither does the envoy suffer delay, nor the petitioner any loss from the slowness of a translator, when both are heard in their native words and are addressed with an answer in their father's tongue. Conjoined to these qualities, as though in an extraordinary diadem, is a priceless familiarity with literature, through which, since it teaches the wisdom of the ancients, her royal dignity is ever increased. **8.** But although she rejoices in such fluency in languages, she is so demure in public events that it may be credited to disinterest. She dissolves tangled litigation with a few words; she settles seething quarrels with calm; she manages the public weal in silence. You do not hear proclaimed what is openly adopted, and, with miraculous restraint, she accomplishes surreptitiously what she knows must be done in great haste. **9.** What similar distinction has antiquity produced? We have learned of Placidia:[9] celebrated by reputation across the world, glorious in a line of a number of *Principes,* she was devoted to her purple-clad son, whose *imperium* diminished shamefully because she administrated it carelessly. At length, she purchased a daughter-in-law for herself by the loss of Illyricum, and the union of rulers was accomplished through the lamentable division of provinces.[10] She also sapped the military with excessive inactivity. Warded by his mother, he endured what an abandoned child would hardly be able to bear. **10.** But with this matron, who follows as many kings as she has kinsmen, with God's blessing, our army terrifies foreign peoples: the army is balanced by provident policy, neither ground down with constant campaigning nor again enervated by long peace. Furthermore, at the very beginning of the reign, when novelty always tests uncertainties, she caused the Danube to be Roman against the will of the eastern *Princeps.* **11.** What the invaders suffered is well known, on which account I judge it must be passed over, lest the spirit of an allied *Princeps* retain the shame of defeat. For what he felt concerning our territories was made known when, having been beaten, he conferred a

9. Galla Placidia was the daughter of Emperor Theodosius I, the sister of Emperor Honorius, and the mother of Emperor Valentinian III, during whose early reign she ruled as regent, much like Amalasuntha.

10. This was the marriage of Valentinian III to Licinia Eudoxia, the daughter of the eastern emperor Theodosius II. Its negotiation had involved the cession of the province of Illyricum, previously attached to the administration of Italy, to the eastern empire.

peace that he was unwilling to grant others when prevailed upon. It is added that he has furnished so many embassies to us, which we rarely sought, and her unequalled excellence has diminished the awe of eastern grandeur, so that she elevates the masters of Italy. **12.** Even the Franks, so able in victories over barbarians—how they were thrown into disorder by that great expedition![11] They, who always wage war on other nations by sudden assault, when challenged, feared to enter battle with our soldiers. Although an arrogant nation, they declined confrontation, but they nevertheless failed to avoid the death of their own king. For that other Theoderic,[12] long glorified by a mighty name, died, to the triumph of our *Principes,* overcome by torpor, rather than in battle, I believe by divine arrangement, lest wars between relations by marriage pollute us, or lest a justly raised army not enjoy some retribution. Well done, sword-girt Goths, more welcome than any good fortune, you who felled a royal host at the head and endured the death of not the least soldier. **13.** Indeed, the Burgundian too,[13] in order to regain his own territory, has become devoted, surrendering himself completely, while he received something meager in return. Indeed, he decided to obey with territory intact, rather than resist in a diminished state. He then defended his kingdom more carefully when he set aside his arms. For he recovered by entreaty what he lost in battle. Blessed are you, matron, in resounding fame, for whom every pretext for conflict is removed by divine favor, when you either conquer adversaries of the republic through heavenly favor or join them to your *imperium* by unexpected generosity. **14.** Rejoice, Goths and Romans alike, at what all may call a proper marvel. Behold, by God's favor the fortunate matron has achieved what both sexes consider extraordinary: for she has reared a magnificent king for us, and she defends the broadest *imperium* with strength of spirit. **15.** So much of this pertains to war, as it has been reported. But if we want to enter the

11. The campaign to eject Franks and Burgundians from southern Gaul after the death of Alaric II in 507.

12. This can only be the eldest son of Clovis, Theuderic I, who inherited the Frankish kingdom of Austrasia in 511 and attempted to reclaim Gothic Gaul before his death in 533 (see Gregory of Tours, *Decem Libri Historiarum* 3.21, 3.23).

13. Probably Godomar, son of Gundobad. His kingdom of Burgundians was incorporated into the Frankish realm in 534, a year after Cassiodorus became praetorian prefect.

halls of her devotion, hardly "a hundred tongues and a hundred mouths"[14] would be able to suffice: for her, purpose and justice are equal, but kindness is greater than power. Therefore, let us speak inadequately about weighty matters, a few words about many things. You know how many blessings she has bestowed on our order from heavenly kindness: nothing is in doubt where the Senate is witness. She has restored the stricken to a better condition, she has elevated with offices the unaggrieved, whom she protects with universal care, and she has lavished blessings on each. Even now what we declare has increased. **16.** For behold the patrician Liberius,[15] a man practiced in military affairs, beloved by the public, distinguished with merits, attractive in form, but more handsome for his wounds, possessed of the rewards of his own toil, and moreover the prefect of Gaul: a double honor adorns this outstanding man, so that he would not lose the prefecture which he has managed so well. Acknowledged for merits, for him one reward alone does not suffice. For he has even received the dignity of attending at court,[16] lest one well deserving be thought unwelcome for his long absence from the republic. **17.** Oh, the admirable goodwill of the rulers, which has extolled the aforementioned man so greatly that, with the grant of offices, it even deemed his patrimony must be enlarged, which was thus gratefully received by the public, as though everyone believed themselves, rather, to be enriched by his reward, because whatever honor is granted to a deserving man without doubt is felt to be shared among the many. What may I say, therefore, concerning the resolve of her mind, by which she surpasses even widely celebrated philosophers? For an advantageous discourse, and promises abiding in assuredness, issue from the mouth of our matron. **18.** What we say, conscript fathers, is not unproven by us: the one who praises is a true witness, experienced in her virtues. For you know what wishes conspired against me: neither gold nor powerful appeals

14. Virgil, *Aeneid* 6.625.

15. An influential figure in Ostrogothic public life. This interpolation in a panegyric for Amalasuntha is difficult to reconcile, except perhaps as a statement of recent realignment in support of the Amals at that time.

16. *Praesentaneam dignitatem:* there were a number of honorary ranks that would provide access to the court, and it may be that Liberius assumed the same privilege as the king's honored advisor that Cassiodorus's father had received after completing his prefecture.

prevailed; all things were attempted in order that the glorious constancy of our most wise matron should be proven.[17] **19.** Formal expression demands a challenge to the display of ancient empresses by comparison to her contemporary example. But how would feminine examples be able to compare to one for whom all the fame of men yields? If the royal cohort of her ancestors beheld this woman, they would immediately see their own celebrated qualities, as though in the most refined mirror. For Amalus basked in his good fortune, Ostrogotha in patience, Athala in kindness, Winitarius in equity, Unimundus in beauty, Thorismuth in chastity, Walamer in trust, Theudimer in duty, her illustrious father, as you have already seen, in wisdom. When each individual cause for fame is rightly unable to compare itself with a host of virtues, they would happily confess her to be superior, certainly because, in her, they would recognize each of the whole to be her own. **20.** Think what joy they would have from such an heir, who was able to surpass the merits of each. Perhaps you expect to hear of the good qualities of the *Princeps* separately: one who praises the parent proclaims the child abundantly. Next you should recall the exceptional saying of that most eloquent Symmachus, "Happily observing the growth of his virtues, I defer praising his beginnings."[18] Assist me, conscript fathers, and, by acting on my behalf, satisfy my debt to our shared masters with your assent: for just as one man is not capable of satisfying the wishes of all, thus are many able to fulfill the requirements of one.

17. Cassiodorus's appointment was controversial, possibly as a result of his earlier elevation as *Magister Officiorum,* an office made vacant by the death of Boethius, a prominent senator and scholar. Boethius had been slandered by rivals at court and executed on (likely spurious) charges of treason.

18. Q. Aurelius Symmachus, consul of 391, was known for eloquent orations; the passage quoted by Cassiodorus does not survive independently.

Section XI

Law, Order, and Conflict

*Letters Describing the Court's
Approach to Criminal Charges
against Individuals*

The political theology of the Amal court projected strong attachments to a traditional constellation of Roman virtues, and the exercise of justice (*iustitia*) forms one of the more prominent thematic strands of the *Variae*. The state position on crime manifests in a wide range of cases here, concerning property theft, sorcery, grave robbing, murder, and administrative corruption. In each case, the letters that Cassiodorus selected demonstrate what must have been thought of as the most appropriate responses (mild or severe) to each offense and the most appropriate personnel (civil or military) to handle each occasion. Deference to long-established Roman legal tradition is universal throughout the collection, but, perhaps because of this, direct references to Theoderic's *Edictum* (promulgated ca. 500) and Justinian's legal codifications (529–34) are absent. More surprisingly, explicit mention of the early fifth-century *Theodosian Code* is also lacking, although one letter mentions a *Novella* of Valentinian III. The implication is that the Ostrogothic state was harmonized with Roman legal tradition at an ethical and philosophical level, rather than through the pedantic implementation of Roman legal texts. Nonetheless, for all its rhetoric, the portrayal of law and order in the *Variae* reveals a fascinating landscape of how individuals interacted with state authority.

LETTER 1.5 (C. 507–11)

This letter, brief and spare of background details, concerns a property dispute in which Theoderic denied the appeal of a ruling by the local Gothic count, who may have served in the place of a civilian provincial governor.

King Theoderic to Florianus, Spectabilis

1. It is not fitting for a settled dispute to drag on without end. And what if peace is given over to wrangling? Should comfort not be found in lawful decisions? For only one safe haven among tempests of human conjuring is provided, and if men should ignore it with raging willfulness, they will always wander astray into surging tides of brawling. 2. And for that reason, we declare to your excellency in the present proclamation that, insofar as the case remains as it was entreated by those present, the quarrel over the estate at Mazenis has been decided with lawful statutes in the judgment of Count Anna, nor shall anything that has been decided be judged by appeal. 3. Because just as we would not want to deny justice to the oppressed, thus should we not offer assent to unreasonable quarrels. For one who would reject being peaceful on account of his own vices ought to be compelled to be peaceful. Even so does the skilled doctor often cure the uncooperative patient, whose will is unbalanced by burdensome desires, so that the patient grasps after that which is onerous rather than that which is perceived to be a healthful choice.

LETTER 1.11 (C. 507–11)

Instructions to the military commander of the province of Raetia to intervene in the abduction of slaves by the Breones, a people with some connection to local military service. The letter insinuates that liberties taken by the Breones had been tacitly condoned by the addressed duke. The Breones are not otherwise attested as a people.

King Theoderic to Servatus, Duke of Raetia

1. It is fitting that the honor which you bear in title you should demonstrate in habits, so that throughout the province in which you preside you should suffer no violent actions to occur, unless it is urged for the

justice whence our *imperium* flourishes. **2.** Therefore, we have been asked in a petition of Moniarius to stir you with the present statement, as it seems you have been aware that the Breones have unreasonably borne away slaves that are legitimately his. These Breones, being accustomed to military service, are said to threaten civil harmony with arms, and, on account of this, they despise yielding to justice, since they continually direct themselves toward warlike acts. While I know not for what reason, it is difficult to preserve a measure of good conduct with these people constantly threatening. **3.** Therefore, with that impudence which can be adopted on the presumption of strength having been removed, cause the aforementioned property to be restored by them without hesitation, lest the petitioner be seen to despise his victory on account of the inconvenience of delay by Breones.

LETTER 1.23 (C. 507–11)

This letter assigns two senators of patrician rank to settle a dispute among three other senators. It was standard policy for the Amals to avoid direct involvement in the affairs of Roman senators, as indicated by the paucity of details concerning the case and the great attention to the dignity of senatorial rank.

King Theoderic to Caelianus and Agapitus, Illustres and Patricians

1. It is fitting that concern at a royal height preserve the harmony of the general populace, since it adds to the praise of the one ruling if peace should be loved by all. For what is there that speaks in favor of us better than a peaceful people, a Senate in accord with itself, and the whole republic enrobed in the respectability of our habits? **2.** Hence it is that we have decided by the present dictate that the dignified patricians Festus and Symmachus should, by your judgment, make an end to the case which they claim to have against the *illustris* patrician Paulinus. With these claims taken up according to the measure of the laws and settled, if the extent of the law should permit it, then let Paulinus produce in his own turn whatever case he himself may claim to have against the aforementioned dignified persons. We do not want the judgment with respect to either party to be delayed, but we do want everything to be decided and nothing else remaining between them except what should be owed out of goodwill. **3.** Take heed, therefore, that you have been chosen as arbiters for such a great legal case. Take heed of our expectation to demand fair justice. You would bear a rich bounty of gratitude if this present controversy should not prove those believed worthy to be unequal to the task of judging it. Indeed, there ought to be special care taken with respect to such men, who are able to provide clear examples to junior men. For whoever neglects a legal quarrel that must be eliminated from among the ranks of the highest men encourages others to imitate the same without hesitation.

LETTER 2.14 (C. 507–11)

The great patrician and father-in-law of Boethius, Symmachus is here asked to investigate a case of possible parricide and to exact punishment if necessary. A digression on the nature of duty between children and parents occupies the greater part of the letter, perhaps reflecting the significance of Symmachus's devotion to Boethius, for which he was executed in 526.

King Theoderic to Symmachus, Patrician

1. Who could now find fault with anything else if commitment to familial devotion is deemed to be unfeeling? The man accused of a trivial matter is ignored when a great tragedy of crime clamors, nor does anyone strive to protect what is equitable if the highest order of travesties are seen to escape. The very nature of his intent displays an enemy to be savage; you may even find a colleague more wrathful, but decency does not allow the disobedient son to deflect punishment. **2.** Where is that moral vigor of nature that fastens to offspring in the embrace of kinship? The whelps of wild beasts attend to their parents; shoots do not disagree with their own seedbed; the tendril of a vine serves its own origin; and should a man, once begat, quarrel with his own origins? What shall we say for that kindness which can bind even foreign persons to a family?[1] From infancy, children are tended to, and riches are made and accumulated for them. And when anyone should believe that what he possesses abounds for himself, when to that point it had been acquired from fathers, he sins more on behalf of

1. Slaves are implied here.

the new generation. Oh, the grief! Do we not deserve the affection of those for whom we would not refuse to undergo utter ruin? The cares of a father do not flee from the very ocean when it is stirred by savage storms, so that he might attain through foreign commerce what he may leave behind for his offspring. 3. The very birds, for whom life is continually concerned with food, do not defile their own nature with perverse behavior. The stork, continually the harbinger of the returning year, expelling harsh winter and leading in the delights of the spring season, provides a great example of devotion. For when the wings of a parent become weakened with ripening age and it cannot suitably find the necessities of its own sustenance, the offspring restore warmth to the cold limbs of the parent with their own plumage and revive its weary bodies with victuals. And until the elderly bird returns to its former vigor, in a dutiful change of roles, the young return what they had received as children from their parents. And therefore, those who do not abandon the responsibilities of devotion rightly preserve a long lifespan. 4. Moreover, it is the custom with partridges to replace a broken egg with one taken from another mother, so that by the adoption of an alien offspring they amend the misfortune of their bereavement. As soon as the hatchlings begin to confidently move about, they venture into the fields with the foster parent; but when they are stirred by the call of the natural mother, they would rather seek the birth mother of their egg, even though they were reared by others as stolen hatchlings. 5. Therefore, how ought men to behave, when this devotion is recognized also in birds? And so, bring to our court this Romulus, who, tainted by the egregiousness of his own deed, befouls the name of Romans. And if it is determined that he laid hands upon his own father, Martinus, let him immediately feel the lawful punishment. Thus we have chosen your probity, since you would not be able to spare the cruel, not when it is a kind of piety to confound those who are shown to have involved themselves in criminal acts against the order of nature.

LETTER 2.35 (C. 507–11)

A curious letter, illustrating concern for Roman cities by ordering an investigation into the loss of a public statue at Como. The nature of the statue is not discussed, merely its importance to antique heritage, and its loss provoked an edict (*Variae* 2.36, not included in this volume). The addressee of the letter was probably a count. Compare a similar concern for public statues in Rome elaborated at far greater length in *Variae* 10.30 (see Section 13).

King Theoderic to Tancila, Spectabilis

1. It is exceedingly grievous that the accomplishments of the ancients diminish in our times, we who desire to increase the adornment of cities daily. Wherefore, we urge in the present command that, with full devotion, you carefully inquire after the bronze statue in the city of Como which happens to have been lost. Promise even one hundred *aurei* if anyone will see fit to expose this disrespectful theft, so that the promise of our kindness may invite those anxious for hope of forgiveness, which an edict sent to you also explains. But nonetheless, after you have published the command, if the crime has remained secret thus far, after Sunday bring together the craftsmen from all the shops, to inquire from them under threat by what assistance the crime was accomplished. For the overturning of a statue would not be accomplished easily by those unskilled in these matters, unless the help of experience had dared to change its location.

LETTER 3.46 (C. 507–11)

This letter delivers a verdict in a case involving the abduction (and presumed rape) of a young woman. The petitioner claimed that his confession of guilt was extracted under duress by the governor. In response, the letter reduces his sentence to temporary exile and revokes his loss of civil rights (*infamia*). Although the defendant's rank is not mentioned, the length and elaboration of the letter suggest a person of some importance.

King Theoderic to Adeodatus

1. The formal charge of a crime is the stuff of glory to a *Princeps*, since compassion would have no place unless the opportunities for errant behavior should arise. For what wholesome resolutions could be arranged if the probity of good morals settled everything? Parched thirst longs for the blessing of moistening rain. Firm health does not require salubrious hands, unless when sick. Thus, when one succumbs to feebleness, the cure may be suitably granted. Therefore, in cases of harsh misfortune, governance must be offered for the praise of justice, so that we neither allow the punishment to exceed the sin committed nor permit an unpunished crime to outrage the laws. **2.** And so, you have alleged in submitted entreaties that, oppressed by the bitter hatred of Venantius, the *spectabilis* governor of Lucania and Bruttium, and suffering for a long time in a place of confinement, you were coerced to confess the abduction of the young woman Valeriana, because a man will more gratefully expect the prospect of a quick death than endure the cruelties of torture. For amid the utmost constraints of suffering, the desire is to perish, rather than to live, since the wretched feeling of punishment excludes anticipation of sweet relief. Moreover, what is least amenable to justice, you claim further that the protection of legal representatives, so often demanded, was withheld from you, while your adversaries, being eloquent by nature, were able to bind you, as yet an innocent man, with the nooses of the law. **3.** This petition effectively set upon the inclination of our devotion and gradually bent the laws toward mercy, although a report sent from the governor of Bruttium has arrived, which enfolded the personal allegation of tragedy in his own voice, denying that a deceptive supplicant should be believed in opposition to public trust. **4.** And therefore, in our leniency we have softened the harshness of the punishment, ruling that, from the day of the sentence's publication, you should endure exile for six months, so that, after our verdict, in no way may it be permitted for the stigma of infamy[2] to oppose you under any sort of interpretation, when it is the endowed right of the *Princeps* to scour away the stains of a rapist's reputation. But with this period of time completed, restored to your home and all properties, you may have every right of free men that you first possessed, since we deem that you, whom we have decided to detain in temporary exile, should not groan with the brand of disgrace.[3] We threaten anyone who attempts to violate our present decision, by either obstructing or misinterpreting it, with the penalty of no less than three pounds of gold.

2. The phrase *crimen infamiae* likely refers to a reduction in the defendant's civil status that would have otherwise attended conviction.

3. *Maculosa nota* and *adustio probri* refer to branding that convicted criminals could endure as part of their *infamia*.

5. But since we do not want this decree to extend all the way to the innocent, lest the ignorance of anyone seem to have benefited them not at all, by this present dictate we free from fear those who have been unknowingly involved in this case at any time or place. For one who has no knowledge of criminality resembles a man not present.

LETTER 3.47 (C. 507–11)

This letter sentences a town counsellor to permanent exile on a remote volcanic island for the murder of his municipal colleague. It presents an interesting study in contrasts with *Variae* 3.46 (above), which similarly exiles a man, but under less severe terms. Also of note is the interest in the providence of nature, volcanism, and the habits of the salamander, which offer philosophical justifications for the sentence.

King Theoderic to Faustus, Praetorian Prefect

1. A softened punishment is a reflection of devotion, and one who mitigates a due penalty with considered moderation punishes out of kindness. The governor of Lucania and Bruttium[4] reports to us that the town counsellor Jovinus has been stained with the shedding of human blood. Having been incited to this in the passion of a mutual disagreement, he escalated a verbal altercation to the punishable death of a colleague. But being aware of his guilt in the deed, he refused to entrust himself to the punishment prescribed by law and fled into the precincts of a church. We have condemned him by permanent banishment to the Vulcan Islands, so that we may be seen to maintain respect for the holy building; nor may such a criminal, who is himself believed to be unforgiving of the innocent, avoid punishment entirely. **2.** Consequently, because he would be overcome by deadly heat, let him lack a paternal hearth there, where the bowels of the earth do not extinguish, when they are perpetually devoured for all time. Indeed, such earthly flame, which is nourished by the diminishment of some substance, if it does not consume, is extinguished. The interior portion of the mountain continuously seethes, unexhausted, among the waves,

---

4. This may or may not be the same governor, Venantius, of *Var.* 3.46 (above): although here "governor" is given as *corrector* and in *Var.* 3.46 the title is *praesul,* these terms could be used interchangeably.

nor is that diminished which is known to have been released. It is certainly on account of the inexplicable agency of nature that however much devouring flame reduces, an increase of stone restores. For by what means may stone remain intact, if it always melts away without increase? 3. Indeed, divine providence thus causes the wonder of contrary natures to be perpetual, so that what purposes to remain fixed for all time, having been openly consumed, is reborn from the most obscure origins. Certainly, when other mountains boil forth with billowing clouds, they are not known by corresponding names. Therefore, it must be thought that this mountain is acclaimed by the name of Vulcan because it burns so severely. 4. Hence, let the man condemned to capital punishment be sent to the aforementioned place. Let him lack the world that he enjoys, from which he has cruelly banished another man to exile, so that the one surviving would receive that which he inflicted with the result of death. He will follow the example of the salamander, which commonly passes its time in fire, for it is constrained by such a native coldness that it finds burning flames to be temperate. It is a slender and sparing animal, related to the worm, and clothed in a yellowish color. It enjoys a life of heat that consumes all other mortal creatures. 5. The conservators of ancient ages recall, however, that some many years ago this island erupted from deep within with a fearful churning of waves, at the time when Hannibal himself contended with his own veins at the court of Prusias, king of Bithynia, lest so great a leader come to the derision of the Romans.[5] Thence, it is more remarkable that a mountain burning with such a great gathering of flames would be held concealed under currents of the sea, and that heat should thrive there without end, which such great waves were known to overwhelm.

LETTER 4.27 (C. 508–11)

This letter, about an interesting case of legal guardianship gone awry, orders the arrest of a *saio* for attacking and extorting his delegated ward. The addressee, another *saio,* is ordered to work with a count (and likewise *saio*) to resolve the matter.

5. Hannibal committed suicide sometime between 183 and 181 B.C. rather than be handed over to Roman authorities.

King Theoderic to Tutizar, Saio

1. Any insult is certainly detestable, and whatever has been permitted contrary to the laws is justly sentenced to condemnation. But where the harm of every wickedness is deemed to have reached the furthest extent, there assistance is believed to advance. For diverted cruelty heaps blame upon the hostile party, and an unexpected betrayal is a greater burden for the accused. **2.** And so the *spectabilis* Peter has complained to us in a remarkable deposition that the protection of the *saio* Amara,[6] which we granted to him against violence, has instead been twisted about, such that only the intervention of doors could stop the blow of a sword from being plunged into him. He has been subject to a wound of the hand, which, as it had not been completely severed, the hard wood of the doors prevailed against further blows. Even when the attack had been exhausted, the extreme condition of his body attested to the glittering sharpness of the blade. **3.** O execrable crime! His own protection assaulted the man, and, with the beneficial comfort of protection removed, harm increased from his defense. He even affixed a more grievous crime to this, almost as though hostility came at a price; his own crime was thus appraised with an enormous tribute. And therefore, the wrath of our devotion justly rises up against such men, who have transformed liberal commands into a savage practice. For what refuge is there for supplicants if even our favors cause wounds? **4.** Thence, we have decided in the present order that whatever the above-mentioned Amara received in the name of payment for the representation of the same petitioner, bound by you as though he himself were the unwanted assailant, let him be compelled to pay double to Peter, since it is proper that what happened to be extorted by means of willful impudence should be restored as a punishment. **5.** Moreover, concerning the blow that the brash outlaw inflicted with a drawn sword, let him come, by your compulsion, for a hearing at the court of Count Duda, also appointed a *saio,* so that it may be settled without any delay following the precedents of edicts that clarify the crime committed. Indeed, you will demonstrate protection for one requiring it against unlawful attacks, with civil harmony preserved by our injunction, not

---

6. The term *tuitio* in this instance indicates that the protection of the *saio* was a legally formalized patronage.

with the example of one condemned, but with the thoughtful consideration of one properly delegated.

LETTER 5.34 (C. 523–26)

This letter offers a vivid indictment of a former official convicted of embezzling public funds, whom the praetorian prefect is ordered to arrest. Of particular interest is the mobilization of natural history in building a case against the culprit.

King Theoderic to Abundantius, Praetorian Prefect

1. It was reported to us in frequent claims that Frontosus, a testament to his own name,[7] had frittered away no small amount of the public funds. We caused the man to be examined in just investigation by various judges, lest perhaps, as often happens, not the truth but rather prejudice condemn him. Having confessed the crime, that man claimed he was capable of restoring everything, if the judges should grant him a generous period of time. With judges frequently exhausted, unmindful of his own promise, he hastens ever unprepared to the agreement, not even knowing how to flee, but ignorant of his own guarantee, forgetful when he fails, trembling when he is apprehended. He changes words, varies the arrangements; not satisfied with the nature of his own promises, he alters them with a diverse array of ploys. **2.** Rightly should he be compared to the chameleon, which, similar in form to a small serpent, is distinguished only by a head of gold and in the rest of the body by pale green. This creature often attracts human attention, and since the speed of flight is denied it, confused with excessive timidity, it alters its own colors with a many-sided nature, so that it is possible to be found now light blue, now vermilion, now green, and now dark blue. **3.** Whence it is a marvel to behold such diversity in one likeness, which, not without merit, we have said to be very similar to a sparkling gem,[8] in which it is not possible to contain but one brilliance. When the stone is held still, it fluc-

---

7. A *frontosus* was a shameless person, related to *fronto,* a person with a bulging forehead; Cassiodorus here reveals his fascination with the moral import of physiology, as seen, for example, in his *De anima.*

8. The type of gem named (*pandia*) is not otherwise attested.

tuates with wavering appearances. For what you see at one time, if you inspect more closely, you presently change to something else. Thus, what you know no man has laid hold of you nonetheless believe to have changed. 4. The mind of Frontosus is found to be similar to these considered permutations, a mind that does not hold faith with its own claims, which will produce as great a variety of words as it contains. Rightly, he must be associated with the stories of Proteus, who, once seized, never maintained the form of his own substance. In order to conceal his human form, he either roared as a lion, hissed as a snake, or was dissolved into ripples as a liquid. 5. And thus, since he is well known, when he should present his face at your court, first harry him, lest he promise anything, then threaten him, lest he decide upon anything, since it is easy for the character of a fickle mind to promise what it does not plan to fulfill. Having been confined, let him pay then, without any delay, whatever he will be able with considered fairness, since, after so many falsehoods, his own cleverness will be able to reflect upon what he knows he has so frequently ridiculed.

LETTER 11.8 (C. 533)

Clothed as a general edict, this letter to the provincials acts more as an oration declaiming Cassiodorus's intent to pursue justice, including a brief introductory disquisition on the nature of law. Few specific issues are targeted; rather, the accessibility of the praetorian prefect is elaborated, as is the expectation that the provincials will remain obedient to the laws.

Edict of Praetorian Prefect Senator to the Provinces

1. It was the custom of the ancients to decide new laws, so that they would append whatever seemed lacking for the following generation; now, however, it is sufficient enough for a good conscience to observe the decrees of the ancients. Formerly, the nature of man was roused by this novelty, when they recognized the governance of their own lives to depend on the will of another; but then each law became fixed, because it was not doubted to be soundly constituted by antiquity. Therefore do the laws suffice for us, if their intent should not be exceedingly unclear. What cries of the herald, what troublesome sentences of judges do you attend with expectant ears? 2. Whoever knows

himself to be practiced as a judge of his own character imposes the manner of an upright life. Pay attention to the good acts of all men and you will know nothing that must be dreaded. Refuse the ardor for illicit presumptions: cherish living peacefully; always act without harm. Why would you confound honest things with litigation? Why would you cause what you would immediately fear? If you seek gain, you should instead avoid litigious losses. Nonetheless, if any civil contest should arise, be content with the laws of the fathers: let no man hasten to rebellious behavior; let no man seek refuge in violence. It is a kind of madness to pursue a disorderly purpose in a peaceful age. **3.** But even if this is not true with respect to our magistrates, nevertheless, an understandable hesitancy arises when an untried authority instead attracts fear; it is so much to my purpose, with the blessing of God and of the rulers of the state, to promise you that everything will be just and moderate. First, because it especially discredits a judge, corrupt bribery will be unknown to me. For my words are not sold in the manner of garments on display. Only a lack of resources, not the cunning of venality, will prompt us to desire anything from you. Nonetheless, where circumstance mitigates, the policy will be moderate; we do not demand what may be purchased, nor do we sequester for appraisal property that is not considered necessary. **4.** Be engaged only in customary practices, untroubled by novelty, since we judge something to be an advantage to us only if, with the Lord's blessing, we preserve you unharmed. No public official will disturb you for his own sake; no collector will burden you with additional exactions. We will keep not only our own hands innocent, but also those of our staff. It is otherwise useless to be a good judge when one refuses personal gain but offers license for it to many others. For they do not thus depart from our policies, so that the practices permitted by others would seem proper. For the favors that, up to this point, used to increase to the detriment of all have diminished with your love. **5.** We exercise self-restraint in actions, so that, with God's blessing, we can require it without shame from public servants. For a declaration that is not supported by example lacks authority, when it would be dishonest to demand good behavior and not to have acted in the same way. Therefore, our administration looks only to the public weal, not to private theft. We know what prayers you poured forth on our behalf, with what anxiousness you have been in suspense. It would be unseemly for us to do such things that would cause you to celebrate with less joy. **6.** By the grace of God, our ears are open to receiving the wishes of petitioners. The litigant must be free to see us with his own eyes; he will speak, not with a bribed tongue, but with his own. For neither will a subordinate dictate to us, nor will nobility deserving respect be exhausted by us in court fees. No disgrace, then, will enter our court; no man will leave us less wealthy than he had come. Our personal household knows no difference from the court chambers. Whoever observes me will find me a judge in each. **7.** Mindful of shame, and with God's blessing, we desire to act according to the mandates we have received from the masters of the state. Be dutiful to everything just, so that you would cause me to be a father to the provinces rather than a judge, since the latter grows even more wrathful the less he is given to deeds of impropriety. For if you have offered service to scandalous persons, what should you extend to one whom you know to toil greatly for you? Do not let the established conveniences be denied to the toiling servants of our office, since the very man who does not permit just rewards to be paid opens a way to excess. **8.** Moreover, show obedience to our precepts with equal restraint. Let each man comport his intentions with reason, lest armed terror compel you. The man who recoils from just commands brings hatred upon himself. I will not love one whom I have already compelled. Thus do we want to explain everything that must be done, so that we would not cause you to be diminished by anything compulsory. We desire that the blessings granted to you by rulers long ago be preserved without anything reduced on account of detestable illegality. We want you to experience our elevation only with congratulations and for you to seek blessings from rulers who are known for granting your desires. **9.** Now live in celebration of a fitting security. It will not be necessary to compel one whom you have been able to oblige with willing pledges of good conduct. For whoever hesitates to promise just things under oath to God wants to have the freedom, which is not guaranteed, to change. Hold, therefore, this suitable assurance of my vow, a mirror of my intention, the likeness of my desire, in which, since I am not known by face, may I become recognized by the nature of my character. Behold me instead in this report, by which our presence is concealed. My absence is not a loss to you; it is more useful to know a judge in the mind than in the body.

LETTER 11.40 (C. 533–38)

This letter serves as a dispensation or amnesty, a general edict ordering the release of prisoners. An exploration of ethics and natural history provides material for the justification of the order, including an address to the personification of Indulgence. A reference to what may have been a religious holiday focused on redemption suggests that the edict could have been prompted by Easter celebrations. The theme of redemption makes it a pair with the last letter of Book 12 (see Section 4), which focuses on fiscal remission.

Indulgentia

1. Although the very title of judge would seem to speak of justice, and we may bid the course of the entire year to tread on paths of equity, nonetheless, on these days we rightly turn aside from duty to the household, so that we may approach the redeemer of all men along the path of forgiveness. Indeed, from this virtue we pluck the sweetest fruit, and by freeing others do we save ourselves. For we, who are harshly just, always forgive in a time of security. Therefore, we renounce punishment, we condemn torture, and we are then truly a judge. 2. Rejoice, Indulgence, you who are exceptional and who unbind. You, the patroness of humanity; you, the unique medicine for those afflicted by circumstance. Who is not in want of your service, when sinning is a universal condition? You assault hardship for all, when that hope of freedom is claimed under you which was not had under justice. For while you may share the grace of heaven with three other sisters, and you are bound together in a loving embrace, and although they too are virtues, they honorably yield everything to you when they recognize you to be the salvation of humanity.[9] But how do we proclaim such a thing in earthly discourse? It is piety that rules even the heavens. Oh, if it were permitted to reside with you for a longer extent of time![10] Every man accused would be excused, and it would happen that, by being forgiven, he was given leave to forgive. 3. But most providently, such a

9. Although it would be easier to equate Indulgence with either Hope or Charity of the three Graces, the reference to three other sisters suggests that Cassiodorus had in mind the four cardinal virtues (Prudence, Temperance, Fortitude, and Justice), in which case he may have intended Indulgence to serve as Justice.

10. Another reference to what was probably a Christian holiday.

sacred service seems to be granted only at certain times, so that the world would receive this blessing more gratefully, because it rejoiced for the unexpectedness of the thing. Therefore, O lictor, refrain from the hated ax, by which it is permitted to commit with impunity what you would see punished in others; love for a short while steel that is polished, not gory. Let your chains, moistened with tears, cheerfully take on rust; lock away what was instead accustomed to confine. Let the sound of feral voices be exchanged for a better condition. Thus, in a real sense, you would preserve a title without grief to others.[11] Why do you continually labor in the dungeons? Even you must occasionally serve the heavens. An act of clemency means leisure for you. Let kind piety disarm him for whom it is necessary to keep vigil over ceaseless justice. 4. And therefore, the chambers of groaning, the house of sadness, a place blinded with perpetual night—let them shine with a flood of light, among those beyond the hospitality of Pluto, where not a single condemned man endures torment. He is thought to be lost to heavenly assistance even before he may meet a violent end. First the fetter cripples with the unbearable suffering of heaped chains; groans and lamentations of other men torment the hearing; long fasting debilitates the taste; pressing weights fatigue the touch; vision obscured with continual darkness becomes enfeebled. There is not just one death for the confined; one tormented in the squalor of the prison is killed by multifarious death. 5. Now, therefore, set free those condemned to your Avernus;[12] let those who have suffered infernal things for a long portion of the year return to heavenly things; let your halls be filled with emptiness. May a place formerly of endless tears lose its native sadness. Those people are happy who are not there, where there would be a kind of grace if it would appear abandoned. Come forth, prisoners, men growing ever pale with death's company; return to the light, those whom the depths of darkness possessed, those for whom nothing could be better than a merciful death, except that you were already dead. 6. But you who ought to be deceived by no ambition now, forsake crime with the chains, be absolved by the blessings of these days. Live honestly now, you who have learned to prevail over death. Learn

11. Here *nomen custodis* has the double meaning of "you preserve the title" and "title of jailor."

12. Hell.

how good habits may be beneficial: one manner of living knows how to bestow splendid liberty; the other confers foul prison. The one offers such things as you would want to enjoy; the other grants such that you would now choose to perish. If the laws bind you, no man will imprison you further. Take fright at hidden chambers; come into the forum without trepidation. 7. You justly flee that by which you had come to sadness. Let free men marvel at you, whom they saw condemned. You should despise what led you to death. Even cattle know to avoid what they have learned will harm them; they do not follow again those paths where they have fallen into snares. The cautious bird avoids tangling snares, and those perceiving the glue of lime do not perch. The pike buries itself in soft sand, so that it may avoid the entanglements of weighted lines; since the above-mentioned nets scrape across its back to no effect, it leaps nimbly into the waves and, now free, acknowledges the joy of the avoided danger. 8. The wrasse lured by bait, when it begins to enter its reedy prison, as soon as it recognizes that it is being led to its own death, glides back tail first, gradually retracting itself from the narrow confines. If another of the same species recognizes the entangled fish, it draws its tail by the teeth, so that the fish unable to help itself in captivity may be shown to escape with the assistance of another. Thus too, a clever species of mackerel noted for their speed, when they have driven themselves into snares, knit themselves together into a kind of rope and then, drawing backward with full strength, attempt to free their captive companions. There are many examples, if such are sought. Indeed, everything that has an enemy would easily meet its ruin if it lacked the means of its own salvation. 9. To you, master jailor, we repeat our words: open your penal chamber and be innocently hidden. You are indeed tormented because no man is afflicted; you derive grief from public rejoicing, when for you alone, behaving with raging jealousy, shared grace is not a pardon. You, who experience happiness at the affliction of many, endure your loss from the safety of all. But so that we may also console your lamentation, claim entirely for yourself those whom the welcome law of devotion may not free, lest, when it would spare the most savage men, it would open the way for the most grievous deeds. Let us, therefore, absolve all those fettered for secular offenses. Let each man suffer the company of those who hasten to escape the dangers of bondage. Let the cells disperse convicted men; let us loosen the bonds of impure intent.

Intellectual Culture

Letters Pertaining to Aspects of Late-Antique
Intellectual Culture

As seen with regard to the law (Section 11), the *Variae* present an intellectual landscape that everywhere shows reverence for habits of mind received from antiquity. A colorful panoply of literature informs the legal, administrative, and even diplomatic positions that Cassiodorus takes in his collection. He cites Greek and Roman authors with equal frequency, and "folk" literary traditions that by his day were probably detached from specific authorship similarly shaped his mental world. The deployment of learned excursuses on a variety of topics (law, the liberal arts and sciences, nature and geography) is a carefully managed substratum in the collection. These digressions appear in select letters of each book and often overwhelm a fuller understanding of the given letter's original purpose. For all that the collection portrays obedience to (and dependence upon) received intellectual and literary tradition, it is precisely the inclusion of such material that makes the *Variae* a unique and innovative specimen of Roman administrative writing.

LETTER 1.10 (C. 507–11)

One of several justifiably famous letters addressed to the philosopher and senator Boethius. Here concern for timely and proper payments to the palace guard, reported to Boethius presumably during his tenure as master of offices, opens an opportunity for a lavish excursus on mathematics. The other letters to Boethius (*Variae* 1.45 and 2.40, below) are similarly propaganda pieces.

King Theoderic to Boethius, Illustris *and Patrician*

1. It is fitting for the people that justice must be weighed out to all in common, by which it thus obtains dignity in the meaning of its own name, if it delivers measured equity to the powerful and humble; nonetheless, those who do not shun service in the palace more boldly expect this equity. For it is something bestowed with leisurely ease from the beneficence of a *Princeps;* the habit, moreover, is expected as a kind of payment by those serving faithfully. **2.** The palace guards of both the foot and horse divisions, who are known ever to keep vigil in our palace, because it is customary to arise out of serious grievances, have complained to us loudly in a unanimous petition concerning their accustomed salary that they do not receive *solidi* of full weight from the treasurer of the prefecture and they incur upon themselves a severe loss in value of coin. Therefore, let your wisdom, learned as it is from well-read instruction, cast out this criminal falsity from the company of truth, lest anything be profitable in detracting from the integrity of truth. **3.** For that which is called arithmetic has established a sure rationale among the uncertainties of the world, just as we know it has in the heavens: a visible ranking, a sweetness of arrangement, a recognizable simplicity, a changeless body of knowledge, which both serves the earthly and gives dimension to the celestial. For what is there that has not measure or transcends weight? Each thing has compass, all is measurable, and hence the universe attains a sublimity, since we recognize everything by its own measure. **4.** It delights to observe in what manner the measure of the *denarius* both revolves upon itself in the manner of the heavens and is never found lacking. Its calculation always increases according to its own amount, by adding itself back with each change, so that while the *denarius* does not seem to be diminished in itself, it has the capacity to combine boundlessly into a greater amount. This process may be repeated often by bending the fingers on the hands and continued indefinitely by reextending the fingers. Unfailingly, the calculation leads back to its own beginning in amount, just as it increases all the more by the same. Sands of the sea, drops of rain, stars of the clear sky are each delimited within a quantifiable number. Indeed, every created thing is enumerated from its own beginning, and whatever comes into existence is unable to transcend such a condition. **5.** And since it delights us to speak on such mysteries of learning with knowledgeable persons: although coins by themselves seem base from their frequent use, nonetheless attention must be given to the extent of reason with which coins were amassed by the ancients. They intended six thousand *denarii* to equal one *solidus*—namely, so that the circularity formed with shining metal should correspond suitably to the ages of the world, like a golden sun. In fact, the *senarius,* which, not without merit, learned antiquity defined as perfect and indicated by the name of the ounce, which is the primary base of measurement, with twelve reckoned in a pound, would similarly correspond to the twelve months computed in the course of the year. **6.** O revelation of the wise! O foresight of the ancients! Such a thing is carefully worked out, which both naturally adorns human usage and so symbolically contains the secrets of nature. Thus scales are rightly called *libra,* which weigh with such consideration of matters. Therefore, does it not seem a cruel and wretched mangling of truth itself to want to so confound certitudes of nature and to violate such mysteries? Let an exchange of value be practiced in commerce, let people buy cheaply what they sell even more dear, but let the weights and measurements remain credible to the people, since everything is thrown into disorder if rectitude becomes mingled with deceit. **7.** Certainly, what is given to those toiling ought not to be corrupted. Rather, the compensation by which faithful service is solicited should stand out as inviolable. Give a *solidus,* by all means, and thence draw away from it if you are capable; hand over a pound and diminish it if you can. The provision against such an act would remain fixed in the name itself:[1] whether you would give pure or not, you may not unbind it from that by which it is called. This is in no way possible. You may not bestow the name of purity and also effect criminal reductions. Therefore, see to it that the custodian of the treasury maintains his own just practices and that what we intend for those deserving well they obtain through uncorrupted reward.

LETTER 1.45 (C. 507)

The second of three addressed to Boethius by Cassiodorus, this letter asks that he prepare clocks to be delivered by envoys to the Burgundian

---

1. That is, reducing a *solidus* or a pound changes its name and value.

court of Gundobad. As in *Variae* 1.10 (above), this request provides an opportunity for an elaborate disquisition, here on engineering. And like the third letter addressed to Boethius (*Variae* 2.40, below), about preparations for envoys to the Frankish court of Clovis, this one says less about Ostrogothic diplomatic culture than about interest in Boethius's legacy as a philosopher. It is also worth noting that this letter is far longer than the letter to Gundobad (*Variae* 1.46, in Section 1), on whose behalf Boethius was being consulted. A similar disproportion prevails in the next pair of letters, respectively to Boethius and Clovis (*Variae* 2.40 and 2.41).

King Theoderic to Boethius, Illustris *and Patrician*

1. Favors requested out of presumption by foreign kings should not be scorned, since acts of little consequence may succeed in accomplishing far more than the greatest riches would be able to obtain. Indeed, what arms often fail to accomplish, the pleasantries of kindness impose. Therefore, while we seem to trifle, it is also on behalf of the republic. For in this way we seek after delights, so that we may accomplish something earnest. **2.** And so, the master of the Burgundians has avidly requested of us that clocks, one that observes limits by the rhythmic measurement of flowing water, and one that designates completed hours with the illumination of the full sun, be sent to him with instructors for such devices. With the enjoyment of such sought-after delights, what is quotidian for us seems miraculous to them. Indeed, it is fitting that they should desire to gaze upon what has astounded them in the reports of their own legates. **3.** We have discovered that you are known as one gorged with great learning, so that those arts which men commonly practice without understanding, you have imbibed from the very source of their instruction. For you, having abided long in the schools of Athens, entered into them, mingling the toga with the crowds of Greek tunics, so that you made Greek philosophy become Roman learning. Indeed, you have learned in what depth speculative theories may be considered in their own categories, by which each is learned within its respective division by active reasoning, passing on to the senatorial heirs of Romulus everything extraordinary about the world that the heirs of Cecrops have produced. **4.** In your translations, the Italian reads Pythagorean poetry and Ptolemaean astronomy, the Ausonian hears the arithmetic of Nicomachus and the geometry of Euclid, the children of Quirinus discuss the theology of Plato and the logic of Aristotle; you have even given back to the Sicilians a Latinate mechanics of Archimedes. And whatever learning or arts Greek eloquence has produced through multiple men, Rome has received in its native speech from your single authorship. To those famous men you have restored such a great splendor of words; to men already remarkable you have added such great suitability of language that those who have read both works would be justified in preferring yours. **5.** You entered upon the aforementioned art, known from famous teaching, by way of the fourfold doors of mathematics. Situating these matters in the inner sanctum of nature, summoned forth in the books of authorities, you have come to know clarity of spirit, you whose purpose it is to know difficult practices and to display wonders. It is stirring to display that which men have come to wonder at, and in a marvelous manner this phenomenon draws faith in an event from the reversal of nature, even while it offers proof to the eyes. Such knowledge causes water drawn from below to fall headlong, fire to course with its own weight, instruments to sound out with unnatural voice, and fills pipes with traveling wind, so that trifles may bewitch by their very artifice. **6.** By its means, we have seen the fortifications of once tottering cities suddenly rise up with great strength, so that the despairing man is rendered greater who finds strength with the assistance of machines. Buildings steeped in seawater are drained, while what is firm may be loosened by ingenious contrivance. Metal objects bellow, a Diomedes trumpets heavier in bronze, copper snakes hiss, the likenesses of birds chirp, and that which is known not to have its own voice is proven to emit the sweetness of chatter. **7.** We shall mention a little concerning that by which it is lawful for the heavens to be imitated.[2] Here Archimedes caused a second sun to traverse its sphere; here he forged another zodiac wheel, by human deliberation; there with artifice he showed the moon, restored from its own waning illumination; there a small machine pregnant with the world, a portable heaven, an abbreviation of the universe, a mirror to the likeness of nature in the upper world, flies with its own incomprehensible movements. Thus a constellation, for which we are permitted to know the course, we nevertheless do not discern to advance before deceived

2. The famous astrolabe of Archimedes of Syracuse.

eyes: standing, it crosses through the stars, and what you know by true reason has coursed swiftly along you would not behold moving. **8.** How wondrous is it for humanity to devise that which is hardly able to be understood? Because published fame in such matters adorns you, send the clocks to us at public expense and without any loss to yourself. Let the first be one where the indicator is designed to show the hours by its own slender shadow. And so a small and motionless spoke, accomplishing what that wondrous span of the sun traverses, matches the flight of the sun, whose motion it always ignores. **9.** If the stars were sentient, they would envy such an accomplishment, and would perhaps turn away from their own courses, lest they be subject to such ridicule. What unique miracle is in the light of approaching hours if even a shadow reveals them? What is the distinction of an unfailing rotation if even a metal device that remains continually in place accomplishes it? O the inestimable excellence of the craft which succeeds in making the secrets of nature common, when it claims only to play! **10.** Let the second clock be where the hours are recognized without the radiance of the sun, dividing even the night into portions, because, as though owing nothing to the heavens, it converts the reckoning of the heavens instead to the flow of water, by which it shows with motion what revolves in the heavens; and by bold presumption, artifice confers measure upon the elements, which a stipulation of creation denied. All of the disciplines of learning, every endeavor of the learned, as far as they are able, seeks to know the power of nature; it is only mechanics that attempts to imitate nature by contrary means, and, if it is proper to say so, to a certain extent it even strives to surpass nature. For this is known to have made Daedalus fly; this caused the iron Cupid to be suspended in the temple of Diana without any fastenings. It is this art that today causes mute objects to sing, the inanimate to live, and the immovable to be moved. **11.** The engineer, if it is proper to say, is practically a colleague of nature, revealing secret things, controlling the palpable, tinkering with the wondrous, and thus simulating the sublime, so that what is known to have been arranged by craft is nonetheless valued as real. Since we know you have studiously read in this art, hasten as quickly as possible to send the aforementioned clocks to us, so that you would make yourself noted in that part of the world, where otherwise you would not be able to travel. **12.** Let foreign nations recognize in you the kind of nobles that we have, who are chosen as authorities. How will they manage to disbelieve what they have seen? How often will they attribute this reality to a pleasurable dream? And when they have recovered from their stupor, they should not dare to call themselves equals with us, in whose presence they know learned men have pondered such ingenious devices.

LETTER 2.40 (C. 507)

Among the lengthiest in the collection, this letter requests Boethius to select a cithara player to accompany envoys to the Frankish court of Clovis. Boethius does not seem to have had formal office at the time, but his reputation for learning commended him for the task. The digression on music (the bulk of the letter) blends natural history, philosophy, mythology, and Christian ethics. It is noteworthy that this request to Boethius is far more elaborate than the letter to Clovis (*Variae* 2.41), on whose account Boethius was being consulted.

King Theoderic to Boethius, Patrician

1. While the king of the Franks has sought from us the player of a cithara with great entreaties, being allured by the fame of our banquets, we have promised this to be fulfilled for the sole reason that we know you to be accomplished in the learning of music. For to select one so instructed falls to you, who with great effort have been able to attain station in the very same discipline. **2.** For what art is more outstanding than this, which keeps time with celestial mechanics by means of sweet resonance and encompasses the arrangement of nature, dispersed everywhere, with the grace of its own virtue? For anything of measurable dimension that arises into being does not draw back from the moderation of harmony. Through this we think properly, we speak sweetly, and we move pleasingly. However often it reaches our ears, it directs melody according to the law of its own discipline. **3.** When heard, the practitioner of music changes dispositions, and this most powerful pleasure, while it advances from the mystery of nature, it is the queen of the senses adorned with her own melodies; she causes everything to divert course and other thoughts to disperse, so that she would delight that only she is heard. The musician brings pleasure to hurtful grief, disperses swollen rage, caresses cruel savagery, excites the idleness drunk with lethargy, returns healthful rest to the sleepless, calls spoiled chastity back from shameful love to an ardor for honor, restores a weary mind ever adverse to good thoughts, turns pernicious hatred into grateful assistance, and, what is a blessed kind of restoration, expels the maladies of the mind with the sweetest of pleasures. **4.** He softens the incorporeal soul by means of a bodily sense, and by merely being heard he leads to what he wants, to accomplish what would not prevail by word. Silent, he calls out by the hands, he speaks without voice, and, by the obedience of unintelligible notes, he succeeds in exercising mastery over the senses. Among men, this is accomplished entirely by five scales, which are named according to the individual provinces where they were discovered. Indeed, while divine compassion made everything for its own greater praise, it sprinkled favors on specific places. The Dorian mode bestows foresight and is the author of chastity. The Phrygian excites aggression and inflames the will of rage. The Aeolian calms the agitated mind and lends sleep to those already agreeably disposed. The Iastian sharpens the intellect for the dull minded, and as the agent of blessings grants an appetite for heavenly things to those burdened with earthly cares. The Lydian acts against excessive cares of the soul, and it was discovered that it may restore fatigue with rest and enliven amusement. **5.** A corrupt age caused this scale to be noted for dances, turning an honorable remedy to shame. In truth, the five scales are arranged into three divisions. For each scale possesses a high and a low; moreover, each of these is joined to a middle range. And since they are unable to exist without each other, each returning back to another in alternating changes, musical theory was profitably invented—that is, discovered by the work of musicians on various instruments—by which the fifteen modes are arranged. **6.** Adding something greater to these properties, human ingenuity assembled through learned inquiry across the world a certain agreement of sounds, which is called a diapason, evidently from all the modes assembled, as though virtues, which together are able to constitute melody. In this, a marvelous unity is bound. Hence Orpheus, by being heard, persuasively directed inarticulate animals and enticed wandering herds from disdained pastures to the banquet instead. By that song, the Tritons came to love dry earth, Galatea danced on firm land, ambling bears deserted the forests, lions at last abandoned the thicket of reeds as a home, prey rejoiced beside its own predator. Contrary natures were gathered together into one assembly, and with the lyre singing in faith, every creature entrusted itself to its enemy. 7. And so, Amphion, conqueror of Dirce,[3] is said to have built the Theban walls by singing to strings, so that when he would rouse men enfeebled by toil to a zeal for the work's completion, the very rocks were thought to have abandoned their craggy purchases. The powerful tongue of Virgil celebrated even Musaeus, the son of Orpheus in both craft and nature, saying that he had a fortunate eminence among the dead because he delighted happy souls throughout the Elysian Fields with the thrumming of seven strings, indicating that the loftiest reward is to be enjoyed by one who happens to feast upon the sweetness of this discipline. 8. But all these things are seen to be accomplished by human fondness for music produced by the hands. The natural rhythm, however, of the living voice is recognized as its accompaniment, which then governs fair melody when it remains silent at the right moment, when it articulates appropriately, and when it follows with a suitably arranged voice a path marked by musical feet. And even the forceful and captivating speech of orators was invented for the purpose of stirring the mind, so that judges might either become incensed at criminals or have pity for mistakes. And whatever the eloquent man can bring about, it is no doubt attained by the glory of this discipline. 9. Moreover, according to the testimony of Terentianus,[4] to the poets have been attributed the first two principle meters, the heroic and the iambic, of which the one rouses, while the other soothes. From these, diverse means have arisen for amusing the attention of the audience, and just as with the scales of a musical instrument, so too in the human voice does a pregnant meter give birth to various emotions of the soul. 10. The inquiries of antiquity claim sirens to have sung in a wondrous fashion, and although the waves would direct ships away and the wind would billow the sails, those soothingly charmed would choose to rush upon the crags, lest they suffer being torn away from such sweetness. Among these, only the Ithacan evaded the snare, who adroitly blocked the seductive song from the hearing of his sailors.[5] This most prudent of

---

3. Here given as *Amphion Dircaeus;* according to Euripides's now lost *Antiope,* Amphion and his brother executed Dirce for tormenting their mother.

4. The Roman poet Terence.

5. Odysseus, or Ulysses.

men contrived a felicitous deafness to the dangerous charm, and thus, what the sailors would not have overcome by understanding, they prevailed over all the more by not turning their attention to. But he bound himself with tight knots to an immovable beam, so that he could test the famous song with unfettered ears, and having been conquered by the dangers of the charming voices, he nonetheless escaped from the grasping waters. **11.** And indeed, that we might pass beyond such temptations, in the example of the wise Ithacan, let us speak concerning that psalter descended from heaven which a man worthy of song throughout the world so composed and measured for the salvation of souls, that by these hymns the wounds of the mind might be healed and the singular grace of divine authority might be sought. Behold what this age should marvel at and believe: that David's lyre drove forth the devil, the sound commanded the spirits, and by singing to a cithara, a king was restored to freedom who had been shamefully possessed by an internal enemy.[6] **12.** For it is fitting that many instruments of such delight have been tested; nonetheless, nothing more efficacious to stirring the soul has been discovered than the pleasing reverberations of the hollow cithara. Moreover, we believe that chord to be notable which easily moves the cords of the heart.[7] Here so many voices are gathered under a diverse harmony, so that once the cord has been struck, it spontaneously causes trembling in the neighboring cords, which nothing has touched. For such is the force of harmony, that it causes an insensate object to move itself, since its partner happens to act. **13.** From here come diverse voices without language; from here the most pleasing chorus produces a variety of sounds. This one is exceedingly sharp with tension, that one heavy with a certain laxity, the middle most pleasing from an adjustment at the neck of the instrument. Even men may not succeed at attaining such unity among themselves, such a social concord, which these strings arrive at while lacking reason. For here a certain string sounds out sharply, another heavily, one harshly, another with purity, and others with diverse differences, which are assembled together as though in one ornament, even as a diadem shines before the eyes with a variety of gems: thus it is pleasing for the cithara to be heard with a diversity of sound. **14.** The

---

6. A reference to David's ministrations to Saul in 1 Samuel 16:14–23.

7. *Chordam . . . corda.*

loom of the Muses speaks, with copious warp and singing thread, on which is woven with a lively pick that which is sweetly heard. Thus, Mercury is said to have invented this in imitation of the variegated tortoise, which, because of its utility, astronomers have supposed must course among the stars, since they believe music to be celestial, when they are able to perceive the shape of the lyre located among the constellations. **15.** Indeed, the harmony of the heavens cannot be explained adequately in human speech. Reason has given this only to the soul, but nature has not transmitted it to the ears. For they say it ought to be believed that heavenly beatitude is to be fully enjoyed through those pleasures which neither finish at an end nor falter with any kind of interruption. Indeed, the celestial beings are said to live in the presence of this sensation, the heavens to enjoy these very allurements; and those heavenly beings cleaving to such contemplations are enclosed in their delights. **16.** They would indeed have considered rightly if they had been able to assign the source of heavenly beatitude, not to sounds, but to the creator, where there is truly joy without end, ever abiding eternity without any weariness, and the mere contemplation of divine authority brings it about that any greater happiness is not possible. This truly bestows everlasting life, this heaps up pleasures, and just as no creature may exist outside that very authority, so too it is not possible to possess an unalterable happiness without it. **17.** But whereas this digression is pleasurable for us, since it is always pleasing to discourse on learned matters with knowledgeable men, let your wisdom select at this time the one whom we said had been requested from us, the best cithara player, who will accomplish something like Orpheus when he tames the savage hearts of foreign people with sweet sound. And however much this will have been pleasingly done for us, just as much will be returned in our fair compensation to you, who both obey our command and accomplish what is likely to make you famous.

LETTER 3.51 (C. 507–11)

An order to confirm the salary of a charioteer, this letter has a carefully crafted digression on the history of and customs associated with chariot races at Rome's Circus Maximus and ends with a subtle nod to the political expediency of continuing spectacles in Rome. It is noteworthy that a similar letter (*Variae* 2.9, not included in this volume) to the same praetorian prefect, ordering the increase of a charioteer's salary, is far shorter, presumably having warranted far less of Cassidorus's attention.

King Theoderic to Faustus, Praetorian Prefect

1. However rare constancy and respectable inclination may be among performers, it is so much more valuable when genuine goodwill is demonstrable among them. For it is precious for a man to have discovered something laudable where he had not thought to find it. Now, not long ago, a reasonable portion of public rations was bestowed by our consideration upon the charioteer Thomas, who arrived from eastern regions, until we should judge his bravery and skill. But since he is known to hold first place in this contest and, after he abandoned his own country, his inclination has chosen to support the seat of our *imperium,* we have reckoned that he must be confirmed in a monthly allowance, lest we now make an ambiguous return to him, who we know has elected the dominion of Italy. 2. For as a victor, this man flutters in the talk of diverse throngs, conveyed more by reputation than by chariots. He immediately supported that faction of the people in decline and to whom he himself had brought grief, labored to once again return them to a more fortunate state, surpassing other charioteers by means of his skill, just as he bypassed them with the speed of horses. Sorcery is often said to make him victorious, and it is known to be a great mark of distinction among them to have attained such an accusation. For it is unavoidable that a victory which cannot be ascribed to the merits of the horses should be attributed to the perversity of witchcraft. 3. Spectacle expels respected manners, invites frivolous disputes, makes honorability hollow: a spring watered with brawls, which antiquity even held sacred, but which contentious posterity caused to be ridiculous. For it is said that Oenomaus of Asiatic Elis was the first to have brought them into the world, which afterward Romulus, not having yet founded his city, presented to Italy in a rougher mode at the abduction of the Sabine women. 4. But the master of the world Augustus added an undertaking to his own prestige, raising up in the valley of Murcia a structure wondrous even to the Romans, so that he delimited a massive structure, girt firmly around

with mountains, where symbols of great importance were enclosed.[8] They positioned twelve gates for the twelve signs.[9] These were thrown open abruptly in unison by ropes weighted with herms, proclaiming, as they used to suppose, that everything was guided by design there, where the image of the head is known to have influence. **5.** Moreover, the colors were contrived in a fourfold division, following the seasons. Green was said to be for the verdure of spring, blue for the clouds of winter, russet for the heat of summer, and white for the frost of autumn, so that the entire year was signified, progressing as though according to the twelve signs. Thus it happened that the offices of nature were imitated in the ordered confabulation of the spectacles. **6.** The two-horse rig was invented as though in imitation of the moon, the four-horse rig of the sun. The horses of the acrobats, whose names the attendants of the circus, having been sent out, would proclaim as they were about to be released from the gates, mimicked the swiftly advancing course of the morning star. Thus it happened that, when the public thought themselves to worship the constellations, the performances simultaneously profaned their own religion. **7.** Not far from the gates, white lines were drawn on both sides of the podium, as though by a straight ruler, from which the contest between the chariots might spring at the outset, lest, while they attempted to hastily thrust out between one another, they deny the people the pleasure of watching. The whole contest completed seven courses, in simulation of the recurring seven-day week. The very circuits themselves follow the zodiacal divisions,[10] holding three markers, past which the chariots speed, just like the sun. **8.** Stars of the East and of the West designate the boundaries.[11] A channel imparts the likeness of the glassy sea, where sea-loving dolphins pour water. Also, the great lengths of the obelisks have been raised to the heights of the heavens, but the greater

8. The Circus Maximus, located in the valley between the Palatine and Aventine Hills, was sometimes referred to with the name of Murcia, an ancient goddess whose temple was located nearby.

9. The twelve signs of the Zodiac.

10. The *decani zodiaci* were based on astrological practices that divide each sign of the Zodiac into thirds.

11. The unusual *Eoae Orientis et Occidentis* may also refer to images of two of the horses that pulled the sun's chariot.

is dedicated to the sun, the lesser to the moon; on them, as though in letters, the sacred rites of the ancients are indicated in Chaldaean symbols.[12] The partition barrier[13] depicts the fate of unfortunate captives, where Roman generals treading upon the backs of the enemy receive adulation for their labors. **9.** Now, the napkin that is seen to give the signal for the races converged with custom in this way. While Nero reclined at his meal, and the people, eager to see the spectacles, as was accustomed, demanded haste, he ordered the napkin with which he had wiped his hands to be cast from the window, and in this way unleashed the demanded contest. Hence it has continued that the openly displayed napkin should be seen as a promise of races to come. **10.** The circus is so called from its circuitous course, and the *circenses* as though circuits of swords, on account of the rusticity of ancient times, which had not yet brought the spectacles into the adornments of buildings, when they were held on green swards between swords and the river.[14] Nor is it happenstance that the outcome of each contest is decided in twenty-four heats, so that with that very number the hours of the completed day and night would be included. Nor should it be thought without significance that the completion of courses is marked by the removal of eggs, when the very act, pregnant with many superstitious beliefs, openly confesses itself about to give birth to something, after the example of the egg. And therefore, it is made clear that the flighty and inconstant behavior that applies to mother birds is engendered at the circus. **11.** It would require a long explanation to recount everything else concerning the Roman circus, especially when everything seems to pertain to separate causes. Nonetheless, we find it bewildering in every case that here, more than at any other spectacle, the passion of madness is embraced, with seriousness left unheeded. Should the Greens prevail, part of the populace mourns; if the Blues lead, a crowd of citizens is stricken all the sooner. They hotly cast insults, achieving nothing; they are grievously wounded,

12. A reference to the hieroglyphs etched onto the obelisks brought to the Circus Maximus from Egypt: the first was erected by Augustus in 10 B.C. and the second by Constantius II in 357 A.D.

13. The *spina* running down the center of the course; the *euripus*, or water channel, probably flowed down its middle.

14. Cassiodorus here provides an etymology based on *circus* (a circle) and *ensis* (a poetic word for a two-edged sword).

having endured nothing. And they thus fall to petty contentions, as though it were a labor for the standing of an endangered homeland. **12.** It is rightly understood that this has been dedicated to a multitude of superstitions, where one happens to depart from respectable behavior. We cherish the games, necessitated by the demands of a threatening people, whose wish it is to gather for such an event, where they are delighted to cast aside sober thoughts. **13.** For reason leads few, and a commendable purpose pleases even fewer. The crowd is led instead to what was clearly invented for escape from cares. For it is thought that whatever must pertain to its enjoyment also decides the happiness of the age. Therefore, while we grant the expense, we do not always give out of better judgment. It is at present advantageous to act foolishly, so that we are able to restrain the rejoicing desired by the people.

LETTER 3.53 (C. 507–11)

This letter instructs the count of private properties to offer a water surveyor a public salary, so that he could see to the needs of the region surrounding Rome. More attention, however, is given to the art of water divining than to the requirements or role of the surveyor, who, curiously, is not named.

King Theoderic to Apronianus, Illustris *and Count of Private Properties*

1. We have learned in the report of your greatness that a water surveyor has come to Rome from the provinces of Africa, where that skill is cultivated with great eagerness owing to the dryness of the region. This man is able to offer deeply hidden waters to arid lands, so that he may cause a region dry from excessive drought to be habitable from its own abundance. **2.** Know this to have been pleasing to us, inasmuch as this craft had come to us already approved, having been set forth in the books of the ancients. Indeed, he properly infers the proximity of water by the signs of green growth and by the height of trees. For in those lands where fresh waters are not far underground, the fruitfulness of certain shoots always responds favorably, such as water-thriving grass, the hollow reed, the hardy blackberry, the happy willow, the verdant poplar tree, and other kinds of trees which, nonetheless, grow abundantly to a height fortunate beyond their own natures. **3.** These and other things are the evidence of this skill. When, with night's approach, dry wool is placed on ground already chosen and is left, covered with an unglazed pot, then, if the proximity of water is sufficient, the cloth will be found moist in the morning. Moreover, even areas under a clear sky are observed by careful practitioners, and where a swarm of the smallest gnats are seen to fly together above the earth, there they promise with rejoicing what has been sought. They also add that a sort of slight vapor will be visible in the likeness of a column, which they recognize as extending to a height that will be equivalent in measure to the depth at which the waters lay hidden, so that it is miraculous how, through this and other diverse signs, a definite measurement is predicted for the depth at which the sought water should be expected. They even predict the taste of the water, so that bitter waters should not be sought with wasted labor, nor that sweet and advantageous waters should be disdained. **4.** This knowledge was passed down fittingly to subsequent scholars by a certain man among the Greeks,[15] and by Marcellus among the Latins, who carefully treated, not only subterranean streams, but also the location of wells. For they claim that the waters which spring forth to the east and the south are sweet and clear, and found to be wholesome in their lightness. But whatever waters flow to the north and the west are deemed exceedingly cold, and also unbeneficial from the density of their own weight. **5.** And therefore, if your wisdom will detect in the aforementioned man that which is indicative both of the reading of treatises and of experience in the science, you shall alleviate his poverty and his travel with the appropriate salary deducted from the public funds. The man accepting this fee will bestow the gifts of his own art. **6.** For although the city of Rome abounds with irrigated waters, and it may be felicitous in springs and in the abundant flow of aqueducts, nonetheless, many suburban estates are found that clearly need this skill, and one is rightly employed who is acknowledged as essential for this region. Nevertheless, an engineer should be closely involved, so that the waters which the surveyor will find, the engineer may raise, and by his art may bring support for that which is unable to rise naturally. Therefore, let this water surveyor be reckoned even among the masters of other arts, lest the city of Rome be unable to maintain under us what would be deemed desirable.

15. The precise identity of this author is not given.

LETTER 4.51 (C. 507-11)

The last and most elaborate of Book 4, this letter addresses the father-in-law of Boethius, who would later be implicated in the treason trial against Boethius and executed. Here the patrician is asked to undertake the restoration of the Theater of Pompey (originally built in 61–55 B.C.), although the main purpose of the letter seems to be a learned disquisition on theater architecture and arts. The skepticism about the moral content of the theater may be understood in terms of either the parroting of traditional ethics or the parodying of how a great Roman senator ought to allocate his patronage. A similar attitude may be seen in *Variae* 5.42 (Section 7) with respect to wild animal hunts (*venationes*) staged in the arena.

King Theoderic to Symmachus, Patrician

1. Since you have so devoted your attention to private buildings that you may behold a kind of city having been made in your own home, it is right that you should be known for clothing Rome in the same marvels with which you have charmingly adorned your houses, you who are a distinguished founder of buildings and an outstanding embellisher of the same, since arranging their foundation aptly and adorning existing ones agreeably both derive from wisdom. **2.** For it is noted with how much commendation you have drawn Rome into its own suburb, so that one who happens to enter these buildings does not feel himself to be beyond the city, until he recognizes himself to be in the midst of the pleasantries of the country. A most attentive imitator of the ancients, you are the noblest instructor of moderns. The buildings indicate your character, since no man is acknowledged for being attentive to them except one who is found the most steeped in their nature. **3.** And therefore, we believe that the structure of the theater, unfastening itself into a shapeless mass, must be strengthened with your advice, so that what was granted by its founders as an adornment to the homeland should not seem diminished under a better posterity. For what may old age, which has already shaken such a strong structure, not unravel? It is reckoned that the mountains would give way more easily than that this solidity would be disturbed, so that, since the entire mass was thus derived from cliffs, except for the addition of refinements, it would also be considered to be natural. **4.** We would perhaps be able to deny this, if it had not happened that we saw such a thing: those apsidal entrances of vaulting stonework thus arranged with structural supports concealed in a stately manner, so that you would believe them to be the grottos of lofty mountains more than you would think them to be anything fabricated. The ancients made a place equal to so great a people, so that those who were seen to obtain mastery of the world would have the most preeminent spectacle. **5.** But since we deem this to be discourse with a learned man, it is fitting to trace back how it is read that rough antiquity founded these structures. When, on festal days, the cultivators of fields would celebrate the rites of diverse divinities throughout the groves and villages, the Athenians first gathered a rustic beginning to the urban spectacle, naming the place for observing with the Greek word *theater,* so that the gathering crowd might see without any hindrance to those standing at a distance.[16] **6.** However, the front of the theater is called a *scaena,* from the dense shadows of the grove, where songs of various sorts were sung by the herdsmen at the commencement of spring. There, musical acts and the words of the wisest age flourished. But gradually it happened that the most honored disciplines, fleeing fellowship of a more degraded sort, withdrew themselves out of consideration for modesty. **7.** Tragedy is named for the vastness of the voice that seemed to produce the type of sound strengthened by hollow echoes, so that it could scarcely be believed to come from a man. It is, however, based on a goat's meter, since anyone among the herdsmen who pleased with a voice of such quality was given a goat in reward. Comedy was so called from the country village, for the country village is called the *comus,* where playing rustics used to mock human activities with joyful songs. **8.** To these was added the troop of garrulous pantomimes: talkative fingers, silent clamor with soundless expression, which is said to have been discovered by the Muse Polymnia when she demonstrated that men could even declare their will without speech of the mouth. Indeed, in the eastern tongue the Muses are spoken of as *homousae,*[17] because, just like the virtues, they may be seen to be reciprocally necessary to one another. Therefore, peaks of gentle feathers are depicted on their brows, since their perception

---

16. Cassiodorus here supplies a definition for the Greek θέατρον, "a place for seeing."
17. Of the same substance.

meditates on lofty matters, uplifted with speedy thought. **9.** Then, when the pantomime, named for his many-faceted imitations, first advances on to the stage, invited by applause, the harmonious chorus, skilled in various instruments, assists him. Then the hands of sensation display before the eyes a song of melodies and through composed signals teach the appearance to the audience as though by a kind of writing, in which they read the meaning of things, and not by writing do the hands accomplish that which texts clarify. The same body depicts Hercules and Venus, a woman present in a man; it makes a soldier and a king, renders an old man and a youth, so that in one person you would believe there to be many, each distinctive by means of various performances. **10.** Moreover, the mime, who is now considered only with derision, was devised with such great care by Philistio that his performance was set down in writing, to the extent that with trivial thoughts it would calm a world seething with consuming cares. **11.** And what of the jingling of the castanets? What of that melody carried on the varied strokes of sweet sound? It is listened to with such esteemed pleasure that, among the other senses, men consider hearing to be the highest gift conferred upon them. Here the subsequent age has dragged this to vice, mixing the invention of the ancients with obscenities, and impelled what was discovered for the sake of honorable delight to the bodily pleasures of rash minds. **12.** The Romans, inanely incorporating these rites, just like other customs, into their republic, founded an edifice conceived from a lofty idea and wondrous generosity. It is rather from this that Pompey is not undeservingly believed to have been called the Great. And therefore, whether so great a building could be held together with inserted rods or renewed with the application of new construction, we have taken care to send the funds to you from our private treasury, so that the fame of a fortunate undertaking may thus be acquired by you and antiquity may seem pleasingly renewed by our reign.

LETTER 7.5

This *formula* appoints a director to care for the physical fabric of the palace, probably at Ravenna. Much like a general contractor, the director was charged to supervise the contributions of various artisans to its maintenance, with the difference that he was expected to be versed in architectural theory handed down from the ancients. For an example, see *Variae* 2.39 (Section 13).

Formula *for the Caretaker of the Palace*

1. Just as our palace is known to have been constructed by skilled planners, thus ought the precautions of learned men be diligent in its care, since that wondrous grace, if it is not continually restored, may be destroyed by creeping senescence. This is the delight of our power, the charming face of *imperium,* the proclaimed testimony of those ruling; it is demonstrated to legates with admiration, and, at first sight, the kind of man the lord is believed to be is confirmed by his residence. And therefore, it is a great pleasure for a prudent mind to continually rejoice in the fairest of habitations and amid public cares to refresh an exhausted spirit with the charm of buildings. **2.** The Cyclopes in Sicily are said to have first established the most ample residences in an expanse of caves, after which, in the cavern of a mountain, Polyphemus suffered the wailing bereavement of his single eye on account of Ulysses. It is read that, thereafter, the skills of building were transferred to Italy, so that what was discovered by such great and remarkable founders that emulator posterity might safeguard for its own advantage. **3.** Hence it is that we deemed that you, a *spectabilis,* ought to receive the care of our palace for the present indiction, so that you may both maintain in brilliance the ancient things of former men and produce new things similar to those of antiquity. Just as it is fitting that a decorous form is clothed in a single color, thus ought the same brilliance extend to all the rooms of the palace. You will thus be found apt for this if you would often read the geometrician Euclid, planting in your mind's contemplation those plans of his, described with such marvelous variety, so that in time full knowledge may serve your recollection. **4.** Archimedes too, that most discriminating artificer, with Metrobius may ever assist you, so that you, who should be esteemed as learned in the books of the ancients, thus fully prepared, may be assigned to new things. For it is not the least concern that has been delegated to you, when you are recommended to satisfy with the assistance of your art the eager desire in our heart for building. For if we should want either to restore a city or to found a new fort anywhere, even if the charm of building a lodging should flatter us, what is found in our thoughts is produced for the eyes by your design. It is a stewardship of elegance to set a wholly glorious accomplishment in such long ages, whence admiring posterity may be able to praise you. **5.** For whatever the builder of walls, the sculptor of marble, the caster of bronze, the turner of vaults, the plasterer, or the mosaic worker may not know, he wisely asks you about, and that great army of builders rushes back to your judgment, lest it consider anything ill advised. Behold, therefore, how much one who is able to instruct so many ought to know. You will certainly receive a rich reward for your careful plans, since you will be praised for their labor if you meticulously demonstrate their accomplishments to them. Therefore, we want whatever pertains to you to be explained so fittingly and so clearly that only the newness of the buildings should distance them from the work of the ancients. **6.** You make this possible only if our gifts are not misused by any greed. For one who does not permit the worker to be cheated of his proper payment controls the workers effectively. A generous hand nourishes the genius of the arts, when one who has no anxiety over his sustenance hastens to fulfill orders. Consider also what you will accomplish with their obliging behavior, so that, decorated with a golden wand, you might be seen to process first before the royal feet, among a throng of attendants, and so that, by the very testimony of proximity to us, we acknowledge that the palace has been entrusted to you.

LETTER 9.21 (C. 533)

This letter was warranted by apparent reductions in the salaries and benefits given to professorial chairs of grammar, rhetoric, and law at Rome. The Senate was been made responsible for ensuring the continuation of these endowed chairs.

King Athalaric to the Senate of Rome

1. We are known to release the duties of sons to the legal authority of their fathers, so that they may consider the advancement of their sons, for whom it is important to succeed in studies at Rome. For it is not credible that you would be unconcerned about that by which the adornment of your family increases and the deliberation of your assembly advances with unremitting reading. Indeed, as regards our careful concern for you, we have recently learned through certain murmurings that the teachers of eloquence at Rome do not receive the rewards established for their labors and that, by the haggling of some, the payments assigned to masters of schools have been diminished. **2.** Therefore, since it is manifest that rewards nourish the arts, we have judged it scandalous to reduce anything for those teachers of youth, who instead must be encouraged to honorable pursuits through the increase of their emoluments. **3.** For the initial study of grammar is the noblest foundation of the literary arts, the glorious mother of learning, which knows to be attentive to praise and to speak without fault. Thus, it recognizes the discordant blunder in the flow of oration, even as good conduct abominates crime as alien to itself. For even as the musician creates the sweetest melodies from a harmonizing chorus, thus the grammarian knows how to chant balanced meter with well-arranged accents. **4.** Grammatical mistress of words, ennobler of the human race, who is known to assist our counsels through training in the most refined reading of ancient authors. Barbarian kings do not employ this; it is known to remain unique among law-minded rulers. For other nations have arms too; eloquence is found only in obedience to masters of the Romans. Thence the jousts of orators sound the battle call of civil law; thence the most refined speech commends all leading men; and, so that we may put it to rest, it is from this whence we speak. **5.** For which reason, conscript fathers, we bestow this concern upon you and, by divine grace, this warrant, that a successor to the school of liberal studies, whether a professor of grammar, rhetoric, or law, may receive from those responsible the emoluments of his predecessors without any reduction. Once a professor has been confirmed by the authority of the first rank of your order and by the rest of the full Senate,[18] provided he is found suitable for the assigned work, he may not suffer improper suit from anyone concerning the transfer or reduction of his public rations, but he will enjoy the security of his emoluments by your arrangement and patronage, no less than by the protection deputed to the urban prefect. **6.** And lest anything be left undetermined for the caprice of those paying him, immediately after six months have passed, let the aforementioned masters obtain half of the decreed amount, and let the remaining span of the year be concluded with the payment of the public rations owed; let those for whom it is a sin to have wasted even a moment of an hour not be com-

18. Members of the Senate actively holding office, followed by the rest of the *illustres*.

pelled to wait upon the aversion of another. **7.** Indeed, we want what has been decreed to be observed only in the strictest sense, so that if anyone should have an interest in deeming that this must be deferred, as though a tax, let that very individual who, with punishable avarice, has refused just payment to those commendably laboring bear a payment in the amount given to moneylenders.[19] **8.** For if we bestow our wealth on actors for the delight of the people, and those affairs not thus regarded as necessary are carefully funded, how much more should be offered, without any delay, to those through whom honorable conduct advances and eloquent talent flourishes at our palace! **9.** Furthermore, we order this to be made known to the current masters of studies by your respected assembly, so that just as they acknowledge our concern for their welfare, thus will they know that we require the strenuous advancement of young men from them. Now, let that opinion of teachers appropriated from querulous satire die off, since the sources of talent should not be occupied by two worries. Look, they are now proven to have tolerable accommodations, whence they may now rightly concentrate continually upon a single concern, being transported with the full vigor of the mind to studies of the good arts.

19. The payment of interest, probably at the current market rate.

Nature

Letters That Provide Literary Perspectives on the Natural World

This section is more properly a subsection of the intellectual interests of the *Variae:* as a theme, nature often accompanies the presentation of law, administration, and governmental ethics and is frequently intertwined with the study of arts and sciences. Hence, the separation and grouping of these letters pertaining to animals and geography is entirely arbitrary, although it does reveal the importance that Cassiodorus placed on nature, whether as a manifestation of his philosophical leanings, a heuristic device, or both. Most of their examples of animal behavior can also be found in Latin sources such as Pliny's *Historia naturalis* or Ambrose's *Hexameron,* although most such cases probably represent the recycling of favorite literary tropes rather than the deliberate copying of known authors.

LETTER 1.2 (C. 507–11)

A directive seeking to redress the delayed shipment of costly royal garments dyed with the *purpura* (scarlet ink) of harvested shellfish. The recipient is otherwise unknown, although his senatorial rank as *spectabilis* suggests a notable from Calabria who held a monopoly on shipments of royal vestments from workshops in Hydruntum (modern Otranto). Of interest is the elaborate natural history provided for *purpura* production and its relation to imperial authority, which frames a notable contrast to the deference given to eastern authority in *Variae* 1.1 (Section 1).

King Theoderic to Theon, Spectabilis

1. We have learned through the report of the Count Stephanus[1] that the production of royal vestments, which we wanted to be completed with necessary haste, has instead been suspended by disrupted labor, for which reason, by detracting from recurring practice, you will become aware that neglect brings what instead must be avoided. For we believe that someone has caused this neglect, for either those milky fibers, having been steeped at least two or three times in the fleshy draughts, would glow in the lovely saturation, or the wool will not have absorbed the costly substance of the prized murex. **2.** For if the huntsman of the sea[2] at Hydruntum had stored the purple dye with careful consideration at the proper time, that harvest of Neptune, the begetter of an ever-purple bloom, the raiment of regal power, having been steeped in plenty of water, would have released a princely rain of fiery liquid. The pigment abounding with exceeding pleasantness, a darkness blushing red, distinguishes the one ruling with ensanguined blackness; it makes the master conspicuous and demonstrates this to humanity, lest it be possible to mistake the *Princeps* on sight. **3.** It is amazing that this substance exudes a bloody matter made from its own death after such a long period of time, because it is accustomed to flow from wounds in living bodies. For, when the substance has been separated from the vital strength of its preferred sea for even six months, it fails to disturb perceptive noses, and naturally, lest noble blood breathe something repulsive. As soon as this substance adheres, I know not how it can be removed without destroying the garment. **4.** But if the quality of the shellfish is constant, if there is a vintage from its press, the blame will undoubtedly lie with the workers, from whom the supply has not arrived. However, when a skilled worker tinctures white strands of silk in those reddened fonts, it ought to have the most faultless purity of body, since the inner nature of such a substance is said to flee from pollution. **5.** If all of these conditions remain unaltered, if regular practice is overlooked in no way, I marvel that you do not at all recognize your own peril, when it would be sacrilegious to stand accused of negligence and to sin against such vestments. For

1. Probably count of the sacred largesse, who was traditionally responsible for imperial regalia.

2. A flowery phrase for a professional diver (*perscrutator maris*).

what have so many workers to do, so many crowds of sailors, so many troops of rustics? You, who also command so many for transport to the count, defend yourself with the presumption of the very title, so that, while you are believed to conduct royal business, you are seen to command citizens in many affairs. **6.** Therefore, your inactivity both neglects that for which you were commissioned in the province and has managed to come to the noble attention of the *Princeps*. But if anxiety has not thus far deprived you of your ability to act, since the outcome touches upon your health, make ready to come with haste before the appointed day, to bring yourself with the purple, which you have been accustomed to deliver to our chamber each year. For now we send to you, not a supervisor, but one to exact punishment, if you should believe this a matter worth delaying in mockery. **7.** Indeed, it is read how the substance was discovered with such ease and short work! When a dog, excited with hunger, crushed in his jaws the shellfish cast upon the Tyrian shore, his mouth, overflowing with the ensanguined moisture, was naturally stained with the wondrous pigment.[3] And so it is that the occasion led men to an unexpected skill, and those following this example made the substance to give *Principes* an honored distinction which is known to have a humble source. Hydruntum is for Italy what Tyre is for the East: producing royal wardrobe not only preserves ancient rule but continually supplies the new. Therefore, beware if you suffer yourself to accomplish anything less than what you know us to expect as necessary.

LETTER 2.39 (C. 507–11)

A fascinating letter that orders the court architect to supervise the restoration of baths at Aponus and digresses at great length on the healing and spiritual qualities of the natural springs there.

King Theoderic to Aloisius, Architect

1. If we want to join the wonders heard of the ancients to praise for our clemency, with nothing diminished under our care, since fame is the prosperity of a king, with what zeal should that which often happens to come before our eyes seem fit to be restored? Indeed, it is a delight

---

3. Julius Pollux attributed this to the hound of Hercules (*Onomasticon* 1.45–49).

to recall the efficacy of health-bearing Aponus.[4] For this reason, as
you know, we desire to make new what has not been able escape our
memory. **2.** We have beheld the cerulean spring, seething with the
shape of the curved mouth of a wine jar, and the burning craters of
exhaling waters wreathed round with polished rim in the fitting
arrangement of nature. As befits warm water, these exhale a billowy
vapor, which nevertheless reveals such a pleasant transparency to
human inspection that any person would desire to reach for its
charms, all the more since it knows not how to burn. Domes of water
in the likeness of spheres swell beyond their own bounds in the ample
openings, whence the smooth waters flow so tranquilly, as though
gliding along with great stillness, so that you would not think them
moving, except that you noticed something passing thence with a
hoarse murmur. **3.** The waters pass from such boiling heat along cooling channels, so that, after winding lengths that have been made more
extensive by engineering, they return the fullest warmth. O the ever-
miraculous genius of its creator, that the heat of a natural passion
should thus be restrained for the advantage of the human body, so that
what would be capable of causing death at its source, thus moderated
by learning, should bestow both health and delight! It delights to
behold a mystery: fluids exhaling burning clouds, harmless burning
issuing unfailingly from waters, and heat coming from a coursing
stream, whence it is customarily extinguished. The philosophers
rightly speak of the elements, which are known to war among themselves in a variety of oppositions, as being bound to one another in
changing combinations and united by miraculous alliance. **4.** Behold,
a wet substance arranged to produce a fiery cloud, which then travels
to the comely buildings of the baths; the tumultuous waters decreasing
in heat warm even the air with their own attribute and become more
manageable to the touch when they have been received in bathing
pools. Whence not only a charming pleasure is attained, but also so
many caressing medicinal cures are conferred. One hears of cures
without pain, remedies without torture, health exempt of penalty, and
baths opposed to the diverse ills of the body. Therefore, antiquity has
called this blessing Aponus in the Greek language, so that the ill
should recognize it as the source of so much relief, since no doubt

4. Hot springs located near modern Padua.

could be had concerning such a name.[5] **5.** But among the other blessings of this very place, we have learned something else that must be marveled at, that waters with one nature are seen to be suitable for diverse ministrations. For by continually coming into contact with the rock, the churning waters of the first chamber absorb a quality that produces sweat. From there they descend, having exchanged the threat of scalding for soothing warmth, and soften to a gentler temperature. The water thus produced winds about in the area with some delay and cools to a much more alluring temperature, until, finally forsaking even its very warmth in the Neronian pool, it attains a coldness as extreme as the heat first felt. **6.** Not unduly sharing a name with its author, the pool is festooned with the green of gems, so that the very greenness too would stir the waters to a kind of trembling with the transparent stillness of a glasslike substance. But even as this very pool becomes calmer, arrested as though by the discipline of restraint, the waters, by which men may be refreshed, if a woman should enter them, boil over. And on that account, the appropriate display of either one or the other sex has been assigned, evidently, lest they not believe the place to have the most enriching of hot waters, whence so many blessings are bestowed, if both sexes should make use of one gift at the same time. **7.** This constancy of the water provides evidence of its perception, by flowing from a great depth, by secret courses, through heated veins of the earth, the refreshing purity of the boiling waters bursting forth in breaths. For if it were a fire of natural origins, it would not exist without being extinguished by the consumption of its substance. But the sentient substance of the water, just as it attracts foreign heat, thus easily returns to its native cold. **8.** And this strength offers another kind of medical assistance. For, near the head of the shimmering fountain, provident nature has formed a certain path for itself. Here, above its established seat, which is pierced through in the likeness of an arch of human contrivance, it takes up the harmful product from the interior moisture. While the weak will repose here in great weariness, refreshed by the delight of these vapors, the enfeebled flesh of the body is restored and harmful elements are leached from the beneficial humors by an infusion of vital dryness, and, as though from some desirable nourishment, the ailing are

5. *Aponus* literally means "without suffering."

immediately restored and made more vigorous. Thus, that which heats by sulfur and that which dries by salt come to the medicinal property of the waters. To not pass such a wonder to posterity is to sin grievously against a whole generation. **9.** For that reason, the ancient stability of the buildings here should be restored, so that should there be something requiring repair, whether in the underground passages or in the baths, it ought to be rebuilt by you immediately. Also, the harmful thickets springing up with impunity should be torn from the lawns and borne away, lest the gradually swelling tendrils of roots penetrate the body of the buildings and nurture offspring with the nature of a serpent, contrary to their own fecundity, whereupon the seams would burst asunder. **10.** Also, strengthen with persistent care the palace that has been shaken by a lengthy old age. Clean away the scrubby woods from the span that intervenes between the public hall and the beginning of the heated pools. Let a comely disposition smile with grassy blossoms in the level areas. Let Aponus, moreover, rejoice in the fertility of warmed waters, and, by wondrous means, while nearby waters produce a sterile salt, let them also nourish verdure. **11.** But not by these benefits alone should Antenorean ground be fruitful;[6] there are others even greater, by which you would be astounded. This soul, as I shall call it, in conversation with the solitude of the mountains, disarms contentious business. For if someone, by chance, should presume to steal a sheep in the fashion typical of local bandits, the stolen pelt, continually immersed in the burning waters, would inevitably boil away before he should succeed in cleaning it. Oh, how the waters must receive due reverence for their secrets, when they not only possess feeling but also stand possessed of righteous judgment, and what fails to be resolved in human altercations is given over to be decided by the equitability of the pools. Silent nature speaks here, and when it judges, it pronounces by certain means a sentence that prevents the falsehood of the one denying the charge. **12.** But who would fail to protect such a place, when he may become soiled more by parsimony? Indeed, what is singularly honored by the whole world adorns the kingdom. And therefore, concerning the money that has been given to you, if you have not been able to complete the work undertaken,

6. Antenor was a character from the Trojan War famous for the number of his children.

indicate to us in a short letter however much you know still must be spent, since we are not burdened by spending in order that we might be seen to watch over so great a city of the countryside.

LETTER 4.50 (C. 511)

This letter requests that the praetorian prefect assess the extent of damage done to agricultural production in Campania by the eruption of Vesuvius (ca. 511). On this basis, he was to reduce the tax burden for the province, although the natural history of volcanism supplied by the letter suggests limited tolerance for revenue reduction in one of the most productive provinces in Italy.

King Theoderic to Faustus, Praetorian Prefect

1. Campanians have poured forth entreating tears to our clemency concerning the devastating violence of Mount Vesuvius, to the effect that, being stripped of produce of the fields, they would be relieved of the weight of the payment of taxes. Our piety acquiesces to what ought to happen deservingly. **2.** But since unsubstantiated misfortune of any kind is doubtful to us, we order your magnitude to send a man of proven devotion to the territory of Nola and Naples, where that crisis threatens like a kind of domestic assault, so that, with the very same fields carefully inspected, the productivity of the landowner may be alleviated in the amount that he has suffered: let the amount of the kindness be conferred, then, in proportion to the measure of harm that is accurately assessed. **3.** For the province, shorn of verdure of the soil, suffers this one evil, bitter fear of which frequently agitates it, which would otherwise enjoy perfect happiness. But this harsh event is not totally unbearable: it sends ahead pregnant signals, so that the adversities may be endured more tolerably. **4.** For the orifice of this mountain murmurs, by nature contending with the great mass, so that, like a kind of disturbed spirit, it terrifies the neighboring region with deep groaning. Then the airs of this place are darkened with noisome exhalations, and it is recognized throughout almost all of Italy when this displeasure is stirred. Heated cinders fly great distances, and, with earth-filled clouds blown aloft, it even rains ashen drops upon provinces across the sea. What Campania is able to endure is proclaimed when its misfortune is felt in other parts of the world.[7] 5. You would behold ash moving as though a kind of river and, just like a liquid torrent, coursing in a boiling and sterile rush of lava. You would stand amazed at the furrows of fields suddenly filled all the way to the highest tops of trees, and at fields, which had been painted with the most graceful verdure, suddenly wasted with doleful heat. But even while this perpetual furnace vomits forth pumice, the fertile earth, which, granted, will be dry and burnt for long, having enclosed seeds, will soon produce varied shoots and restore even this great expanse which only shortly before had been wasted. Is this singular exception the reason that one mountain rages thus, so that it may be known to cause dread by the perturbation of the atmosphere in so many regions of the world and thus to disgorge its own substance everywhere, as though it seems to feel no loss? 6. It bedews with ashes far and wide, although it belches shapeless heaps on nearby areas and a mountain that is exhausted by such great expenditure has been known for so many centuries. Who would believe that such huge chunks, having fallen so far upon the plain, had boiled up from such a deep orifice, and that projectiles, escaping from the mouth of the mountain in the manner of a wind, were spewed as though mere chaff? 7. Elsewhere nearby, great crags of earth are seen to glow with fire; it is given that these fires are noticeable nearly anywhere in the world. Therefore, for what reason should we not believe from the local inhabitants what may be known from testimony across the world? Therefore, as it has been said, let your prudence investigate this remarkable matter, and let you both confer assistance upon the afflicted and not provide grounds for fraud.

LETTER 10.29 (C. 535–36)

A particularly interesting specimen of Cassiodorus's interest in natural history, this letter grants the Count of Pavia a leave of absence from his official duties to recuperate from gout at the natural springs at Bormio. The lurid fascination with the progress of the disease deserves attention, especially in contrast to other letters concerned with the

7. This may be a reference to the eruption of 472, which appears in Constantinopolitan sources such as the *Chronicle* of Marcellinus Comes.

properties of waters, and the Latin is redolent with comparisons of the human body to the body politic.

King Theodahad to Wisibad, Count

1. Although the distinguished nobility of your family and the evidence of your great fidelity had recommended you, so that we believed the city of Pavia must be governed by you in peace as you would have defended it in war, being suddenly taken with an invasion of muddy gout, you have instead asked to seek the drying waters of Bormio, and there deliverance from acute suffering. We fulfill your request with a medicinal injunction, so that we might restore with the blessing of a command that health which we rightly expect to find in you. 2. For it is not right that this disease should disarm such a warlike man with the tyrannies of grievous affliction, a disease which, by miraculous means, forces virile limbs to seize with an infusion of punishing fluid and, growing, fills pliant ligaments with stonelike swelling. When it feels that all other parts have been rendered useless, it seeks the hollow cavities of the joints, where, arresting as though in the mire of a swamp, it creates stones from water, and the wandering disease solidly fastens an unsightly rigidity to what nature had granted the grace of flexibility. 3. This unhealthy suffering and insufferable health binds anything supple, contracts the nerves, and causes a body that has been stricken with no mutilation to shorten. It withers the measure of the body by fastening upon the limbs, and, having departed, it is hardly noticed by those made incapable of feeling. The assistance of the limbs is removed from those who survive; the living body is unable to move and thus reduced to senseless members; a man is no longer able to move by his own accord, but is carried by the motion of someone else. The condition is spoken of as a living death worse than any torment, and one who was unable to survive to the final outcome of such punishment is considered to have had the better lot. 4. For indeed, the sickness departs, but it leaves only a remnant of strength, and, in a novel example of misfortune, the suffering seems to withdraw while the diseased man does not cease to be impaired. Even the weighted limbs of debtors are occasionally freed from torture; but the chains of this disease, once it has been able to fasten onto a captive, are known to not release him for the rest of his life. Departing, it leaves a ruinous token of its presence, and, after the manner of barbarian nations, hav-

ing claimed the hospitality of the body, it protects its own claim with violence, lest a hostile wholesomeness perhaps dare to return there, where such a savage entity has laid hold. This is known to be especially hostile in every possible way to those who flourish through the exercise of arms; firm limbs not softened by the waste of sloth and which were unable to be overcome by a foe from without are instead conquered from within. Therefore, with God's guidance, proceed on your way to the aforementioned place. For it is not right that our warrior should walk at another man's pace. He should be carried on the back of a horse, not by human conveyance, since it is wretched for a brave man to live in this manner, as though unarmed and unable to function. We have related this to you in exaggerated terms, so that you would be seized by an avid desire for pursuits of health. Therefore, use these waters, first in cleansing drink, then in the drying exhalations of the baths, where the indomitable neck of suffering is rightly made to bend, when everything within is cleared away with violent purging, everything outside obtains an unrestrained character, and it is overcome, as though set in the midst of two gathered armies. Let gifts granted by divine authority be loved for this reason. The advantageous qualities of baths have been given as a defense against this conqueress of humanity, and what is not subdued in a period of ten continuous years, what is not alleviated from within by a thousand concoctions, may be avoided here with the most pleasurable remedy. May divine providence offer the best blessing to one whom we ardently desire to avoid anything that detracts from bodily well-being, so that we may come to know the true reputation of this place rather by your health.

LETTER 10.30 (C. 535 OR 536)

This letter, the second of two attributed to Theodahad that demonstrate interest in natural history, orders the urban prefect in Rome to restore a bronze statue of an elephant. Although elephants were prominent as symbols of empire, the timing of the decree, in the midst of political unrest at Rome, seems questionable, as does the letter's fixation on less ennobling aspects of the animal. As in *Variae* 10.29 (above), the natural history of this letter seems to provide an allegory for the living morbidity of the state.

King Theodahad to Honorius, Urban Prefect

1. We learn from the course of your report that along the Via Sacra, which antiquity named on account of many superstitions, the bronze elephants totter near complete ruin, and what would be accustomed to live beyond a thousand years in the flesh seem to endure a lingering death cast in metal. Let your foresight cause the appropriate longevity to be restored to them by strengthening rent limbs with iron fasteners; brace also the sagging bellies with retaining walls, lest those remarkable masses shamefully give way to ruin. **2.** Even for living elephants, which, while in a kind of genuflection, would lend their enormous limbs to the human occupation of felling trees, a false step is dangerous; those with their full bulk lying prostrate are unable to rise by their own strength, evidently because their feet are not articulated with joints, but they stand continually rigid and unbending in the manner of columns. Whenever such a great mass lies on the ground, then you would believe them more to be crafted of metal, because you would behold living creatures unable to move themselves. They lie overcome, as though lifeless bodies: you would deem dead what you should not doubt to be living. And after the fashion of collapsed buildings, they know not how to quit willingly a place that they were able to occupy by their own support. **3.** Such terrible size is unequal to the minutest ant, when it does not enjoy the blessing that is apparently granted by nature to the least animal. They rise with the assistance of humans, by whose skill they are cast down. Even a brute beast, mindful of this favor, knows itself to be restored to its own footing; indeed, it accepts as master the one whom it recognizes as having assisted it. It moves at the pace set by that very governor, willingly takes sustenance from him, and, what exceeds the intelligence of all four-legged animals, does not hesitate to honor on sight the one whom it knows to be the ruler of all affairs; for which reason, if a tyrant should appear, it remains unyielding, nor is it possible to compel this great beast to give to wicked men the attention that it knows to demonstrate to good leaders. **4.** Instead of a hand, it uses a proboscis, and gladly accepts rewards offered by the master, since it knows that it survives by his care. It is in fact the handlike proboscis of the aforementioned beast, as I have mentioned, by which it receives things given and transfers victuals to its own mouth. For while it may be the tallest animal, it is formed with a very short neck, so that, because it cannot crop fodder from the ground, it seems able to satisfy its appetite by this assistance. It always proceeds only with caution, remembering the harmful fall that had been the beginning of its captivity. **5.** Having been coaxed, it exhales its breath, because it is said to be a cure for the human headache. When it approaches water for drinking, as requested, it expels the liquid drawn through its hollow proboscis in the manner of a shower, and thus it acknowledges what is sought, in this way gladly doing what is asked of it. It extends to its master whatever he may demand with diverse movements of the body, and it considers the sustenance of its provider to be its own property. Because if anyone has refused to offer what it wants, it is said to discharge such a flood from the opened reservoir of its bladder that it would seem to eject a kind of river from its innermost chambers, punishing the contemptuous man with its stench. **6.** For it gladly nurses an insult and is said to take its revenge after a long time on the person by whom it feels itself to have been injured. Indeed, it has small eyes, but they move about solemnly. You would believe that its appearance suggests something regal. It despises those playing like fools; anything honest attracts it by its dignity, and you would be correct to judge that trivialities displease it. **7.** Creases furrow its ulcerous skin, from which comes the name for the abominable disease of those denied entrance to cities, and which is toughened to such a hardness that you would think it to be bony. This hide is torn by no force and penetrated by no point of iron, for which reason Persian kings led this beast into battles, in which it never yielded before the onslaught of blows and terrified enemies with its mass. **8.** Therefore, it is most pleasing to regard the statues of these creatures, so that those who have not beheld the creature in life may recognize the fabled animal by such great renditions. And therefore, do not let them perish, when it is on behalf of Roman dignity that the genius of craftsmen stores up in that city the wealth that nature is known to have generated throughout the diverse regions of the world.

LETTER 11.14 (C. 533–38)

A letter responding to complaints about the burden of the public transport system upon residents around Lake Como. The exact nature of the relief to be provided is not specified, but the bucolic delights of the natural geography of the region receive full attention.

Praetorian Prefect Senator to Gaudiosus, Cancellarius of the Province of Liguria

1. Since the city of Como is sought by many roads, its landowners report that they are exhausted from the constant provision of transport animals,[8] so that they themselves are in fact trampled down by the passage of too many steeds. We extend to them the benefit of a royal indulgence to be perpetually maintained, lest that city, attractively habitable because of its location, become depopulated through the frequency of the damage. For, beyond the distant mountains and the vast expanse of the clear lake, it is a kind of wall for the Ligurian plain. Although it is evidently a key defense of the province, it unfolds such beauty that it seems to be formed for pleasure alone. **2.** Beyond protection, it disseminates supplies of the cultivated plains, on account of both its aptness for comfortable travel and its generous supply of food. Along the shore, it enjoys the amenity of sixty miles of sweet water, so that the spirit is gratified with delightful refreshment, while the supply of fish is not driven away by storms. Rightly, therefore, it has received the name of Como, rejoicing in the gifts that make it comely. Here the lake is truly enfolded in the depth of a great valley; exquisitely imitating the shape of a shell, it is dappled with white on its foamy shores. **3.** Around it the beautiful peaks of lofty mountains gather like a crown; its coasts are exquisitely adorned with great and gleaming villas, and are enclosed as though by a belt with the perennial greenery of a forest of olives. Above this, leafy vines climb the mountainsides. But the summit itself, curled, as though with hair, with thick growth of chestnut trees, is painted by adorning nature. Thence torrents that shine with snowy whiteness are hurled downward by the height, and fall to the levels of the lake. **4.** Into its bays, flowing from the south, the River Adda is received with open jaws. It thus takes such a name because, being fed from a double source, it flows down as though into a sea of

---

8. *Paraveredi,* or animals provided at the changing stations of the state public transport system (*cursus publicus*).

its own.⁹ Such is the speed with which it enters the waves of the vast expanse that, retaining its form and color, it pours northward in a swollen-bellied stream. You would think that a kind of dark line had been drawn across the pale waters, and, by miraculous means, the discolored nature of the influx, which is supposed to blend with similar fluids, is visible. **5.** This also happens with the waves of the sea where rivers debouch: but the reason itself is commonly known, as headlong torrents, polluted with muddy filth, differ in color from the glass-clear sea. But this will be rightly thought something astonishing, because you may see an element move at great speed through standing water similar in so many characteristics, so that you would imagine a stream, which is unable to commingle in color with foreign waters, to decant through standing fields.¹⁰ **6.** Therefore, it rightly should be used sparingly, for the residents of these regions, when everything charming is too delicate for toiling and those who are accustomed to enjoy sweet delights easily feel the burden of strain. Therefore, let them enjoy a royal gift in perpetuity, so that, just as they rejoice in native luxuries, thus may the munificence of the *Princeps* cause them to celebrate.

LETTER 11.38 (C. 535)

This letter orders the award of a pension, to be paid from the taxes of Tuscany, to an unnamed administrative assistant. It also offers one of the most unexpected digressions in the collection: a natural history of papyrus, intended to remind the addressee that all public affairs are documented.

Praetorian Prefect Senator to John,
Canonicarius *of Tuscany*

1. The governess of all affairs, antiquity, diligently prepared so that the abundant supply of documents should not fail, since our archive must

9. The Adda rises in the Alps, runs south into Lake Como, and then continues south until joining the Po. Although Cassiodorus does not directly mention the river's Alpine source, he may have had both it and the lake in mind as the "double source" to which he refers to supply an etymology for the Latin name Addua ("at two places").

10. The confluence of bodies of water is described in similar terms by Ammianus Marcellinus, *Res Gestae* 15.4.3–6.

be consulted by many people, to the extent that, when magistrates should resolve future affairs for the many, sweet benefactions would not experience hateful delays. This service is granted to petitioners, lest they be constrained by avarice to pay for what is known to be provided from public largesse. Shameless opportunity for extortion has been removed, a benefit that the humanity of the *Princeps* has granted to those whom it removes from loss. **2.** Clever Memphis conceived a worked material handsomely plain, so that what the delicate work of a single place has woven should clothe every archive. On the Nile rises a forest without branches, a grove without leaves, a watery crop, comely hairs of the marsh, more pliant than a thicket and hardier than grass. I know not how, but the material is filled with emptiness, and light in its length, containing an absorbent tenderness, a spongy wood, whose durability, in the nature of an apple, is in the exterior skin. Soft in the interior, tall and slender, but it supports itself, the most beautiful fruit of a filthy flood. **3.** For what crop of such a kind is produced anywhere, which there preserves the thoughts of the wise? Before this, the sayings of the wise, the ideas of ancestors, were imperiled. For by what means would it have been possible to quickly write what could hardly be expressed on the resistant hardness of bark? No doubt the inspiration of the mind endured awkward delays, and when words were distracted, their genius was forced to grow cool. **4.** Hence, antiquity named the works of the ancients *libri,* for even today we call strips of green wood *libri.* It was unseemly, I confess, to entrust learned tracts to rough tablets and to impress on unrefined, woody scraps what exquisite sensitivity was able to discern. With hands burdened, few were inspired to record, nor would one to whom such a page was offered be enticed to say much. But this was becoming to primitive times, when a rude beginning ought to use such a contrivance that would challenge the ingenuity of those following. The sweet allure of documents is amply attested where there is no apprehension of a shortage of material. **5.** For this uncovers a field for eloquent composition on a white surface, it always supports abundant writing, and, by which means it becomes easily manageable, it gathers into its own roll, although it may be unfolded into great treatises. Joined without seams, it extends by reducing; the white interior of green reeds, a face for writing, accepts black ink for adornment, where, with elevated letters, the transplanted crop of fertile words returns the sweetest fruit to the mind, as often as it strikes the reader's fancy: faithfully preserving a testimony of human deeds, hostile to forgetfulness, it speaks of past events. **6.** For even if our memory retains material, it changes the words: but there the memory reposes secure, because it may always be read in the same terms. Therefore, we order you to offer to the administrative assistant x the assigned amount of *solidi,* from the third payment of taxes of the province of Tuscany, charged to the accounts of the thirteenth indiction, to the end that the public archive preserve in commendable perpetuity the integrity of its own trustworthiness. Because, not knowing the failure of mortal affairs, the public archive ever increases with annual accumulation, constantly receiving new materials and preserving the old.

LETTER 12.12 (C. 533-38)

This letter requisitioning a particular cheese and a certain wine for royal banquets is an homage to the gustatory delights of Cassiodorus's home province. What it lacks by way of explaining the administration of the region it more than compensates for as an explanation for Cassiodorus's later retirement there.

Praetorian Prefect Senator to Anastasius,
Cancellarius *of Lucania and Bruttium*

1. While we dined at a formal event with the lord of state, the various provinces were praised for their individual delicacies, and the conversation, continuing as is its wont, arrived at the wines of Bruttium and the sweet cheese of Sila, which, by benefit of the grasses there, is produced with such natural pleasantness that you would not believe a flavor that you observe as unmixed with any substance should lack honey. There, slight coaxing expresses milk from pipelike udders, and, from the richness of nature, when collected in flasks, as though into second stomachs, it does not rain in drops, but pours almost in rapid torrents. It emits a sweet and complex odor; the nose detects the pasture of cattle, which, scented with diverse qualities, is thought to exhale something similar to frankincense. **2.** With this, such richness is combined that you would deem that something similar to Pallas's liqueur[11] flowed, except that it is distinguished from the olive's meadow-green by its snowy whiteness. Then, that miraculous supply received by the delighted herdsman in wide-open jars, when by admixture[12] it begins to thicken and harden to a tender solidity, is fashioned into the shape of a beautiful sphere, which, when stored for a short time in an underground storehouse, causes the substance to be long-lasting cheese. You will send ships loaded with this cheese as soon as possible, so that, by a small gift, I may be seen to satisfy royal wishes. **3.** Search too for the wine that antiquity called Palmatianum,[13] wishing to confer praise because it is not dry or bitter but pleasing with sweetness. For although it may seem the most remote among Bruttian wines, it has nevertheless been made distinguished in almost universal opinion. For there it is considered equal to Gazan and similar to Sabine, noted for its weighty aroma. **4.** But since it has claimed the noblest reputation for itself, let the choicest vintage in this wine be selected, lest the wisdom of the ancients seem to have named something inappropriately. For it is gently dense with rich sweetness, full and lively, with a forceful bouquet, also white and clear, and diffuses such flavor in the mouth that it rightly seems allocated a name from the palm. **5.** It binds faltering bowels, dries weeping wounds, restores a weary breast; and what a skillfully brewed remedy barely succeeds in treating, this accomplishes naturally and unaccompanied. But take care that you send the exact varieties described above, since we, who recall this with patriotic integrity, cannot be deceived; for up to this point, we have offered what was desired from our own cellars. You, however, will produce at your own risk anything dissimilar to what you know is still held in traces.

LETTER 12.22 (C. 537–38)

A letter ordering an increase in taxes in kind from the province of Istria, owing to the bounty of cultivation there and presumably because, with the advance of the Gothic War, the court had lost control of tribute-paying regions in central and southern Italy. Addition-

---

11. Olive oil.
12. Of rennet.
13. "Award winning."

ally, the letter directs the delivery of gold to pay for the portion of the crop greater than what was usually required as taxes. Instructions to officials tasked with executing this directive follow in *Variae* 12.23 and 12.24 (not included in this volume).

Praetorian Prefect Senator to the Provincials of Istria

1. Public expenses, fluctuating with diverse variations throughout the year, can be held in check by this means: if the appropriateness of demands accords with the yield of each region. Certainly, collection is easy there where profit is more bountiful. For if the indication of sterile poverty is ignored, then the province is harmed and the desired result is not obtained. Consequently, we have learned from the attestation of travelers that the province of Istria, so named with praise for three outstanding crops, rejoices in fertility this year, being laden by divine gift with wine, oil, and grain. And so, let the mentioned commodities, given in payment of taxes in the amount of x *solidi*,[14] be charged to you for the current first indiction; but the remainder we leave on behalf of the customary expenses of a loyal province. **2.** But since an amount greater than what we had stipulated must be obtained from you, we have also sent x *solidi* from our treasury, so that the necessary goods may be productively gathered without loss to you. For often, when you are compelled to sell to strangers, you are accustomed to experience a loss, especially at a time when the foreign purchaser is suddenly absent, and it is rare to receive gold when you know merchants are not on hand. But how much better it is to obey your rulers than to provide for distant people, and to pay taxes with crops than to bear the contempt of purchasers. **3.** We have caused, moreover, from a love of justice, what you would want to suggest to us, since, while we are not burdened by furnishing ships, we would not tamper with the price. For your region is situated the closest to us across the gulf of the Ionian Sea, covered with olive groves, adorned with grain fields, abundant in vines, where all crops flow forth in optimum fertility, as though from three teats of surpassingly rich generosity. Not without warrant is the region called the Campania of Ravenna, the storehouse of the royal city, an exceedingly pleasurable and delightful retreat. **4.** Being set in the north, it enjoys an admirable commingling of climates. It even has its own Baiaes of a

---

14. The amount is not given.

sort[15]—I do not claim this recklessly—where the turbulent sea enters inlets of the shore, calming to a lovely surface with the quality of a lake. These places also furnish much fish sauce, and they glory in the bounty of fish. Not just one Avernus is located here.[16] Conspicuous are the numerous Neptuniae,[17] in which oysters spawn everywhere, unbidden with even lax diligence. Thus, it is proven that there is neither effort in nourishing nor uncertainty in catching with these delicacies. **5.** You may perceive extensive residences scattered far and wide, shining like pearls, so that here it may reveal what kind of discernment was had by the ancestors of this province, which is known to be adorned with such buildings. Moreover, added to the shore is the most beautiful arrangement of islands, which are positioned with lovely utility, both warding ships from danger and enriching cultivators with great fertility. The region clearly restores the attendants of our *comitatus;* it adorns the *imperium* of Italy; it feeds leading men with delicacies and the humble with its payment of stores; and what is produced there is possessed almost entirely in the royal city. Let the loyal province offer its abundance more willingly now; let it obey fully when this is desired, since it used to produce gladly when it was called upon the least. **6.** But lest any uncertainty proceed from our commands, we have sent with the present directive the most proven gentleman, Laurentius, approved by us in great toil for the republic. Thus, according to the brief attached below, he may unhesitatingly accomplish what he knows to be separate from public taxes. Now procure what has been ordered. For you make public service loyal when you freely undertake a command. **7.** But I shall publish the prices determined for you[18] on a subsequent occasion, when the bearer of the present letter has estimated by sent report the measure of your harvest. For nothing can be justly appraised for taxes unless the amount of resources can be clearly investigated. It is indeed an unfair assessor who produces a judgment in ignorance, and one who decrees without deliberation is shown to be aware of his own bad character.

15. Cassiodorus returns to the comparison of Istria with Campania, where Baiae was a famous seaside resort.

16. A lake in Campania famous for villas and vineyards.

17. Salinated ponds for preserving fish.

18. Prices at which the inhabitants of Istria could sell their surpluses after surrendering the portion owed in taxes.

LETTER 12.25 (C. 536)

This letter was directed to the deputy assistant of the praetorian prefect to order the storage of additional foodstuffs in light of the effects of an unidentified volcanic eruption on crop production. Much of it is a poignant meditation on change and the natural order. Because the deputy assistant acted as the prefect's representative in Rome, it is also possible that this letter was a response to the rupture in food supplies to Rome occasioned by the advance of the Gothic War in southern Italy. In that case, *Variae* 12.22 (above), concerning the requisitioning of commodities from Istria, may also have been a response to exigencies in Rome. This letter's enumeration of the eruption's impact on winter, spring, and summer places it in the autumn of 536, before Belisarius entered Rome that December.

Praetorian Prefect Senator to Ambrosius, Illustris and Deputy Assistant

1. Those who observe the changing order of the world frequently become agitated, since such things often presage what is shown to be contrary to habit. For nothing happens without provocation, nor does the world operate by casual accident, but whatever we see reach a conclusion is known to be a divine plan. Men are held in suspense when kings alter their own policies, and if problems should proceed other than how their practice had prepared them.[19] But who would not be troubled with great curiosity about such events if, in a way contrary to precedents, something mysterious should seem to come from the heavens? For just as there is a certain comfort in observing the course of the seasons in their own particular succession, thus are we filled with great curiosity when such things are thought to be altered. 2. What does it mean, I ask, to gaze intently upon the most conspicuous star[20] and not witness its usual brilliance, to observe the moon, the splendor of night, in its full circumference but absent its natural luster? Together, we all still perceive a kind of sea-colored sun; we marvel that physical bodies lack shadows at midday and that the strength of

19. This may be a reference to Witigis's decision to abandon Rome after Theodahad's assassination earlier in 536.
20. The sun.

the sun's fullest exposure attains only the dullness of a cooling tepidness, which has happened not in the momentary lapse of an eclipse, but for the duration of almost a full year. **3.** What a terror it is, therefore, to endure daily what usually frightens people only in the swiftest moment! And so, we have had winter without storms, spring without mingled weather, summer without heat waves. How is it now hoped to possibly attain the proper season when the months that had ripened crops before have cooled intemperately with the northern winds? For what may produce fertility if the earth does not warm in the summer months? How may buds appear if the progenitress, rain, does not resume her place? Of all the elements, we find these two opposed, a perpetual chill and a difficult drought. The seasons have changed by not changing, and what usually happens with the commingling of showers cannot be procured through dryness alone. **4.** And therefore, let your prudence overcome future scarcity with previous stores, since there was such blessed abundance in the previous year that provisions may suffice for even the coming months. Let everything that is needed for food be stored. The private citizen will easily find necessary things when public provision has been completed. **5.** But, lest the present circumstance torment you with great hesitation, return to a consideration of the nature of things, and let what seems uncertain to the gaping crowd become understandable by reason. For it is known to be thus disposed by divine arrangement: just as the stars of the current year have assembled in their own domains for cooperative administration, thus winter has been rendered colder and drier than usual. Hence, air laden with snow from excessive cold is not converted to dryness by the heat of the sun, but, abiding its acquired density, it blocks the heat of the sun and deflects the view of human frailty. For matter of the middle air governs our ability to see, and we are able to see through this substance only as much as the thinness of its matter allows. **6.** For this great void, which spreads in the manner of a liquid element between heaven and earth, truly extends our vision, provided it happens to be pure and washed with the brightness of the sun. But if it is condensed with some mixture, then, as though with a kind of taught membrane, it allows neither particular colors nor the heat of celestial bodies to penetrate. This has also happened frequently in other eras by means of a cloud cover. Hence it is that the rays of stars have been darkened daily by strange color, that the reaper dreads the novel cold, that fruits have hardened with the advance of time, and that the ripening of grapes on the vine is bitter. 7. But if this is ascribed to divine providence, we are not to fret, since, by command of that very power, we are forbidden from asking for prodigies.[21] Nevertheless, we are certain that this is hostile to products of the earth, when we no longer see proper foods nourished according to their own demands.[22] Accordingly, let your solicitude behave so that the unfruitfulness of one year may not appear to disturb us, since it was foreseen by the founding rector of our office[23] that the abundance of a previous year would suffice to soften the penury to follow.

21. A reference to the biblical treatment of portents in Matthew 16:1–4.

22. *Lege propria* may also be translated as "natural law," although it may be important that Cassiodorus did not simply use *ius naturale* or another more common variant for this term.

23. The biblical Joseph, for whom see also *Var.* 6.3, 8.20 (neither included in this volume), 12.28 (in Section 4).

GLOSSARY

annona	Regular payments made to soldiers, primarily in the form of food, fodder, clothing, etc.
cancellarius	A personal agent of the praetorian prefect (q.v.), often assigned on an ad hoc basis to execute the prefect's orders pertaining to legal or administrative matters.
canonicarius	A magistrate sent annually from the office of the praetorian prefect (q.v.) to work with local municipal officials to collect taxes.
clarissimus	The lowest grade of the senatorial order's three grades; *clarissimi* obtained senatorial rank by birth but did not attend the assembly of the Senate at Rome. Compare *illustris; spectabilis.*
comitatus	Originally the body of officials, both military and civil, who attended the Roman emperor on his travels; in sixth-century Italy, the term signified, more generally, the king's court.
comitiacus	Lower-ranking officials of the king's *comitatus* (q.v.) who were delegated administrative and judicial assignments on an ad hoc basis much like the *saiones* (q.v.), but often at the command of the praetorian prefect (q.v.).
consiliarius	A legal aide assigned to a public official.

consul	Among the oldest political offices of the Roman Empire, the consulship was held by two appointees annually—from the fifth century, one for Rome and one for Constantinople, largely as a diplomatic means of signifying détente between Italy and the eastern empire, since consulships at that time were ceremonial only.
count	A *comes* usually held a military command, in the Ostrogothic context often that of a city garrison or a field command in a province; it was expected that counts would defer to civil officials in matters of judicial and administrative practice.
count of private properties	A senior administrative official, the *Comes Rei Privatae* was part of the *comitatus* (q.v.) of the king and played a fiscal and administrative role similar to that of the count of the patrimony (q.v.), the primary difference being in the classification of the lands over which they exercised authority: owned by the king for the count of the patrimony and from private sources—through individual bequests, intestacy, or confiscations by judicial procedure—for the count of private properties.
count of the patrimony	A senior administrative post, the *Comes Patrimonii* was part of the *comitatus* (q.v.) of the king and managed the resources produced on royal properties—that is, properties in Italy owned by previous emperors which had come under Theoderic's control; more than an estate manager, this was a fiscal office that could direct resources to various needs of the state (especially military). Compare *count of private properties.*
count of the sacred largesse	A senior administrative post, the *Comes Sacrarum Largitionum* was part of the *comitatus* (q.v.) of the king and may be thought of as the state's senior treasurer: he controlled the mints; funded, at the king's discretion, the largesse allocated to various public celebrations; and disbursed military salaries, which could be paid either in kind (as the *annona*) or in coin (often as the donative), that had been collected as taxes.
curia	The physical assembly of the Senate at Rome; also, a name for the municipal assemblies of local town counsellors (q.v.).

curule	Of or relating to the regalia associated with senior public offices, such as the consulship.
duke	A *dux* held a military command—often a field command assigned to a campaign—usually subordinate to that of the military counts but could also function similarly to counts (q.v.) in frontier provinces.
fasces	Originally the bound rods and axes that served as emblems for public offices possessing judicial authority; in sixth-century Italy this was a general term for the authority of a senior magistrate.
illustris	The highest of the three grades of senatorial rank; the *illustres* constituted the body that convened as the Senate at Rome, with membership dependent on either imperial or royal appointment to a military or civilian senior post. Compare *clarissimus; spectabilis.*
imperium	Generally, the authority of an emperor or king; the term also conveys the sense of the sovereignty of the realm ruled by an emperor or king.
indiction	A particular year within a fiscal cycle of fifteen years.
Magister Militum	The commander-in-chief of the military forces assigned to a prefecture (a group of provinces).
master of offices	A senior administrative post, the *Magister Officiorum* was part of the *comitatus* (q.v.) of the king and supervised the personnel of the royal or imperial court; because this personnel included secretaries responsible for official correspondence, the office also directed the receipt and dispatch of envoys and thus shared authority over the public post (q.v.) with the praetorian prefect (q.v.).
modius	A dry measure of approximately 2.25 gallons; most frequently used in reference to the collection of grain for taxes.
monopolium	The exclusive right to farm taxes on a particular commodity, awarded by the royal court.
praetorian prefect	The *Praefectus Praetorio* was the highest nonmilitary office in the Ostrogothic kingdom and the highest appellate authority below the king, upon whom the

prefect often attended in the *comitatus* (q.v.); Amal rulers appointed two praetorian prefects, one for Italy and adjacent provinces (the original prefecture of Italy) and one for Gaul and Spain (the prefecture of the Gauls), whose duties were often legal and administrative, including the assessment and collection of taxes and their redistribution as the salaries of state officials.

Princeps

A title of supreme distinction without a clear parallel in English, except perhaps "Sovereign"; used in reference to the emperor of the eastern empire or the king of Italy.

public defender

Originally an office designed to provide legal aid to underprivileged citizens, by the sixth century the *defensor* was involved in the assessment and collection of taxes, although this need not preclude the continued practice of its original role, especially as an intermediary between individual citizens and tax officials.

public post

The *cursus publicus* was a transportation system, consisting of a series of way stations (*mansiones*) that provided accommodation and transport animals, for the use of couriers, envoys, and other officials with writs supplied by either the praetorian prefect (q.v.) or the master of offices (q.v.).

Quaestor

The senior official most intimate with the policies of the king and attendant upon his *comitatus* (q.v.), who drafted the language of all official pronouncements; legal as well as literary training was preferred for this post, as much official communication dealt with the state's legal and administrative needs.

saio

A member of a corps of Gothic agents, with some attestation in Visigothic sources, who acted as direct representatives of the king with judicial and military authority, often assigned to mobilize military forces, execute royal commands, or provide legal guardianship to wards of the state; the criteria for recruitment are unknown, although *saiones* were presumably Gothic nobility.

siliquaticum

A form of sales tax, originally levied as 1/24 of the purchase value of major commodities.

solidus   The largest denomination of gold currency commonly
                        used in the eastern empire and most of its successor
                        states; in theory a *solidus* was equivalent to 1/72 of a
                        pound of gold.

spectabilis   The second of the senatorial order's three grades;
                        spectabiles presumably obtained their distinction,
                        higher than the hereditary *clarissimus* (q.v.) rank, by
                        some official appointment which nonetheless did not
                        grant *illustris* (q.v.) rank or a seat in the Senate at
                        Rome.

town counsellors   The *curiales* formed a college of leading citizens and
                        were often the largest landowners of a given munici-
                        pality; they were expected to maintain urban
                        residences and facilitate the local assessment and
                        collection of taxes, at the risk of penalty to their own
                        properties.

tribunus et notarius An honorary title received after completing service in
                        certain administrative bureaus.

urban prefect   In the absence of the king and the praetorian prefect
                        (q.v.), the *Praefectus Urbis* was the highest-ranking
                        authority resident at Rome; often appointed from
                        among *illustris* (q.v.) senators and sometimes from the
                        king's *comitatus* (q.v.), the urban prefect usually
                        presided over meetings of the Senate and was held
                        accountable for maintaining order in Rome and
                        managing the financial resources of the ancient
                        capital.

CONCORDANCE OF LETTERS CITED
IN THIS VOLUME

BOOK 1

BOOK 2

BOOK 3

BOOK 4

BOOK 5

SELECTED BIBLIOGRAPHY OF
RELATED READING

STUDIES OF THE *VARIAE*

Barnish, Samuel. *Cassiodorus: Variae*. Liverpool: Liverpool University Press, 1992.

———. "Sacred Texts of the Secular: Writing, Hearing and Reading Cassiodorus' *Variae*." *Studia Patristica* 38 (2001): 362–70.

Bjornlie, Shane. *Politics and Tradition between Rome, Ravenna, and Constantinople: A Study of Cassiodorus and the Variae, 527–554*. Cambridge: Cambridge University Press, 2013.

———. "The Rhetoric of *Varietas* and Epistolary Encyclopedism in the *Variae* of Cassiodorus." In *Shifting Genres in Late Antiquity*, ed. Geoffrey Greatrex, Hugh Elton, and Lucas McMahon, 289–303. Burlington: Ashgate, 2015.

———. "Virtues in a Time of War: Administrative Writing, Dialectic, and the Gothic War." In *The Collectio Avellana and Its Revivals*, ed. Rita Lizzi Testa and Giulia Marconi, 425–62. Newcastle: Cambridge Scholars Publishing. 2019.

———. "What Have Elephants to Do with Sixth-Century Politics? A Reappraisal of the 'Official' Governmental Dossier of Cassiodorus." *Journal of Late Antiquity* 2, no. 1 (2009): 143–71.

Gillett, Andrew. "The Purposes of Cassiodorus' *Variae*." In *After Rome's Fall: Narrators and Sources of Early Medieval History*, ed. Alexander C. Murray, 37–50. Toronto: University of Toronto Press, 1998.

Skahill, Bernard. *The Syntax of the Variae*. Washington, D.C.: Catholic University of America, 1934.

Suelzer, Mary J. *The Clausulae of Cassiodorus*. Washington, D.C.: Catholic University of America, 1944.

Vidén, Gunhild. *The Roman Chancery Tradition: Studies in the Language of the Codex Theodosianus and Cassiodorus' Variae*. Göteborg: Acta Universitatis Gothoburgensis, 1984.

STUDIES OF CASSIODORUS

Barnish, Samuel. "The Work of Cassiodorus after His Conversion." *Latomus* 48 (1989): 157–87.
Croke, Brian. "Cassiodorus and the *Getica* of Jordanes." *Classical Philology* 82, no. 2 (1987): 117–34.
Giardina, Andrea. *Cassiodoro Politico*. Rome: Erma di Bretschneider, 2006.
Halporn, James W., and Mark Vessey. *Cassiodorus: Institutions of Divine and Secular Learning; On the Soul*. Liverpool: Liverpool University Press, 2004.
Momigliano, Arnaldo. "Cassiodorus and the Italian Culture of His Time." *Proceedings of the British Academy* 41 (1955): 207–36.
O'Donnell, J. *Cassiodorus*. Berkeley: University of California Press, 1979.

STUDIES OF OSTROGOTHIC ITALY

Amory, Patrick. *People and Identity in Ostrogothic Italy, 489–554*. Cambridge: Cambridge University Press, 1997.
Arnold, Jonathan. *Theoderic and the Roman Imperial Restoration*. New York: Oxford University Press, 2014.
Arnold, Jonathan, Shane Bjornlie, and Kristina Sessa, eds. *A Companion to Ostrogothic Italy*. Leiden: Brill, 2016.
Barnish, Samuel. "Pigs, Plebeians and *Potentes*: Rome's Economic Hinterland, c. 350–600." *Papers of the British School* 55 (1987): 157–85.
Barnish, Samuel, and Federico Marazzi, eds. *The Ostrogoths from the Migration Period to the Sixth Century: An Ethnographic Perspective*. Woodbridge, Suffolk: Boydell, 2007.
Bjornlie, Shane. "Law, Ethnicity, and Taxes in Ostrogothic Italy: A Case for Continuity, Adaptation and Departure." *Early Medieval Europe* 22, no. 2 (2014): 138–70.
Jones, A. H. M. "The Constitutional Position of Odoacer and Theoderic." *Journal of Roman Studies* 52 (1962): 126–30.
Lafferty, Sean. *Law and Society in the Age of Theoderic the Great: A Study of the Edictum Theoderici*. Cambridge: Cambridge University Press, 2013.
Marazzi, Federico. "The Destinies of the Late Antique Italies: Politico-Economic Developments of the Sixth Century." In *The Sixth Century: Production, Distribution, and Demand*, ed. Richard Hodges and William Bowden, 119–59. Leiden: Brill, 1998.

Moorhead, John. "Cassiodorus on the Goths in Ostrogothic Italy." *Romano-barbarica* 16 (1999): 241–59.

———. *Theoderic in Italy.* Oxford: Oxford University Press, 1992.

O'Donnell, J. "Liberius the Patrician." *Traditio* 37 (1981): 32–71.

———. *The Ruin of the Roman Empire.* New York: Ecco, 2008.

INDEX OF INDIVIDUALS

INDEX OF CONCEPTS, PEOPLES, AND TERMS

urban prefect, 1.6, 1.32–33, 1.41, 2.6, 2.34, 3.30, 3.51, 4.16, 4.51, 5.38, 6.18, 7.5, 9.15, 9.21, 10.30

Vandals, 1.4, 1.15, 5.43, 9.1
vicar, 3.16–17, 3.41

Visigoths, 3.1

Warni, 5.1
women, 1.7, 2.10–11, 3.14, 3.46, 4.1, 5.32–33, 5.43, 7.40, 9.1, 9.4, 10.10, 10.23, 11.1

INDEX OF PLACES